Law in the Age of Pluralism

By
Andrei Marmor

OXFORD
UNIVERSITY PRESS

OXFORD
UNIVERSITY PRESS

Oxford University Press, Inc., publishes works that further Oxford University's objective of excellence in research, scholarship, and education.

Published by Oxford University Press, Inc.
198 Madison Avenue, New York, New York 10016

Library of Congress Cataloging-in-Publication Data

Marmor, Andrei.
Law in the age of pluralism / by Andrei Marmor.
p. cm.
Includes bibliographical references and index.
ISBN: 978-0-19-533847-8 (alk. paper)
1. Law—Philosophy. 2. Pluralism. I. Title.
K230.M356L39 2007
340'.1—dc22

2007017535

Note to Readers:

This publication is designed to provide accurate and authoritative information in regard to the subject matter covered. It is based upon sources believed to be accurate and reliable and is intended to be current as of the time it was written. It is sold with the understanding that the publisher is not engaged in rendering legal, accounting, or other professional services. If legal advice or other expert assistance is required, the services of a competent professional person should be sought. Also, to confirm that the information has not been affected or changed by recent developments, traditional legal research techniques should be used, including checking primary sources where appropriate.

(Based on the Declaration of Principles jointly adopted by a Committee of the American Bar Association and a Committee of Publishers and Associations.)

Table of Contents

III. Rights and Equality

Introduction

The essays collected in this volume are organized in three groups. The first group is about democracy and the rule of law. The second is about the nature of law and adjudication, and the third group comprises essays on the nature of rights and equality. Overall, these essays cut across moral, political, and legal philosophy. There is nothing new or surprising about this; morality, law, and politics are very closely entwined both in practice and in theory. Political institutions determine what the law is, and the law shapes our political institutions. Both are morally important and should be subject to moral scrutiny. Thus the idea that these three domains are closely intertwined is obvious. The idea that in theorizing about these issues we should make an effort to disentangle them is less obvious and more controversial. It is, however, part of what I aim to do in this volume. I try to follow in the footsteps of a well-established analytical tradition, which has taught us that in trying to understand complicated issues, the first step is to take the building blocks apart and carefully analyze them one by one. Once we have a clear view of the elements, we can begin to reconstruct the complicated structures.

There are many issues discussed in this volume of essays. I would not be telling you the truth if I suggested that there is one major issue or argument uniting these diverse topics. There is no such thing. But there are three closely related themes that motivate the discussion. First, as the title of the volume suggests, I firmly believe that we should take the idea of value pluralism very seriously, and see how it informs a morally acceptable vision of law and politics. Why pluralism? Because I share Rawls's view that pluralism is the most significant moral aspect of the social-political world we live in. This is both an observation and a value judgment. It is a fact that we live in a world in which different segments of society have deeply conflicting views about the good and the just. And it is a moral judgment that many of these differences are reasonable and ought to be respected.

That I share Rawls's views about the main challenge does not mean that I share his solutions. In several chapters I raise some doubts about Rawls's conclusions, in particular, about his ideal of neutrality and the concept of public reason. In fact, doubt is the second underlying theme here. The close connections between law, morality, and politics have led many influential writers to suggest rather grand unifying theories of law and state. Some of these theories tend to glorify American Constitutionalism, suggesting that if we can only come to see the correct moral principles of the Constitution, we will have gained both the vision and the mechanism for implementing the ideal of a liberal state. I am skeptical about these grand theories, and I am very skeptical about the glorification of Constitutionalism. Both are at odds with due respect for value pluralism—or so I argue in some of these essays.

Those who see Constitutionalism as the heuristic vision of a liberal state tend to be very doubtful about the conceptual possibility of separating law from morality. The idea that what the law is, and what the law ought to be, are conceptually separate, is famously associated with the legal positivist tradition in jurisprudence. There is no necessary connection between constitutionalism and anti-positivism, but with very few exceptions, these two philosophical views tend to go hand in hand. Though not necessary, this connection is understandable. If you hedge your bets on the idea of constitutional morality, you are unlikely to favor the view that what the law is does not necessarily depend on what it ought to be. But this separation is precisely what we need to maintain, I argue here, both in method and in substance. A philosophical account of the nature of law should not be tainted with moral-political visions about what the law ought to be. And what the law is does not necessarily depend on morality either. A defense of the legal positivist tradition constitutes the third theme of this volume.

All this is very vague, so let me provide a very brief outline of what the reader should expect to find in each of the chapters of this book. The *first chapter* is about the rule of law. The challenge for any theory about the rule of law is threefold: to explain what the rule of law is, why it is good, and to what extent. This chapter proposes a comprehensive analysis of the rule of law, articulating the conditions that the law has to meet in order to be able to fulfill its pivotal functions in guiding human conduct. The chapter advances two main theses about these conditions of the rule of law. First, although the virtues of the rule of law are essentially functional, they are also moral-political virtues, enhancing a range of goods valued in a pluralistic society, in addition to their functional merit. Second, the essay comprises detailed arguments purporting to show how legalism can be excessive and demonstrating that upholding the rule of law virtues is never costless, morally, politically, and otherwise. Within contemporary jurisprudence, this essay takes an intermediary position between Lon Fuller's account of the rule of law as exhibiting the "inner morality of law" and Joseph Raz's functional account.

Chapter two challenges the widely held view that legislative integrity is a distinct political ideal. According to this ideal, lawmakers should try to make the total set of laws they enact as morally coherent as possible. There are two types of arguments advanced against this ideal. First, it is shown that the ideal of legislative integrity is directly at odds with the value of pluralism and the commitment of a liberal state to respect reasonable pluralism. Second, the essay looks at the main causes of the failure of legislative integrity in democratic legislatures, arguing that there is nothing regrettable about these causes; on the contrary, they manifest commendable aspects of democratic lawmaking.

But is democracy really valuable? Is it intrinsically valuable? The purpose of *chapter three* is to show that considerations of fairness play an essential (but not exclusive) role in the justification of democratic decision procedures. The first part of the chapter argues that considerations of fairness form an essential part of a practical authority's legitimacy. Moreover, in the political context, those considerations of fairness entail a principle of equal distribution of political power. Subsequently, the essay elaborates on the kind of equality that is required in democratic procedures, showing that different principles of equality should apply to the deliberation and the decision stages of democracy. Finally, the chapter concludes with a few suggestions about the possible relations between considerations of fairness and soundness of democratic procedures.

The common theme of chapters two and three is that democratic legislation, messy and morally problematic as it often is, has great value and commands our moral respect. In *chapter four*, I go one crucial step further and argue that constitutional constraints on democratic legislation enforced by judicial review are morally problematic, perhaps illegitimate. Following a preliminary outline of the main features of (what I call) "robust constitutionalism," the chapter presents some of the main moral concerns about the legitimacy of robust constitutions, particularly those issues posed by the challenge of respect for pluralism. It then considers in detail several arguments that purport to answer those concerns, arguing that they all fail to meet the challenge. The essay concludes with a brief outline of some of the moral implications of this failure and some suggestions for constitutional reform.

It is very tempting to think that the moral-political ideals of constitutional democracy and the rule of law should find their way into a philosophical account of the nature of law, of what the law, in general, is. Indeed, it has become increasingly popular to argue that even legal positivism is actually a normative theory, and that it cannot be purely descriptive and morally neutral as H.L.A. Hart has suggested. *Chapter five* aims to disprove this line of thought. It argues that legal positivism is best understood as a descriptive, morally neutral theory about the nature of law. The essay distinguishes among five possible views about the relationship between normative claims and legal positivism, arguing that some of them are not at odds with Hart's thesis about the nature of jurisprudence, while the others are wrong, both as expositions of legal positivism or as critiques of it. Legal positivism does not necessarily purport to justify any aspect of its subject matter, nor is it committed to any particular moral or political evaluations. And this, I argue, is precisely as it should be. H.L.A. Hart's insight that a philosophical account of the nature of law should be a descriptive account, general in application and morally neutral, is quite right.

Chapter six moves from method to substance: It is an essay on the conventional foundations of law. The essay consists of three main arguments. First, that between Hart's view on the *rules of recognition* and Kelsen's view on the *basic norm*, Hart's account is more plausible. Second, it argues that the rules of recognition are not coordination conventions, as some commentators have claimed, but conventions of a different kind. Finally, the paper draws a distinction between *deep* and *surface* conventions, arguing that there are deep conventions determining what law is, and surface conventions of recognition determining what counts as law in a particular community. This distinction between deep and surface conventions is employed to solve some of the puzzles about the conventional foundations of law.

One of the more common mistakes in jurisprudence is to assume that a general account of the nature of law, such as H.L.A. Hart's or any other, must also settle various issues in a theory of adjudication. After all, if we know what *law is*, we should also know how judges are to figure it out when, for some reason, it is not entirely clear what the law prescribes in particular cases. But this is a mistake. When we come to understand what law is, we realize that the law cannot possibly settle in advance every dispute that reaches the courts. What the courts should do in such cases remains an open question, one that needs to be settled by normative, sometimes straightforwardly moral, arguments.

Chapter seven deals with one example of such a normative dilemma that judges may face in common-law adjudication: are there any good reasons to treat previous judicial decisions as legally binding in similar cases, just because they are similar, even if the underlying reasons for the previous decisions underdetermine the result? This is the relevant question raised by the principle of "treating like cases alike." There are two possible rationales that may justify an affirmative answer: the principle that justice should be *seen* to be done, and the principle of protected expectations. Both answers are criticized as overinclusive and only partly defensible. It is not always desirable to treat like cases alike. Finally, the essay concludes with a suggestion that there are two modes of analogical reasoning in adjudication, and that one of them may rationalize one type of cases in which like cases should be treated alike.

When the law is not clear and it needs interpretation, normative questions become inevitable. But a theory of adjudication, particularly in the context of statutory interpretation, necessarily involves some issues about the nature of language as well. Before we interpret the law, we must know what the relevant part of the law actually says. And what the law says is first and foremost a matter of understanding language; a philosophical account of this aspect of adjudication must therefore be informed by a philosophical account of linguistic communication. Unfortunately, however, judges tend to have rather confused views about the nature of language, and, as I argue in *chapter eight*, sometimes they use a mistaken view of semantics to advance a political agenda. Of course, it is the currently fashionable theory of textualism that I have in mind here. This short essay argues that textualism, as a doctrine of statutory interpretation, is inherently deceptive and therefore immoral. Textualism is typically presented by its adherents as an interpretive practice that is motivated by respect for democracy and respect for the authority of the legislature. But, in fact, textualism's preoccupation with ordinary meaning and literal application of statutes is motivated by a desire to constrain the legislature's ability to pursue broad regulatory policies. Authorities do not want to be understood literally. Authorities purport to govern, and governance requires cooperation in the spirit of its goals, not strict adherence to the letter of its directives.

Chapter nine (the oldest essay in this volume) is about the politics of rights. The main purpose of this essay is to demonstrate that rights discourse in a pluralistic society is based on a very thin layer of consensus. Widespread consensus on how to resolve conflicts between rights (and between rights and other goods) is possible only in a framework of a shared culture of moral and political values. However, typically in such cases rights have actually little political and cultural significance. If rights discourse is prevalent in a certain society, it is precisely because there is very little agreement on anything else, in particular, on the basic values people hold. The argument is based on an analysis of the interest theory of rights, explaining the functions of rights in light of their unique nature as intermediary conclusions in practical arguments.

Some of the moral implications of this view about the nature of rights are explored in *chapter ten*. The essay explores the question of whether people can have a right to common goods, such as the flourishing of their culture or national heritage. It first explains the concept of a common good and its distinction from similar concepts, such as collective and public goods. Second, it argues that individuals ought not to have a right to common goods, unless a particular distributive principle applies to the good in question, and that then the individual's right is the right to a certain share in that common good. Finally, the essay explores the question of how this analysis applies to group rights, with respect to other groups and to members of the group itself.

Chapter eleven is a very short essay on the question of whether people should have a right to their pretax income. More precisely, I argue that the main insight of Liam Murphy and Thomas Nagel's book, *The Myth of Ownership*, that people have no right to their pretax income, is not supported by their claim that the right to private property is not a natural right. The non-naturalness of the right to private property is irrelevant to their moral argument. The plausibility of their moral conclusion derives from the thesis (which they also seem to endorse) that people have a right to the fruits of their labor, maintaining, however, that there is no possible conception, morally speaking, of what the fruits of one's labor are, independent of a system of legal and social norms that constitute the terms of fair bargaining, pricing, etc. People can only have a right to a fair assessment of the added value of their labor, and the latter cannot make any moral sense independent of the entire system of norms prevailing in the relevant society. The main point of this essay is that this last conclusion is not affected by the nature of the right to private property.

The concluding essay of this collection, *chapter twelve*, is about the value of economic equality. Harry Frankfurt and Joseph Raz, among others, have argued that economic equality is not intrinsically valuable. Their argument rests on the claim that what we should care about is the satisfaction of people's needs, not their relative position *vis-à-vis* others. If people have enough of what they need, it does not matter whether they have more or less than others. This chapter contends that economic equality is intrinsically valuable precisely because we should care about people's needs, mostly due to the fact that sufficiency is profoundly relative to the possessions of others. The first part of the essay purports to establish this basic relativity of needs; the second part explains why this is an argument for the *intrinsic* value of equality; finally, the essay concludes with a few remarks on what principle of equality is justified by this argument, drawing on a distinction between two general types of moral ideals.

With the exception of chapters nine and twelve, these essays have been written in the last few years. In the course of these years, I have gradually moved to the U.S. and I have had the opportunity to discuss my work with many friends and colleagues. Perhaps no physical proximity could be more rewarding than the proximity of Scott Altman's office to mine; Scott has read the drafts of most of these essays, always forcing me to make a greater effort to convince him. Though I am sure that Scott is still unconvinced, my work has benefited greatly and I am very grateful to him. My wife, Elizabeth Garrett, has been somewhat more understanding, yet equally helpful. Her detailed comments on many of these chapters helped me to avoid numerous mistakes. I have also greatly benefited from her work on direct democracy and theory of legislation and, in general, from her extensive knowledge, both practical and theoretical, of American politics. Joseph Raz has also commented on some of these essays. As always, if the papers see the light of day, it is only because I tell myself that Joseph cannot be *always* right. In the back of my mind I know that my assumption is false, but without it, this book would have been much shorter. Words cannot express how grateful I am to everything I have learned from Joseph. I have also benefited greatly from the comments of Jeremy Waldron and many conversations we have had over these years. Both our agreements and disagreements are clearly manifest in this collection. We share a very similar view about political morality, and we disagree about the nature of law and legal philosophy. Whether we agree or not, a discussion with Jeremy is always a pleasure and intellectually rewarding. In the course of preparing this collection for the book, Martin Stone read many of the chapters and gave me detailed comments. Skeptical and insightful as usual, Martin has helped me to avoid some errors and forced me to clarify some of my arguments. I am very grateful to him. Many other people have commented on various essays and I have tried to express my gratitude to all of them in each specific chapter.

Acknowledgments

All the essays in this volume have been published in journals or anthologies. I am very grateful to the editors and publishers for their permission to use the articles for this volume. Below is the list of the original publications of these essays.

"The Rule of Law and its Limits," *23 Law & Philosophy*, (2004), 1.

"Should We Value Legislative Integrity?," in R Bauman & T Kahana (eds.), *The Least Examined Branch, The Role of Legislatures in the Constitutional State*, Cambridge University Press, (2006), pp. 125–138.

"Authority, Equality, and Democracy," *18 Ratio Juris* (2005), 315–345.

"Are Constitutions Legitimate?," *XX The Canadian Journal of Law and Jurisprudence*, (2007), 69–112.

"Legal Positivism: Still Descriptive and Morally Neutral," *26 Oxford Journal of Legal Studies*, (2006), 683–704.

"How Law is Like Chess," *12 Legal Theory*, (2006), 347–371.

"Should Like Cases Be Treated Alike?," *11 Legal Theory* (2005), 37–48.

"The Immorality of Textualism," *Theories of Statutory Interpretation*, Symposium Issue, *38 Loyola L Rev*, (2005), 2063.

"On The Limits Of Rights," *Law and Philosophy*, Vol. 16 (1997), pp. 1–18.

"Do We Have A Right To Common Goods?," *XIV The Canadian Journal of Law and Jurisprudence*, (2001), 213–225.

"On The Right to Private Property and Entitlement to One's Income," *XVIII The Canadian Journal of Law and Jurisprudence*, (2005), 69.

"The Intrinsic Value of Economic Equality," in Meyer, Pogge, & Paulson, eds., *Rights, Culture and the Law: Essays after Joseph Raz*, Oxford University Press (2003), 127–141.

PART I

The Rule of Law and The Rule of the Many

CHAPTER 1

The Rule of Law and Its Limits

My grandmother used to say that too much, even of a good thing, is bad for you. She was no philosopher, my grandmother; she just used to say this when I asked for another serving of her wonderful homemade jam. Needless to say, she would not have connected her thoughts about the good with the rule of law. In fact, I think she lived her ninety-odd years without knowing what the rule of law is. She lived through most of the twentieth century in Romania, where "rule of law" was not a very popular political slogan. Nowadays, however, when the Eastern European countries have freed themselves of communism and wish to join the Western world, implementing the rule of law is one of the main social changes that they seek to establish. Perhaps nowhere is the rule of law so cherished as in those places where it was largely ignored for decades. Indeed, at least in the Western world, the rule of law has long been associated with the idea of a well-ordered society. We criticize countries which do not strictly adhere to the rule of law, and we take pride in having it.[1] In spite of its popularity, however, the various ideas associated with the rule of law are often conflicting and not infrequently rather confused. When a complicated idea becomes a popular political slogan, this is not surprising.

The most common mistake about the rule of law is to confuse it with the ideal of the rule of good law; the kind of law, for instance, that respects freedom and human dignity.[2] But of course, understood as a general ideal of good law, the rule of law is no longer a unique ideal but a whole moral-political philosophy about what the

---

1 Needless to say, admiration of the rule of law is not universal; Marxists have been traditionally hostile to the rule of law, and more recently, other critical theories have come to share this hostility. See, for example, C. Sypnowich, "Utopia and the Rule of Law," in D. Dyzenhaus (ed.), *Recrafting the Rule of Law: The Limits of Legal Order*, 179.

2 In spite of his awareness of this danger, it is difficult to avoid the impression that Hayek fell into this trap. See: Friedrich Hayek, *The Road to Serfdom*, Ch 6.

law should achieve and the values it should uphold.[3] Thus, the challenge for any theory about the rule of law is to articulate a much narrower interpretation of the rule of law that avoids this mistake. Namely, we must focus on what legalism, *per se,* means, and then ask why it is a good thing to have. Not less importantly, however, we must also realize that legalism can be excessive. Even if the rule of law is a good thing, too much of it may be bad. So the challenge for a theory of the rule of law is to articulate what the rule of law is, why is it good, and to what extent.

Let us assume, then, that the essence of the ideal of the rule of law is that people ought to be governed by law. This general ideal has at least two main components. First, it requires that governments, namely, *de facto* political authorities, should rule—that is, guide the conduct of their subjects—by law. Second, it requires that the law by which governments purport to rule should be such that it can actually guide human conduct.[4] Interestingly, it is the second component of the rule of law that has attracted most of the scholarly attention and, as I shall argue, rightly so. But let us take up these two components of the rule of law in this order.

A. Basic Principles

1. Governments *Should* Rule by Law

This first aspect of the rule of law is less obvious than it seems. Many people associate it with the familiar slogan of "government by law, not by men." But it is difficult to understand what this slogan actually means. As Raz rightly noted, we must be governed by human beings, not just by law. It is human beings, namely, legislators, judges, and countless other officials, who make the law and apply it, and this is, presumably, as it should be.[5] Thus, this slogan cannot really mean what it literally states. Perhaps sometimes it is meant to suggest that those people who are assigned the role of making laws should be subject to the laws they enact. But this is, at best, a very rough generalization. Whether the lawmaker should be

---

3 J. Raz, *The Authority of Law*, 211.

4 See Raz, *The Authority of Law*, 212–214. Some commentators assume that the rule of law also requires the subjects to obey the law. In one sense, this is clearly true; unless the law is by and large obeyed, it cannot function as a means of social control. But of course, it should not be assumed that the rule of law entails a general *prima facie* obligation to obey the law. The question of whether there is such a general obligation to obey the law is clearly a moral one.

5 See Raz, *ibid.*

subject to the particular law it enacts is bound to vary according to the kind of law it is. (Nothing would be wrong, for example, with an act of parliament prescribing that no other institution can alter the laws parliament enacts; by definition, this is a kind of law that applies to every institution except the legislature that enacted it.) Furthermore, even if the lawmaker exempts herself, as a private person, from the law she enacted in her public role, we could only say that it is a bad law, unless it was enacted for very good reasons.

Finally, the slogan of "government by law, not by men" is sometimes meant to suggest that all governmental actions should be authorized by law. But, as Raz rightly noted, this is a tautology: "Actions not authorized by law cannot be the actions of the government as government."[6] It is true, of course, that any governmental agent might perform a specific act that purports to be authorized by law but, in fact, is not. Raz's point is not to deny that there are actions which are legally *ultra vires*. The point is that governmental acts without legal authorization are by definition illegal, and therefore if governmental agents act without legal authorization, they simply fail to obey the law.[7]

So we are back to the question of what it means to suggest that governments *ought to rule by law*. This can be answered only if we have an idea of what would violate this ideal: How could a government rule if not by law? By sheer terror, perhaps? Or just through haphazard, whimsical orders? Would that be a form of governance? In other words, can we observe any sustained form of governance which is somehow achieved without law? This question is surprisingly difficult to answer, partly because the answer depends on a theory about what law is, and what kinds of means of social control are legal. For example, according to a somewhat crude version of the command theory of law, any order backed by sanction of the *de facto* sovereign would be law, by definition.[8] Therefore, once we have a group of people actually governed by a sovereign, the governance is bound to be legal regardless of the exact form of the sovereign's commands. On the basis of such a command theory of law, it would be very difficult to think of a case where *de facto*

6 *Ibid.* 212.

7 To be more precise: there is a technical legal sense in which lack of authority is not equivalent to illegality. A governmental action can be *ultra vires* in various respects (*e.g.* wiretapping without legal permission) without also being illegal in the sense of a crime, or tort, or other violation of the law. Nevertheless, when a governmental agent acts without the requisite legal authority, he simply fails to obey the law. This is what I mean in the text. I am indebted to John Finnis for this comment (which is not to suggest that he agrees with me).

8 See J. Austin, *The Province of Jurisprudence Determined.*

governance is sustained by means which are not legal. At the other end of the spectrum, if one relies on a traditional natural law theory, and assumes that only those norms which meet certain moral constraints can count as law, one would get the opposite problem—a great deal of what we would normally call legal would not really be law even in a well-ordered legalistic society.

The problem is not confined to particular theories about the nature of law. There is a genuine dilemma here: if we assume that any means of social control which actually amounts to a form of governance are legal, then the ideal that government should rule by law becomes morally vacuous. Alternatively, if we impose some substantive moral constraints on what counts as law, then the ideal that governments should rule by law would amount to the ideal that governments should rule by *good* law, which, as we have already seen, is too broad an ideal. Now, one would be tempted to think that there must be other options between these two horns of the dilemma. That may be right. Still, the ideal that governments should rule by law remains somewhat unclear, as long as we do not have a sense of the alternatives. What this partly shows, however, is that this first aspect of the rule of law actually depends on the second. The idea that governments *should* rule by law must be premised on the assumption that rule by law, regardless of the law's specific content, is to be preferred to governance by other means of social control. And this immediately brings us to the second component of the rule of law, namely, that the law must be such that it can actually guide human conduct, and the further assumption that these necessary features of law embody certain virtues. In other words, unless we can first articulate what is unique about legal means of social control, and explain why those features promote certain goods, we cannot ground the ideal that governments should rule by law. This, I think, is why the second component of the rule of law has rightly attracted most of the scholarly attention.

2. The Law Should Be Such that it Can Actually Guide Human Conduct

Lon Fuller[9], Joseph Raz,[10] John Finnis,[11] Neil MacCormick,[12] and many others who have written about the rule of law all share the view that there are many ways

---

9 Fuller, *The Morality of Law*, mainly Ch. 2.

10 Raz, *The Authority of Law*, Ch. 11.

11 Finnis, *Natural Law and Natural Rights*, 270–276.

12 MacCormick, "Natural Law and the Separation of Law and Morals" in R. George (ed.), *Natural Law Theory*, 105.

in which one can fail to make law. There are certain conditions that the law has to meet in order to be able to fulfill its pivotal function of guiding human conduct. Law's ability, as a social instrument, to guide human conduct necessitates certain features the law must possess in order to fulfill such a function, regardless of its specific contents. Furthermore, there seems to be a fairly wide consensus on what those conditions are. Following is the list of these conditions, roughly along the lines originally suggested by Lon Fuller:[13]

i. Generality

Legal prescriptions must be issued at some level of generality. No legal system can function by addressing its prescriptions to individuals, one by one, or by addressing each particular act separately.

ii. Promulgation

For law to be able to guide human conduct, it must be promulgated to its subjects. People can only be *guided* by rules or prescriptions if they know about the existence of the rule or prescription. One can act *according to* a rule without being aware of the rule one actually follows, but then it is not the case that one is guided by the rule. It is, in a sense, the essence of *following* a rule that one is aware of the rule one follows.

iii. No retroactive rules

For the law to be able to guide human conduct, it must prescribe modes of behavior prospectively. Retroactive rules, namely, rules purporting to affect behavior which had already occurred prior to the rule's promulgation, cannot achieve the purpose of actually guiding human conduct.

iv. Clarity

Rules or prescriptions can only *guide* human conduct if the subjects understand what the rule requires. Promulgation is not enough. If you tell me that I ought to do φ, but I do not understand what φ is, or φ strikes me as confused or incomprehensible, then I cannot follow your prescription. A certain level of understanding of the rule is essential for rule-following.

---

13 *The Morality of Law*, Ch. 2.

v. No contradictory rules

For similar reasons, if the rule prescribes one thing and at the same time its contradiction, people cannot follow it. Or, if people are prescribed to do φ by one rule and not-φ by another rule, then there is no way in which they are able to follow both.

vi. No impossible prescriptions

A rule or prescription may be comprehensible and not inconsistent but, in practice, impossible to follow. A rule that people cannot follow is a rule that cannot guide human conduct, even if it is understood perfectly well. Suppose that you order me to fly without any mechanical assistance. I understand what you say, and I know what following your command would be like, but I just cannot do it. To guide human conduct, rules must require conduct that is possible for the rule subjects to perform.

vii. Stability

It is generally assumed that some level of stability over time is essential for the law to achieve its purposes, whatever they are. The law can change, of course, and changes in the law are not infrequent in any modern legal system, but the assumption is that *if changes are too frequent*, people cannot follow the law. This stems partly from the fact that many of our actions that the law purports to regulate require advance planning, preparation, and a certain level of guaranteed expectations about the future normative environment.

viii. Consistent application

For the law to be able to guide human conduct, it must maintain considerable congruence between the rules promulgated and their actual application to specific cases. In other words, the law cannot guide human conduct if actual deviations from it are not treated as such, namely, as deviations from the rule. This is a very complex requirement which entails a whole range of principles and practices. Generally speaking, it requires that the agencies dealing with the enforcement and application of law to specific cases actually apply those rules promulgated by the law. In practice, given the conditions of society and politics as we know it, this aspect of the rule of law may well require such important things as an independent and professional judiciary, relatively easy access to litigation, reliable enforcement agencies, and so on.

Assuming, then, that this or some other similar list of conditions is a set of features the law must possess in order to be able to guide human conduct, we must proceed to ask: Why is it a virtue of law to have these attributes, if it must have them anyway in order to fulfill its functions? The answer is, presumably, twofold. First, if feature x is functionally necessary for A to fulfill its designated task y, then having x is *functionally good* for A. For example, to the extent that knives are made to cut, and assuming that a knife must be sharp in order to cut, then the sharpness of the knife is functionally good; a sharp knife is a good knife. This must be true of the rule of law as well. To the extent that certain features are functionally necessary for law to guide human conduct, and to the extent that the law purports to guide human conduct, these features of the rule of law make the law good, that is, good in guiding human conduct.

Secondly, it is widely assumed that the law can possess these features to a greater or lesser extent, and the better it scores on each one of them, the better it functions in regulating behavior. The sharper the knife the better it cuts, and thus the better the knife it is.

Both of these points, however, require considerable modifications. Maintaining that the only virtue of the rule of law consists in a purely functional good, as described above, would seem to miss a great deal of what makes the rule of law worthy of our appreciation. After all, as I mentioned at the beginning, the rule of law ideal is closely associated with the ideal of a well-ordered society. We typically employ the rule of law as a critical standard, aspiring to better implementation of it, and criticizing aspects of the law which fall short of implementing it. The rule of law would not seem to deserve such normative attention if its only values were strictly functional, as the above argument suggests. Perhaps, ultimately, there is no more to it than that. Perhaps associating other values with the rule of law virtues will turn out to be a mistake. But at least it is worthwhile to explore the possibilities.

One possibility we should explore is the following. Purely functional values do not have any additional value beyond the value that is instantiated by the function they perform. The only good there is in the sharpness of a knife is that it makes the knife cut better. There is no additional value to sharpness (of a knife) as such. On the other hand, it is arguable that the rule of law virtues, though essentially functional, promote other goods that we value independently of, or in addition to, the function they serve in enabling the law to guide human conduct. For example, the condition of generality may ensure a certain level of impartiality which we value in addition to the fact that it enables the law to function as an instrument of social control. Or, to take another example, it is arguable that the condition of promulgation and publicity make the law politically transparent and open for public deliberation, which again, is something we value independently of law's ability to guide human conduct. Whether these, and similar, arguments withstand closer scrutiny remains to be seen. For now, suffice it to say that there may be complex relationships between the conditions of the rule of law, understood in purely functional terms, and a host of other goods that we value. This would explain why so many people regard the rule of law as an important ideal. They believe that upholding the conditions of the rule of law is likely to promote a whole set of goods that are worth promoting.

With respect to the second point, it is, indeed, quite true that the law can meet the conditions of the rule of law to various degrees. Just as one can fail to make law, one can succeed in making law to a greater or lesser extent. The sharper the knife, the better it cuts. Likewise, most commentators assume that the more a legal system instantiates the conditions of the rule of law, the better it functions in regulating human conduct, and in promoting other values which emerge from adherence to the rule of law. But this, as we shall see as we discuss the details of rule of law virtues, is far from true. Generally speaking, it is not necessarily the case that the more of a good thing, the better, and for two main reasons. First, implementation of ideals is rarely costless because values and ideals often conflict with each other. Promoting one kind of good often comes at the expense of another. Less trivially, however, there are some values or ideals that do not call, on their own grounds, for anything like full or perfect implementation. That is, not because we must give up on their full implementation, but because such values, on their own grounds, set only a *rough* standard whereby gross deviations from it would be wrong.[14]

B. The Rule of Law Virtues (Or, God Is in the Details)

1. Generality

i. Norm-subjects

The feature of generality pertains to two separate aspects of any given norm: the *norm-subjects* and the *norm-act*.[15] Generality is opposed to particular denotation,

---

14 For the distinction between these two types of ideals see Ch. 12, Section 3.

15 The distinction was introduced by G.H. von Wright, *Norm and Action*.

but it also admits of degrees. Let us consider the norm-subjects first. A norm can either be addressed to particular individuals, or addressed at some level of generality to individuals with a certain feature. Consider these two types of norms:

1. Individuals ***A, B, & C*** [particular norm-subjects] ought ***to φ*** [norm-act].

2. ***All X's with feature F*** [norm-subjects] ought ***to φ***.

Thus, **1** is the kind of norm which is addressed to particular individuals, and it can prescribe either a particular act, or some general act-type. For obvious reasons, it would be exceedingly inefficient for the law to be comprised of rules which are addressed to particular individuals. Indeed, exceptions are quite rare. But they do exist, and sometimes it makes sense to address the law to particular individuals.[16] Mostly, however, the law addresses its rules to subjects defined by a certain general feature in the form of **2**, above. Note that the generality of the definition of the norm-subjects does not entail anything about the size of the set of the norm-subjects to whom the rule applies. The size of the set depends entirely on the question of how many subjects actually possess the relevant feature ***F***. Maybe nobody does (as with, for example, "all individuals who have landed on Mars . . . ."), and maybe everybody does. And there are indefinite possibilities in between.

Generally speaking, there is no reason to assume that the size of the set of the norm-subjects is of any particular concern. Some rules should apply to everybody and others ought to apply to a very small set of people (e.g., rules governing the authority of the U.S. president or other officials). It is certainly not the case that the more the better, and I do not know of anyone who has claimed otherwise. But there is a genuine aspect of generality that does raise important and complicated issues. After all, we are not indifferent to the question of who are the norm-subjects of a given legal rule. Rules can be either overinclusive or underinclusive or, actually, both. But what makes a rule over- or underinclusive with respect to its norm-subjects? Essentially, it is determined by the substantive relevance of the feature ***F***, by which the norm-subjects are identified, to the norm-act, ***φ***, that the rule prescribes. The reasons for identifying the norm-subjects by feature ***F*** must be derived from the reasons for prescribing the norm-act ***φ***. For instance, if the

16 For example, the law can authorize a particular individual to act as a negotiator or arbitrator, etc., in a particular dispute. More interestingly, the prevalent use of ballot lists exemplifies that the law can address itself to a huge number of individuals by naming them.

norm is enacted to prevent a certain form of pollution by restricting the activities of the polluters, the characterization of the norm-subjects by feature ***F*** must be such as to capture those, but only those, who are the polluters. Otherwise the law would miss its own target. Needless to say, in practice this is not easily achieved, and numerous laws often end up being either overinclusive, underinclusive or, not infrequently, both.

This essential connection between the reasons for prescribing the norm and the appropriate characterization of its norm-subjects is precisely what is meant by generality (of the norm-subjects) as a rule of law virtue. The assumption is that, whatever the purpose of a legal norm, its purpose will be defeated if it does not address itself to the relevant set of norm-subjects. Let me call this the *generality-relevance principle*. On the face of it, it would seem that the generality-relevance principle is a *pure functional* value of law. Arguably, however, it is more than that. The generality-relevance principle may have valuable aspects over and beyond its pure functional value. To some extent it serves as a safeguard against favoritism or partiality. As opposed to individuals in their private dealings, who may well be justified in acting on the basis of partial reasons, favoring, for example, their family members just because they are family members, the law should act on the basis of general reasons. It is plausible to assume that in the public domain partiality is never justified. When the law favors or disfavors a certain class of people, it may only do so on the basis of general reasons that warrant the differential treatment, and not because the lawmakers or judges simply favor, for example, their relatives or supporters.

It is a truism, but an important one, that favoritism and partiality cannot be judged on the basis of the actual results of decisions and actions. The question is not whether one side ended up favored over another, but whether such uneven results were justified by the right reasons which apply to the case.[17] Compliance with the generality-relevance principle is crucially important in safeguarding against such unjustified favoritism since it requires that the norm's subjects be those who qualify as such only on the basis of the reasons for enacting the norm in the first place. In other words, the generality-relevance principle imposes a certain reason-based identification of the norm-subjects which is essentially general in nature, thus preventing partiality and favoritism of a certain kind. But of course, there are endless possibilities for the law to be biased, or prejudiced, or to unjustly discriminate

---

17 See my *Positive Law & Objective Values*, 150–151.

between groups of people, even if it strictly adheres to the generality-relevance principle. Apartheid in South Africa was quite legalistic in this respect. If the law is based on bad reasons, then the fact that its norm-subjects are identified on the basis of those reasons does not prevent it from being a bad law.

ii. Norm-act

The generality of the norm-act is a different matter altogether, and its connection to the rule of law virtues is much less clear. A norm-act can either be defined in terms of a particular action or omission one is required to perform (or avoid), or else it can be defined in terms of a general act-type. If I tell my daughter, "eat this peanut butter sandwich," I have prescribed a particular act; if I tell her "you should eat peanut butter sandwiches for breakfast," I have prescribed a general act-type. Needless to say, the law generally prescribes act-types, but there is nothing to prevent it from occasionally prescribing the performance of particular acts.[18] Examples of the latter are abundant. The law may authorize, for example, an official to perform a particular act (e.g., the U.S. president to wage war on Iraq), or it may require all public companies to pay a one-time tax on certain income, etc. Usually the law does not work in this way, simply because it is much more efficient to regulate behavior by generalizing actions under types and regulating types of behavior as such.

The level of generality with respect to the act-types prescribed by various legal norms admits of degrees. It has become familiar nomenclature by now to call "rules" those norms which prescribe relatively specific act-types, and "standards" those which prescribe relatively general act-types. This rules-standards distinction is a rather vague continuum where, on the one extreme, we would have very specific rules (such as "all F's must file a tax return by April fifteenth of every calendar year") and on the other, very general standards (such as "act with reasonable care"), with an indefinite number of possibilities in between. The legislative choice between enactment of rules or standards involves a great many complex issues which have, not surprisingly, engendered a considerable amount of literature. For example, it is arguable that the more norms are standardlike, the greater the judicial discretion in applying and interpreting them. Whether this is good or bad depends on the particular legal domain, relative institutional competence of courts, legislatures, administrative agencies, and so forth. We need not go into

18 Why J. Austin insisted otherwise is a bit of a mystery. Surely he was wrong about this. See his *The Province of Jurisprudence Determined*, 19.

this here. Suffice it to say that the distinction between rules and standards would seem to have one main bearing on the rule of law issue. Namely, it may be argued that the more general the norm-act prescribed by the legal norm, the less actual guidance to conduct it provides. If the law tells you to "be good," or to act with "reasonable care," or the like, there is very little that it actually says in terms of the specific behavior you are required to perform.

It may be worth keeping in mind that there is a distinction between the generality of a norm-act and its vagueness. A definition of a norm-act type can be more or less general, and it can also be more or less vague. For example, a rule requiring that we add vitamin C to every meal we eat is fairly general but not vague. However, a rule which prescribes that due care be taken when fixing electric appliances is perhaps less general but quite vague. Most legal "standards," however, are both general and vague.[19] In the context of the rule of law, both generality and vagueness raise the same kind of concern, although I presume that it is, actually, mostly vagueness that people tend to worry about.

But what, exactly, is the concern here? There are commentators who claim that overgenerality, or vagueness, of legal norms is a serious deficiency, and one which violates the rule of law virtues. The law's purpose is to guide human conduct, and if the legislature purports to guide conduct, it must do so in fairly specific manner, so that we can understand what the law actually requires and follow it. Leaving statutes and regulations too general or vague, it is claimed, undermines law's function in guiding conduct.

The problem is that there is an ambiguity here with respect to what "the law" prescribes. When a statute prescribes rather general standards, or when the definition of the act-type is vague, it normally leaves the specification of the details of the requisite behavior to other institutions, such as administrative agencies or the

---

19 See Frederick Schauer, *Playing by the Rules*, Ch. 2. Vagueness should not be confused with ambiguity. Ambiguity is, normally, a deficiency in lawmaking. If the law prescribes that you ought to do φ, but φ can either mean x or y, then it is, indeed, not clear what is it that you should do. To be more precise, there are two types of ambiguity: one word can mean two different things, like "bank," for example, which can mean either a financial institution or riverbank. This is rarely a practical problem since we can normally disambiguate according to the context of the expression. More frequently in the legal context, we face ambiguities that derive from the fact that a certain concept-word has both a narrow and a wide meaning, and it is often difficult to determine which one is meant. For example, the word "drug" can either mean, in its wider sense, any type of chemical substance that purports to have medical use, or it can mean, in the narrow colloquial sense, hallucinatory drugs. A nice example of such ambiguity in the legal context is the famous case of *Rector, Holy Trinity Church v. U.S.*, 143 U.S. 457 (1892).

courts. After all, somebody would have to determine what, for example, "reasonable care" under the circumstances is, and it is normally assumed that eventually administrative agencies or the courts will do that. Thus, from the perspective of the norm-subjects, it is more a question of *who* decides what exactly has to be done: whether it is the legislature, an administrative agency, or the courts. In other words, legal norms are rarely left in their very general, or vague, form; ultimately, some institution must specify in greater detail what the norm requires, and the question is basically one of institutional choice.

Furthermore, there are good reasons, quite familiar to every law student, why the legislatures are often justified in leaving the specification of their statutes to agencies and the courts. To mention just a few examples: consider those cases where the specification of legislative details is better left to administrative agencies due to their relative expertise; or those cases in which the legislature may rightly assume that the law should be developed by the courts, piecemeal, adjusting itself gradually to the specifics of individual cases and changing circumstances.[20] Finally, though perhaps most problematically, there are many cases in which the legislation is a result of a delicate compromise between opposing ideological factions, and a compromise can only be reached at a fairly abstract or general level, thus de facto delegating the lawmaking power to agencies or the courts.

Whether or not any of these, and similar, legislative decisions are warranted is a complicated issue that must be considered on the merits of particular cases. Those who oppose overgenerality, or vagueness, of legislation can make an argument based on considerations pertaining to separation of powers, limits on the delegation authority of the parliament, requirements of democratic decision procedures, or relative institutional competence. But none of this bears on the rule of law virtues.[21] The rule of law requires that the law be such that it can actually guide human conduct. It is indifferent about the question of *who* makes the law.

2. Promulgation

The requirement that the law should be promulgated seems so obvious that it barely needs any elaboration. After all, how can the law *prescribe* human conduct

---

20 As we shall see, judicial lawmaking may give rise to problems about retroactivity, but that is a separate issue.

21 With one exception, namely, the separation of powers. As we shall see later on, some aspects of separation of powers may derive from the rule of law requirements, but in a different context.

if it is kept secret? The law must be promulgated because it must *guide* human conduct. But suppose that this were not the case, and that human conduct could be directed, to some extent, without the awareness of the relevant rule. Suppose, for example, that instead of promulgating a new rule of conduct, the legislature could induce the behavior consistent with the rule by something like very sophisticated subliminal advertising. The rule would not be made public, but we would be "brainwashed," so to speak, to act in accordance with the rule by subliminal TV advertisements. Needless to say, we would find this appalling. But is it a violation of the rule of law? One might be tempted to reply that the answer is no: the rule of law requires only that the law be such as to be able to fulfill its functions. If it can do so by subliminal messages, so be it. To be sure, there are very good reasons to object to this method, but those reasons would have nothing to do with the rule of law virtues. Consider the analogy of the sharpness of knives: We think that a knife has to be sharp in order to cut, but this is just a question of technology. If we invent a new type of knife which cuts better without being sharp (say, with some laser technology), then sharpness will no longer be functionally necessary for knives to cut well. Similarly, if people can be brought to follow the legal rules without possessing an awareness of them, then promulgation would no longer be functionally necessary for the law to guide human conduct.

But the analogy is actually misleading. If the legal rules are somehow inculcated in the subjects by subliminal messages, then it is not really *the law* that guides their conduct, though the "law" makers might. In other words, this is an issue about the concept of law. Not every conceivable mode of affecting human conduct is legalistic. It is part of the concept of law that the law purports to affect human behavior by introducing new norms and changing old ones. The concept of a norm and conduct-guidance by norms is an essential aspect of what the law is. Norms, as such, necessarily purport to provide *reasons* for action. A norm cannot provide a reason for action, however, unless its subjects are aware of the norm and regard it as a reason for action.[22] Just like language, law must be public; its public aspect is an essential feature of its normativity.

But isn't there a puzzle here? After all, most people do not know the vast majority of the laws of their country. In a modern legal system, the sheer size of the law makes it practically impossible to be known by any single person. Not even expert

22 The subjects of a norm need not be aware of the precise formulation of the norm. But they must know that there is such a norm and have at least a rough idea of what the norm requires.

lawyers are familiar with the vast majority of the law of their jurisdiction. At best, they know how to find out what the law is. Even then, there is much less to find out about it than their naïve clients tend to assume.[23]

Perhaps all this is beside the point. Perhaps the rule of law requires promulgation only in a formal sense: it only requires that once a law is enacted, it must be put in the public domain, so that those who want to know what the law is have the opportunity to find out. We do not need to know the vast majority of the laws because most of them do not affect our dealings. And when they might, all we need is access to those agents who can tell us about the law which is relevant to us. Then we will know all that is necessary for our pertinent purposes.

There is, of course, a great deal of truth in this. There is, as it should be, a considerable amount of *division of labor* in the regulation of behavior by law. Different segments of society are entrusted, as it were, with different segments of the law, and various agents provide relevant information when it is needed. Like so many other aspects of our life in a modern society, only a complex division of labor ensures a practical way of regulating behavior by numerous and complex rules. Once again, the analogy with language is not irrelevant: there is also a complex division of labor in the use of language.[24] Nobody knows everything that there is to know about the meaning and the precise reference of all the concepts which comprise natural languages. Nevertheless, we are able to use language correctly and regard its rules as normative because there are numerous experts who know the details. When the practical need arises, we can rely on others who know better.

The conclusion so far is very limited, however. We have seen that the law cannot be a system of norms unless it is essentially public. Publicity is an essential aspect of law's normativity. But this does not entail that each and every norm must be made known to everybody. The desired *extent* of promulgation remains an open question. Many laws could be made available only to their specific addressees without being disclosed to others. It seems, then, that from a purely functional-normative perspective, the law must be promulgated only to those subjects whose behavior it purports to regulate. Sometimes this comprises the population at large, but many

23 First year law students discover this in the first few weeks of classes; they suddenly realize that there is much less certainty about what the law requires than they had assumed when they enrolled for their legal studies. At first students tend to find this discovery utterly frustrating. Later on they realize that this uncertainty is rather conducive to the prosperity of their professional careers.

24 See H. Putnam, *Mind, Language and Reality*, 227–229.

times the addressees of the legal rules are a very small subset of the population. Thus, from a purely functional perspective, there is no reason to assume that all laws must be promulgated to the public at large.

The value of promulgation, however, is not confined to this functional aspect. Making the law public renders it politically transparent and open for public deliberation and criticism, which we value regardless of the law's purely functional aspects. We can have good reasons for criticizing laws even if they do not purport to guide our conduct, even if we are not their intended addressees. Arguably, the less laws are known to the public, the less they would be exposed to critical appraisal.[25] Assuming, then, that the possibility of critical appraisal of the law is a general good, we seem to have good reasons to expect the law to be made widely available to the public at large.

The more the better? Not necessarily. Ignorance of the law is sometimes bliss. Meir Dan-Cohen has argued, very convincingly I think, that in the sphere of criminal law, sometimes partial ignorance of the law is morally desirable.[26] Consider, for example, the relatively recent defense, or quasi-defense, in criminal law referred to as the "battered women's syndrome."[27] In considering whether to recognize such a defense, the law faces a familiar dilemma. On the one hand, values of compassion call for legal recognition of such a defense. On the other hand, there are serious worries about the deterrence-deficit that might result from such legal recognition. After all, the law does not want to encourage women, even if they are subject to serious abuse over the years, to get rid of their abusive husbands by killing them. Thus, it would be ideal from the law's perspective if the law could conceal from its potential addressees that there is such a defense, but then grant the defense whenever it is warranted under the circumstances. Furthermore, the less a particular defendant knew about the defense when she committed the crime, the more credible her reliance on it in court. Needless to say, in practice such an "acoustic separation," as Dan-Cohen called it, is very difficult to achieve, but the law does have certain means of achieving it in part

---

25 See J. S. Mill, *On Liberty*, Ch. 2.

26 See M. Dan-Cohen, "Decision Rules and Conduct Rules: On Acoustic Separation in Criminal Law," reprinted in Dan-Cohen, *Harmful Thoughts*, 37.

27 Experts have come to realize that there is severe cumulative psychological effect on women who are subjected to continuous abuse by their husbands which might reach a breaking point at some stage, even if at that particular stage the abusive husband's behavior does not amount to a grave provocation. As consequence, women have occasionally killed their husbands in act of otherwise almost inexplicable rage. Many jurisdictions have recently recognized this cumulative aspect of provocation, thus giving effect to its consequences by recognizing some sort of defense called the "battered women's syndrome" (usually reducing a murder charge to manslaughter). This is not Dan-Cohen's example but it refers to the same idea.

(more on this later). At least, it demonstrates that some ignorance of the law is not necessarily a deficiency.

How much can we generalize from such examples? That is very difficult to say. As Dan-Cohen carefully demonstrated, the virtues of such partial "acoustic separation" apply to many defenses in criminal law, as well as to the definition of many offenses. Criminal law often faces the difficult dilemma between an *ex ante* interest in deterrence and an *ex post* concern with human compassion. There are numerous things people ought not to do, but under certain circumstances, if they do them, we should partly forgive them and forgo their punishment. In such cases, deliberately creating partial ignorance of the law is a mechanism through which the law can reconcile its conflicting interests in deterrence and compassion. But is this limited to the criminal law? Presumably not. There may be other areas in the law where a similar dilemma, and perhaps a similar solution, exist.

Let me pull some of the strands together. We have seen that in one important sense, promulgation is an essential element of law's normativity. The law is a system of norms, and norms purport to provide reasons for action, so it must be publicized to those whose action it purports to guide. But, as we have seen, such a functional explanation does not fully capture the values we associate with the requirement of promulgation. From a purely functional perspective, many laws need not be made entirely public. To the extent that we have reasons to require a wider promulgation of the law, those reasons must be derived from other, nonfunctional values, such as the need for public scrutiny, open deliberation, and critical appraisal of the laws of our community. In other words, the promulgation of law serves deliberative and critical values over and beyond its role in securing the normative efficiency of the law. On the other hand, it should not be assumed that promulgation is always morally costless. Under certain circumstances, it is better if people are not entirely aware of the laws governing their situation. There is, in such cases, a certain conflict between the political values of promulgation, ensuring public scrutiny and critical appraisal, and considerations of individual justice or human compassion. From a political perspective, perhaps we would always want to put the law under glaring light, but there is something to be said for the need to resolve some subtleties if not quite in the darkness, at least in the twilight.

3. No Retroactive Rules

One may wonder how the law can purport to guide human conduct if it is enacted after the conduct has taken place. Surely, retroactive guidance of conduct is an oxymoron. The fact that retroactive laws do exist, however, and much more abundantly than laypersons often assume, might indicate that guiding conduct is not the law's only function. I do not intend to suggest that retroactive laws are always justified, or even if they are, that they do not raise serious concerns about efficiency and fairness. Far from it. My only suggestion at the moment is to proceed with caution.

Presumably, the bluntest violation of the no-retroactivity requirement of the rule of law would occur in the case of a criminal law creating a new type of offense that has retroactive effect. We would find it appalling, and rightly so, if the law purports to render a certain mode of conduct which has been legal in the past a criminal offense retroactively. Criminalizing something which a person had no reason to think would be a criminal offense when engaging in the pertinent behavior would be utterly wrong. Note that in such blunt violations of the rule of law, our reasons for concern would be twofold: First, the retroactive law would simply fail from a functional perspective. It would fail in guiding conduct since it would attempt to guide conduct that had already occurred. But we would also have other, moral, reasons to object to criminalization of past conduct. We would see it as an affront to human dignity and freedom. People deserve to be treated in a rational and dignified way, whereby the law must set its standards of conduct in advance, standards with which we can either choose to comply or willingly disobey.

There is an important caveat, however, that needs to be mentioned here. It is certainly true that in a relatively just legal system, people are morally entitled to assume that behavior which is not prohibited by law will not become prohibited retroactively. But not all legal systems are even minimally just. If the legal system is profoundly corrupt (as it was, for instance, in Nazi Germany, in South Africa during the apartheid era, and still is in many regions of the world), citizens *are not morally entitled to assume* that whatever is legal at the time is something that they are permitted to do. There is a great deal to be said against the assumption that the law cannot criminalize, even retroactively, wicked behavior just because it had not been prohibited by the law at the time it occurred. Of course, in such cases, the law does not purport to guide conduct retroactively; that cannot be done. The retroactive criminalization of such wrongful conduct is aimed at punishment alone. Its value is mainly expressive, conveying the message that legalism should not be allowed to shield atrocities.[28]

28 A recent example is the criminal prosecution of East German guards who followed orders to shoot-to-kill people who tried to escape to the West over the Berlin wall. See R. Alexy, "A Defense of Radbruch's Formula," in D. Dyzenhaus, *Recrafting the Rule of Law: The Limits of Legal Order*, 15.

Bearing this important exception in mind, however, we should return to consider the problems of retroactivity in legal systems which are at least minimally just. In such cases, it would be fair to assume that retroactive criminalization of behavior is a double failure of the law; both in functional terms, as the law would fail to actually guide conduct, and in moral terms, as the law would fail to treat its subjects with due dignity and respect. There are many other cases of retroactive laws, however, which are much more complex than this, and we should consider them in some detail. In particular, I will consider two types of retroactive laws: those which purport to rectify a previous legal mistake and, mainly, judicial retroactivity in the application of the law.

Retroactive laws are sometimes justified—required, actually—to correct a mistake created by the law itself. Even with the best intentions, the law sometimes inadvertently creates a problem that must be corrected by enacting a law that retroactively nullifies a previous one. Suppose, to generalize from Fuller's example,[29] that the law had made the validity of a certain legal action conditional upon a certain element, say E, assuming that E is readily available to the parties concerned. As it happens, however, it turns out that the assumption was wrong, and E is not available. Furthermore, suppose that the relevant parties were not even aware of the fact that they needed to obtain E for the validity of their transactions and went ahead without E. When the mistake is discovered, the law should correct it, and the only sensible way of doing so would be to enact a new law that retroactively nullifies the requirement of E for the validity of the relevant transaction. In such cases, no harm is done to anyone, and the retroactivity of the law poses no reasons for concern.[30]

Far more pervasive, however, is the retroactive effect of any change in the law which is introduced by judicial decisions. Within the common-law tradition, judges have ample legal tools to introduce changes in the law by their judicial holdings. Previously settled cases can be overruled or, much more frequently, distinguished by later courts. In common-law jurisdictions, higher courts have the

---

29 See *The Morality of Law*, 53–54.

30 What if there is a rule or convention in a certain legal domain that makes it clear to the norm-subjects that retroactive rules might be enacted in that domain? Arguably, a limited convention to this effect exists in U.S. tax legislation. In this context, the function of the convention is to signal to the law-subjects that they should be careful not to exploit legislative errors as they might be corrected retroactively. For obvious reasons, such a legislative policy is generally undesirable since it undermines people's ability to rely on the law as a guide to their conduct. Sometimes, however, reliance on the law is simply unreasonable. (I am indebted to Elizabeth Garrett here.)

power to overrule their previous decisions, and thus change the law quite straightforwardly. Overruling is not done very often, partly, I presume, because its retroactive effect is so obvious to all parties concerned. Distinguishing previous cases, however, is a legal power that can be exercised by all courts, as is often done, thereby introducing gradual, almost surreptitious modifications of previous holdings, typically by narrowing them down to increasingly specific circumstances. Unsettled cases can become settled by judicial innovation or extension of previous rulings by analogy and other familiar forms of judicial reasoning.[31]

All these changes that are introduced into the law by judicial lawmaking have a de facto retroactive effect. The new decision, which changes the law, applies to the parties to the litigation and often to many other parties who behaved similarly under similar circumstances. Thus, any judicial decision which introduces a change in the law actually changes the law in a retroactive manner for the parties concerned.[32] Is this necessarily a problem? Does it give rise to functional and moral concerns?

The main worry about the retroactivity of judicial decisions concerns the frustration of legitimate expectations.[33] One of the main virtues of the rule of law consists in the value that we attach to the predictability of the legal environment. People should be allowed to lead their lives and conduct their business in a way which allows them to plan their conduct. The very idea of planning is only rational, however, if there is a certain level of certainty as to the future normative consequences of one's choices.[34] Thus, once again, we can see that law's failure to create a predictable legal environment would amount to a double flaw: both functional and moral. From a functional perspective, the law would fail to guide people's conduct since it would undermine their ability to plan their conduct in advance.

---

31 See Raz, "Law and Value in Adjudication," in his *The Authority of Law*, Ch. 10.

32 This is not quite accurate: In principle, judges could render decisions which would have only prospective effect and sometimes, though rarely, they have done so. But as a general policy, this would be extremely problematic, both from a political perspective, as it would highlight the legislative role of judges in a manner which is politically problematic, and, mainly, because it would seriously undermine the incentive of potential litigants to bring forth their cases. If litigants knew in advance that their success in court might not result in a decision that affects them, why would they bother to spend their resources on expensive litigation? Some jurisdictions have a practice of referring some hard cases back to the legislature, but these tend to be rare cases not frequently used.

33 To be sure, retroactive legislation is not the only way in which the law can frustrate legitimate expectations. For example, a statute which repeals the mortgage interest deduction for all future interest payments is prospective, but it unsettles the expectations that homebuyers had when they bought homes and committed themselves to paying a certain amount of interest for decades.

34 Not complete certainty, of course; we frequently plan our conduct under conditions of (partial) uncertainty.

And from a moral perspective, such a legal regime would manifest a profound disrespect for people's freedom and autonomy.[35] However, all this is a matter of degree. People ought to have a certain range of legitimate expectations about the future normative environment, but they are not entitled to assume that nothing will change in the future.

The problem with the retroactivity of judicial lawmaking, however, concerns the question of *how* the change in the law is introduced, and not the change itself. Changes in the law that are introduced by the legislature can provide due notice about the expected change, and thus allow the subjects to accommodate their conduct accordingly. On the other hand, when the law is changed through a judicial decision, it is changed retroactively with respect to the particular litigants addressing the court. That is why judicial lawmaking seems to be at odds with the value of protecting legitimate expectations.

The retroactivity of judicial decisions would seem to be much less of a problem in the cases of previously *unsettled* law. When the law is not clear, litigants cannot claim that they had legitimate expectations that the judicial decision frustrates. Of course they may have had expectations, but those expectations cannot be regarded as legitimate in the context of unsettled law. What makes an expectation about the law legitimate is the fact that it relies on the law as it is, and not as the litigant would want it to be. To the extent that the law is not clear, frustrating expectations about it hardly raises a serious concern.

But what about those changes that are introduced by judicial lawmaking in areas of law which had been previously settled? It is difficult to deny that in such cases the judicial decision does, indeed, frustrate legitimate expectations. Presumably, it is the price we have to pay for the social benefit of allowing the courts to improve the law and adapt it to changing circumstances.

Dworkin thought that there is a way around this problem. In fact, he had to produce a solution because Dworkin has long held that all law is, ultimately, settled. The solution derives from his famous distinction between decisions based on *policy* and those based on *principle*. A decision based on policy, Dworkin claimed, is based on collective societal goals. "Arguments of policy justify a political decision by showing that the decision advances or protects some collective goal of the

---

35 Cf. F. Hayek, *The Road to Serfdom*, Ch. 6.

community as a whole."[36] In contrast, a decision based on principle is one which is justified by an appeal to preexisting rights. Thus, Dworkin argued, as long as judges refrain from policy decisions and confine their judicial reasoning to considerations of principle, they would not violate the requirement to avoid retroactivity, because their decisions would simply reaffirm preexisting rights: "If the plaintiff has a right against the defendant, then the defendant has a corresponding duty, and it is that duty, not some new duty created in court, that justifies the award against him. Even if the duty has not been imposed upon him by explicit prior legislation, there is . . . no [more] injustice in enforcing the duty . . . ."[37]

Unfortunately, however, this solution is illusory. To begin with, judicial decisions, like many complex decisions in our lives, are more often than not overdetermined by reasons. A certain change in the law can be justified both because it advances certain societal goals and because it better protects the rights of the relevant parties. An example can illustrate the point. Consider the famous decision by Justice Cardozo in *MacPherson v. Buick Motor Co.*[38], which effectively introduced into American law the doctrine of product liability. Prior to this case, both English and U.S. law had not quite recognized the liability of a manufacturer to the ultimate consumer for damages caused to the latter by their defective products (mostly due to lack of privity of contract). Cardozo, in a rather bold and far-reaching decision, held that manufacturers should be held liable to consumers for any defective product if the producer should have known that the product *could* become dangerous if defective.

It is not difficult to see that Cardozo's ruling lends itself to an analysis both of a decision based on principle and one based on policy. On the one hand, it can be described as a decision which recognizes the right of consumers to a minimal level of safety of the products they purchase. On the other hand, the decision is also based on considerations of policy, reasoning, in effect, that manufacturers are the best cost-avoiders of accidents potentially caused by their dangerous products. These two types of reasons (if, indeed, they are two distinct types) are not mutually exclusive. It would be rather odd to say, however, that the *MacPherson* decision frustrates legitimate expectations from one perspective but not from the other. Generally speaking, the question of whether legitimate expectations have been frustrated cannot depend on the kind of reasoning that the court employs to

---

36 Ronald Dworkin, *Taking Rights Seriously*, 82.

37 *Ibid.* at 85.

38 217 N.Y. 382 (1916).

justify its decision. It depends on the question of how settled and certain the previous legal situation had been. If the Buick Motor Co. was right to assume that it was not legally liable to consumers for defects in its products, then the *MacPherson* decision caught Buick by surprise. And the question of whether it was right to make such an assumption simply cannot depend on how Cardozo justified his ruling in that case. It can only depend on how settled the law had actually been prior to *MacPherson*.[39]

Judicial decisions, then, must be acknowledged as introducing legal changes which often have, at least with respect to the particular litigants, retroactive effect. Most judges and jurists are quite aware of that, and some of them believe that this in itself is sufficient to warrant a policy of judicial restraint, requiring judges to refrain from changing the law. Introducing legal changes is always better left to the legislature, they say, since the latter can do so prospectively with due warning.[40] Although the concern about retroactivity is a serious one, the conclusion is far too quick, even from the limited perspective of the rule of law virtues. After all, flexibility in the application of the law is partly what makes the law an effective tool of social control. The sheer number and complexity of legal issues in a modern society renders it impossible for any legislature to deal with all the subtleties and legal ramifications of the entire normative system. A modern legal system must rely on other agents, like judges and administrative agencies, to work out these numerous details and adjust the law to specific cases and changing circumstances. Presumably, much more harm will be done by a legal system that does not allow for such flexibility in the application of the law than the harm in retroactivity which could be avoided by it.[41]

4. Clarity of rules

Perhaps there is not much that needs to be said about the requirement of clarity. Surely, a rule can only guide conduct if its putative subjects understand what the rule requires. This doesn't mean, however, that each and every legal rule must be clear to the ordinary citizen. A great many rules are not addressed to ordinary

---

39 It is interesting to note that Cardozo in his opinion is at pains to show how unsettled and uncertain the law had been prior to that case.

40 This was precisely the gist of the dissenting opinion of New York's Judge Bartlett in *MacPherson*.

41 None of the above is meant to justify Justice Cardozo's particular decision in *MacPherson*. There is much to be said in favor of the dissent's position arguing that such an important social and economical change in the law should have been left for the legislature to introduce.

people, but to various officials and legal experts. The requirement of clarity only requires that those who need to understand what the law is should be able to do so.[42] The only question that we need to ask, therefore, is whether it is generally true that the clearer and more comprehensible the law is, the better. The patient reader should not be surprised by now if I propose a negative answer to this question. Clarity, I submit, is not always a virtue. The clearer the law, the more rigid it is, and rigidity is often a deficiency in the law. In other words, it is partly because the law is sometimes obscure that courts and other law application agencies have the flexibility they need to adjust the law to particular needs and circumstances. As I have just noted above, some degree of flexibility in the application of the law is also a rule of law virtue.

In addition, we should also bear in mind that the law is often obscure not because the legislators (or other lawmakers) have made a mistake in its drafting. In a pluralistic, democratic society, legislation is often a result of a delicate compromise between conflicting views and purposes. Sometimes the only way to achieve a compromise is by forgoing maximum clarity. Parties to a dispute may find it easier to agree on a formula which is not entirely clear, hoping (as they often do without too much delusion) that future interpretation will favor their stance. If we could envisage a world in which no level of obscurity in lawmaking is allowed, we might find that world to be one in which the only law enacted is the law supported by a solid ruling majority. A "winner takes all" strategy, as this would entail, is a high price to pay for the advantages of maximum clarity. Whether one thinks that the need to compromise in a pluralistic society is a regrettable fact obviously depends on one's moral-political views about the values of pluralism. I cannot go into this here. Suffice it to say that for those who regard pluralism itself as a virtue, the need to compromise is not necessarily a regrettable fact. To the extent that a certain level of unclarity tends to facilitate desirable compromises, maximum clarity may not always be the objective that we ought to seek. I will say more on this in the next section.

5. No Contradiction

It would be unfortunate, and quite useless, if the law prescribed the performance of one thing and at the same time its exact opposite. But this doesn't happen very often. On the other hand, the law is never entirely coherent. If only because so

---

42 On the possible discrepancy between officials and ordinary citizens understanding of the law, see the discussion of the application of law in sub-section 8 below.

many agents are involved in creating, developing and modifying the law, it can hardly be expected that the entire body of law, even in a particular legal domain, will manifest a coherent set of norms. Surely, there is some level of coherence which the law must have in order to function properly in guiding the conduct of its subjects. But it is equally clear that from a functional perspective, the law can tolerate a considerable amount of incoherence. Whether this is necessarily regrettable is a difficult question to answer, partly because legal coherence is itself a rather complicated idea. The law can manifest incoherence in at least three ways: logically, pragmatically, and morally. Let me explain.

Suppose that the law prescribes that all F's should φ under circumstances C, and, at the same time, that all F's should not-φ under circumstances C. In this case the law is simply inconsistent in a straightforward logical way:[43] it requires its subjects to do one thing and its exact opposite under the same circumstances. Therefore, it doesn't allow for any way in which people can comply with one of the law's requirements without necessarily violating another. This kind of inconsistency is both a functional and a moral failure. It undermines law's ability to actually guide conduct, and it puts people in a morally unacceptable predicament. Since the law is rarely incoherent in such a blatant way, I will not dwell on this further.

Pragmatic inconsistency of the law is a much more frequent and familiar occurrence.[44] The law is pragmatically incoherent when it actually promotes aims, policies, or patterns of conduct which practically conflict. For example, suppose that one part of the law, say, a certain tax exemption, may have the (intended) effect of encouraging people to increase their long-term savings, while another provision of the law, say, setting very low interest rates, may have the opposite effect, encouraging people to spend more of their income on purchases of consumer goods. What happens in such cases is simply the fact that the (intended or unintended) actual ramifications of a legal regime create opposing incentives for people's behavior. Similar practical inconsistencies may arise out of different judicial decisions. For example, in one case, a judicial determination placing product liability on manufacturers may have been driven by the objective of encouraging manufacturers to internalize the accident-costs of their products, while another judicial decision, concerning the interpretation of warranties, could have the opposite

43 Assuming that these are not empty sets. Another example of logical inconsistency would be the following: suppose the law prescribes that "all F's should φ" and that "all G's should not φ," and there are persons who are both F and G.

44 See Raz, *The Authority of Law*, 201.

effect, providing manufacturers with ways of avoiding such costs and transferring them to the consumers. Such pragmatic inconsistencies are often very difficult to detect. Not infrequently, it would be genuinely controversial whether a pragmatic incoherence actually exists or not. It may largely depend on economic, social, or psychological theories which are notoriously inconclusive.

Finally, and most problematically, the law can be morally incoherent. The law is morally incoherent if its various prescriptions and their underlying justifications cannot be subsumed under one coherent moral theory. Or, we could say that in such cases there isn't a conceivable single rational moral agent whose moral point of view could justify the entire set of prescriptions under consideration. I think that this is basically what Dworkin means by the value of integrity in law. Whether we should expect the law to be morally coherent in this way is the topic of chapter two.

6. No Impossible Prescriptions

Generally speaking, the law would fail to guide behavior if it purported to guide it in a way which is simply impossible to comply with. If the law prescribes the impossible, it fails both in its functional aspect, and quite often, in its moral legitimacy as well. The functional failure consists in the fact that the law would not achieve its own purpose in guiding conduct. The moral failure would consist in the fact that the law would not treat its subjects with due respect. Asking someone to do something that he cannot possibly do, especially when you know this in advance, typically involves an offensive message; it is like telling your subordinate that he ought to have been taller, or smarter, or the like. Since you know that he cannot become taller (or smarter, etc.), you are, in effect, criticizing a deficiency over which your addressee has no control; you just manifest disappointment in him. It is no longer a genuine attempt to guide conduct, but an expression of disapproval. In personal relations, such criticism, though perhaps somewhat offensive, is not always out of place. But there are good reasons to hold that, generally, the law should not be in the business of such critical appraisals of its subjects.

There are, however, justified exceptions to this principle. To begin with, "impossible" is too strong a word here. Most instances of conduct which are potentially subject to legal regulation would not be actually impossible to follow but rather just too difficult or costly given the circumstances. The law may require, for instance, investing in such precautionary measures with respect to a certain activity as to render the activity itself unprofitable. But of course, this would not necessarily indicate that the law has failed to guide conduct as it purported to. Perhaps the precautions are so valuable that they outweigh the value of the activity which they would render out of business. These kinds of questions are addressed by various legal agents on a day-to-day basis, and there is very little room here for generalities or *a priori* guidelines.

Similarly, compliance with the law can be morally too costly. It may require the subjects, say, to perform an action that they deem morally imperative to avoid. Once again, it would be difficult to come up with general guidelines about such issues since they involve complicated moral-political questions which vary from case to case. Some of these cases concern the question of the justification and the limits of conscientious objection; others concern the question of the enforcement of morality by law and the moral limits of, e.g., criminal law; at other times the concerns about the moral burden that the law imposes involve difficult questions about distributive justice and equality, and so on.

Furthermore, not infrequently the law is justified in setting standards of conduct which may be somewhat unrealistically high. The law may have, in certain areas, a symbolic or educational function which permits it to set higher standards than those with which some of its subjects could comply. For example, it is arguable that in societies which have a disturbing history of racial discrimination, we should expect the law to impose very strict, even harsh, antidiscrimination laws that in other societies might not be warranted. There is in such cases a symbolic and educational value to setting standards so high, given the past iniquities and their potentially lingering effects. Needless to say, the higher the law sets its standards, the more it runs the risk of noncompliance and failing to guide conduct.[45] But perhaps the risk of a certain functional failure in the law is sometimes a reasonable price to pay for such symbolic and educational objectives.[46]

7. Stability over Time

There is very little that needs to be said about this requirement of the rule of law. The desirable level of the stability of the law over time is a very rough standard.

---

45 The dangers of this were all too apparent in the wake of the famous *Brown v. Board of Education* case, 347 U.S. 483 (1954), requiring the federal judiciary to engage in a very aggressive continuous enforcement campaign which lasted for decades, and was often close to miserable failure.

46 Another familiar example of laws which often set high standards are the technology-forcing laws which explicitly set standards not yet attainable, aiming to force the industry to invest in R&D for purposes of developing new technology.

We know that the law must change over time, and we also know that it would be difficult to follow the law if it changed too frequently. But it would be absurd to assume that we can have a precise notion of the ideal pace of change. This requirement of the rule of law is basically a rough standard, whereby gross deviations from it, in both directions, constitute a deficiency. We can criticize changes in the law if they are too frequent or too slow. But it hardly makes any sense to say that a given change in the law is ever so slightly too fast, or just a little bit too slow. A rough standard of stability over time is what law needs to apply in order to function properly.

8. Congruence between the Rules and Their Application

Perhaps this is the most complicated and intricate requirement of the rule of law. Although the general idea is clear enough, its various ramifications are convoluted and often difficult to evaluate. The general idea is that for the law to function properly, its promulgated rules must be the rules which are actually applied to specific cases by the various law enforcement agencies. Rules cannot guide conduct unless deviations from the rule are actually treated as such, namely, as deviations from the rule. In order to see to what extent the law can fail in this regard we need only observe those legal systems where corruption is rampant and bribery is the standard means of achieving almost any official result. Often enough, we would find that those societies have elaborate anti-bribery laws. It is not the law on the books which measures the law's success in guiding human conduct, but its application in practice. The application mechanisms of the law are therefore crucially important in determining law's success or failure in fulfilling its putative functions. What those application mechanisms need to be obviously depends on the specific circumstances of our social lives and the political environment in which we live. Most commentators agree, for instance, that unless there is an independent and relatively powerful judiciary, little would guarantee that the laws on the books are the laws applied to specific cases. Some commentators go so far as to suggest that this aspect of the rule of law requires a full-fledged doctrine of separation of powers. Whether this is generally the case is somewhat doubtful, but we need not go into this here. Suffice it to say that the judiciary is certainly not the only actor in this game; other law application agencies play a crucial role as well. There are countless officials, including within the executive branch, whose job it is to determine, in various domains, how the law is applied in practice.

Generally speaking, the congruence between the legal rules and their application raises two types of issues. First, there is a whole set of questions about the appropriate institutional design which would be required in order to implement this aspect of the rule of law, some of which we have mentioned above: What is the level of separation of powers appropriate for the relevant society? What kind of administrative agencies are needed, and what is the desired level of their independence? How should judges be appointed and what kind of authority should they have? How easy should the access to adjudication be? And there are countless other questions of a similar type. But in addition to these institutional issues, which I will not discuss here, there is another question that arises with respect to the *desired* level of congruence between the law and its application to specific cases: should we necessarily aspire to a perfect match? The more, the better? Let me explain the question.

Kelsen (in)famously maintained that all laws are actually just fragments of laws, forming part of a long list of conditions addressed to officials and authorizing them to impose certain sanctions when those conditions are met.[47] In other words, Kelsen thought that the law is always ultimately addressed to officials, instructing them how and under which conditions to use force. Those laws which *seem* to be addressed to the general public are only part of the conditions constituting the instructions to officials how to impose the sanction of the law when the appropriate conditions are met. That Kelsen erred in this generalization is hardly deniable. Surely the law cannot be addressed only to officials, since a major part of its function is to guide the conduct of its putative subjects.[48] But it is equally clear that part of the law functions in the way in which Kelsen describes, namely, instructing numerous officials how to apply the law and how to impose official coercion on various parties. But even this modest version of Kelsen's thesis poses the danger of entrenching a misconception: it is all too tempting to think that the part of the law which is addressed to its putative subjects necessarily forms a fragment of the set of instructions to officials about the appropriate application of those legal prescriptions. This is misleading, however, since it is not conceptually necessary that the rules addressed to the putative subjects of the law be the same rules which form part of the instructions to the relevant officials about how to apply the law. As Meir Dan-Cohen convincingly argued,[49] these two sets of rules, namely, the rules addressed to the public and those addressed to officials, need not be the same. Whether they ought to be the same is an open question which needs to be determined on normative grounds.

---

47 See H. Kelsen, *General Theory of Law and State*, 45.

48 See H.L.A. Hart, *The Concept of Law*, 38–42.

49 Dan-Cohen, *Harmful Thoughts*, 38–40.

In order to see this, Dan-Cohen asks us to imagine a world divided into two separate chambers: In one chamber we would have the general public, law's subjects, so to speak, and in the other chamber we would have the various officials who are supposed to apply the law to specific cases. Now suppose that the legislature could announce the law to each one of these chambers separately, and suppose that they are acoustically separated so that the announcements to one chamber cannot be heard in the other. Surely, there would have to be a considerable level of congruence between these two sets of rules, but isn't it clear that this congruence need not be perfect? Some rules announced to the public might be somewhat different from those which are promulgated to the officials' chamber. Perhaps such incongruence would not be desirable, but that is something which needs to be determined on normative grounds.

Needless to say, the real world cannot be divided into two acoustically separated chambers. But some level of a partial acoustic separation is possible, and it exists in practice. The very need for considerable legal expertise in different areas of the law attests to that. What "malice aforethought," for example, means to judges and criminal lawyers is probably quite different from what it means to the general public. The technicalities in legal language and the sheer complexity of the law allow for a certain level of acoustic separation, and raise the possibility of some incongruence between the laws promulgated to the public at large and those addressed to officials. The question of whether such potential discrepancies are desirable or not is, indeed, a normative question, directly pertaining to the aspect of rule of law under consideration.

Dan-Cohen argues, and I think rightly so, that some discrepancy between the content of the rules addressed to the public and those addressed to officials is not always regrettable. On the contrary, it enables the law, particularly in the criminal domain, to accommodate conflicting purposes. For example, the law may instruct judges and other officials to interpret various offences in a very technical and rather restrictive manner, thus making sure that only behavior which is surely and unquestionably wrong would be subject to punishment. At the same time, however, the law would achieve better deterrent effect, and perhaps, on the whole, better social results, if the general public's perception of such offenses is more expansive.[50] After all, the good citizen who wants to be guided by the law would

---

50 But of course, not the other way around: if the public perception of the offense is more restricted than its official understanding, people will think that an action is legal whereas in fact, it is not. That would certainly violate the rule of law. See Dan-Cohen, *Harmful Thoughts*, 90, fn. 106.

want to be on the safe side, avoiding behavior which is on the verge of illegality. But again, in case the citizen happens to stumble and finds himself in front of a court, the judge should also play it safe and convict the defendant only if she is very confident that the conduct was, indeed, legally wrong. Thus, the fact that the rules are understood somewhat differently by the public and the judges enables both to be on the safe side, as it were.[51]

But this is not so simple. Consider a noncriminal case first: Suppose we assume that similar considerations apply to contract law as well. Suppose that it would be better if people believed that their contractual obligations are somewhat stricter than the technical-legal doctrines actually require. The problem with such a situation is rather apparent here: the more there is a discrepancy between general perceptions and legal technicalities, the greater the *relative advantage* of those parties with better access to legal expertise, who are, most often, the wealthier parties or the repeat players (who are usually the wealthier litigants anyway). This situation raises a concern about equality. A systematic lack of congruence between general perceptions of the law and its actual application to specific cases normally plays into the hands of those who can afford better access to legal expertise. The same holds in criminal law as well, though perhaps less disturbingly in those cases in which crime is not premeditated. Thus, even if there is some social benefit to be gained by a certain incongruence between the rules which are addressed to the general public and the rules addressed to law application officials, as Dan-Cohen argues, this benefit must be weighed against the cost in terms of inequality between potential litigants. To be sure, I am not denying the possibility of such a benefit but only its scope. Perhaps the conclusion is that Dan-Cohen's argument should be limited, as it may have been intended to be anyway, to very specific instances in the criminal law area.[52] Nevertheless, the more general point remains valid: in principle, it is an open question whether the rules promulgated to the law's subjects and the accompanying rules addressed to the law application officials ought to be exactly the same, or not. That generally they ought to be identical is hardly disputed, but it is possible that certain exceptions are justified.

---

51 See Dan-Cohen, *Harmful Thoughts*, 56. Note that the idea of trial by juries actually goes against this, but it is mitigated by the detailed legal guidance judges are required provide to the jury.

52 Dan-Cohen is careful to point out that the more there is opportunity for *ex ante* legal consultation, the less acoustic separation the law can maintain; thus, he would not necessarily disagree with the argument in the text. He could still maintain that acoustic separation is beneficial in those mainly criminal law cases in which the relevant parties do not have an opportunity to obtain legal advice *ex ante*.

C. The Inner Morality of Law?

Lon Fuller has made these conditions of the rule of law which we have addressed in the previous pages central to jurisprudence by claiming that they exhibit the "inner morality of law."[53] These conditions which the law must meet in order to function as law, regardless of its specific contents, Fuller argued, are valuable in themselves, in that they instantiate certain moral virtues, and therefore render the law, in its form alone, morally valuable. H.L.A. Hart and Joseph Raz responded that these virtues of the rule of law are merely functional values, not moral ones.[54] Just like the sharpness of a knife, which makes the knife a good one, so the rule of law virtues make the law good, but only in terms of its functioning as a means of social control. Functional good, Hart and Raz argued, must not be confused with moral value.

I hope that our detailed discussion of the rule of law virtues proves Hart and Raz to be wrong about this criticism of Fuller. We have seen in some detail that most virtues of the rule of law, though essentially functional, are also moral-political virtues. In addition to the fact that the conditions discussed are necessary for law to function as a means of social control in guiding human conduct, they also enhance certain goods which we have reasons to value in addition to their functional merit. If the law fails on these conditions, it would not only fail in guiding its putative subjects' conduct, but it would also fail morally. As Neil MacCormick aptly put it, "There is always something to be said for treating people with formal fairness, that is, in a rational and predictable way, setting public standards for citizens' conduct and officials' responses thereto . . . That indeed, is what we mean by the Rule of Law."[55]

Even if it is the case, however, that the rule of law virtues are partly moral in content, Raz claims that these values do not prove that there is necessarily some moral

---

53 See Fuller, *The Morality of Law*.

54 See H.L.A. Hart, *Essays in Jurisprudence and Philosophy*, 349–350, and J. Raz, *The Authority of Law*, 226. Raz qualifies this to the extent that he does admit that in addition to functional values, the rule of law enhances certain goods indirectly, at 225.

55 "Natural Law and the Separation of Law and Morals" in R. George (ed.), *Natural Law Theory*, 105, at 123. The truth is that there may be an exception to this: when the law is profoundly corrupt, it might be better if it also failed in its ability to guide conduct, and therefore, violations of the rule of law virtues may actually do more good than harm. But it is very difficult to generalize. Sometimes, even in a profoundly corrupt legal system, the fact that the law also violates some rule of law virtues, say, in that it is kept secret, or haphazardly applied, may be an additional iniquity over and beyond the law's substantive injustice. It all depends on specific circumstances.

value in law, as such. The rule of law values are essentially "negative values," Raz claims, because the conditions of the rule of law are only designed to "minimize the danger created by the law itself."[56] Thus, Raz concludes, "the rule of law is a negative virtue in two senses: conformity to it does not cause good except through avoiding evil and the evil which is avoided is evil which could only have been caused by the law itself."[57]

Let us take a closer look at this argument. Many moral values consist in the avoidance of evil rather than the direct promotion of a good. Raz is right to claim that not every instance of avoiding evil justifies moral credit to the agent; as he rightly notes, the person who cannot poison another due to his ignorance or inability does not deserve credit for it. Moral agents normally deserve credit for avoiding evil when they would have had both the *opportunity* and the *temptation* to commit the wrong, and they have resisted it. But we should not confuse a theory of moral agency and ethical virtue with the question of what is a good. Even if some people cannot physically commit murder, and therefore would not deserve any credit for it, we would still say that it is good that a possible evil is avoided. Suppose, for example, that we discover a world in which people, who are otherwise similar to us, cannot possibly kill each other. Thus they would not deserve any credit for the avoidance of murder. But we would still be able to say that it is a good world in that respect. The fact that those creatures cannot kill each other is good, in itself, even if it is not a personal accomplishment that they deserve credit for. Similarly, the fact that a properly functioning legal system cannot sanction certain forms of arbitrary force or violation of human freedom and dignity is simply good, even if it is true that the law does not deserve moral credit for it.

Now consider the second prong of Raz's argument: The kinds of evil which the rule of law conditions avoid, Raz claims, are only those which could have been created by the law itself. No evil is avoided by, say, the publicity of law or its prospective aspect, unless there is law, first, which could violate these conditions (to some extent). In other words, the rule of law virtues only mitigate possible evils that the law could create to begin with. If there is no law, then there are no such evils that need to be avoided. Raz's analogy with the wrong of deceit is revealing: there is no way in which I can lie to you unless I communicate with you. It is only because I can talk to you and tell you a lie that my honesty, in the limited sense of avoiding

---

56 Raz, *The Authority of Law*, 224.

57 *Ibid.*

deceit, is a virtue. Honesty, in this limited sense, Raz claims, "does not include the good of communication between people, for honesty is consistent with a refusal to communicate."[58] But what if I have a positive duty to tell you the truth? Surely, the physician who avoids telling her patient that he suffers from a serious disease, simply by not telling him anything, violates a duty to be honest. Similarly, the unfaithful husband who cheated on his wife does not manifest honesty by simply keeping quiet about it. If there is a background expectation to communicate the truth, an avoidance of communication might be deceitful. Raz would surely not deny this general point. But then we must take into account the first component of the rule of law, namely, the idea that governments *ought to rule by law*. If we have good reasons to expect governance by law, the absence of law is wrong just as the absence of communication under certain circumstances is deceitful.

I do not intend to undermine Raz's basic insight here. He is right to insist that if there is anything which makes the law essentially good, it is not the fact that the conditions of the rule of law, by themselves, actually create certain goods. We must first assume that the existence of law is good. Similarly, unless we assume that the institution of monogamous marriage is good, there is no wrong in the silence of the deceitful husband. In this respect, Fuller's argument about the inner morality of law is, indeed, incomplete. But it can be completed by adding the necessary assumption which, in fact, Raz has never denied. The necessary assumption is that we have good reasons to have law in the first place.

As a final comment, let me clarify one point: It is sometimes assumed that this debate about the inner morality of law is a debate between legal positivism and some modern version of natural law.[59] But this is a mistake. The truth of legal positivism is simply not at stake here. The main insight of legal positivism is that the conditions of *legal validity* are determined by social facts. This involves two separate claims which have been labeled The Social Thesis and The Separation Thesis. The Social Thesis asserts that law is, profoundly, a social phenomenon, and that the conditions of legal validity consist of social facts. Early legal positivists followed Hobbes's insight that the law is, essentially, an instrument of political

58 Raz, *The Authority of Law*, 224.

59 Fuller certainly gave at least the impression that his views about the "inner morality of law" form part of his anti-positivist argument. Even recent literature on the rule of law, however, seems to share this characterization of the debate. See, for example, David Dyzenhaus's introduction to the volume he edited: *Recrafting the Rule of Law*, pp. 1–12. See also R. George, "Reason, Freedom, and the Rule of Law: Their Significance in the Natural Law Tradition," 249.

sovereignty, and they maintained that the basic source of legal validity resides in the facts constituting political sovereignty. Law, they thought, is basically the command of the sovereign. Later legal positivists have modified this view, maintaining that social conventions, and not the facts about sovereignty, constitute the grounds of law. Most contemporary legal positivists share the view that there are conventional rules of recognition, namely, social conventions which determine certain facts or events that provide the ways for the creation, modification, and annulment of legal standards. These facts, such as an act of legislation or a judicial decision, are the *sources of law* conventionally identified as such in each and every modern legal system.

Traditional Natural Law denies this insight, insisting that a putative norm cannot become legally valid unless it passes a certain threshold of morality. Positive law must conform in its content to some basic precepts of Natural Law, that is, universal morality, in order to become law in the first place. In other words, Natural Lawyers maintain that the moral content of norms, and not just their social origins, also forms part of the conditions of legal validity.[60]

The Separation Thesis is an important negative implication of this Social Thesis, maintaining that there is a conceptual separation between law and morality, that is, between what the law is, and what the law ought to be. The Separation Thesis, however, has often been overstated, and this overstatement is the source of the confusion here. It has been assumed by Fuller and others that natural law asserts, and legal positivism denies, that the law is, by necessity, morally good or that the law must have some minimal moral content. But the Separation Thesis does *not* entail the falsehood of the assumption that there is something necessarily good in the law. Legal positivism can accept the claim that law is, by its very nature or its essential functions in society, something good that deserves our moral appreciation. Nor is legal positivism forced to deny the plausible claim that wherever law exists, it must have a great many prescriptions which coincide with morality. There is probably a considerable overlap, and perhaps necessarily so, between the actual content of law and morality. Once again, the Separation Thesis, properly understood, pertains only to the conditions of legal validity. It asserts that the

60 Note that contemporary Natural Lawyers have suggested different and more subtle interpretations of the main tenets of Natural Law. For example, John Finnis views Natural Law (in its Thomist version) not as a constraint on the legal validity of positive laws, but mainly as an elucidation of an ideal of law in its fullest, or highest sense, concentrating on the ways in which law necessarily promotes the common good. See his *Natural Law and Natural Rights*. As I explain in the text, however, it is not clear that such a view about the necessary moral content of law is at odds with the main tenets of Legal Positivism.

conditions of legal validity do not depend on the moral content of the norms in question. What the law is cannot depend on what it ought to be in the relevant circumstances. But this is quite consistent with the view which holds that law is essentially good in the simple sense that we have good reasons to have law and be governed by it. And it is also consistent with Fuller's basic insight that the rule of law, properly understood, promotes certain goods which we have reasons to value regardless of their purely functional merit.[61]

---

61 I am indebted to Scott Altman, Meir Dan-Cohen, David Enoch, John Finnis, Chaim Gans, Elizabeth Garrett, and Alon Harel for invaluable comments on earlier drafts.

CHAPTER 2

Should We Value Legislative Integrity?

"We have two principles of political integrity:"—Dworkin suggests in *Law's Empire* —"a legislative principle, which asks lawmakers to try to make the total set of laws morally coherent, and an adjudicative principle, which instructs that the law be seen as coherent in that way, as far as possible."[1] In this essay I will be concerned with only the first of these two principles. My arguments here aim to show that legislative integrity is not an ideal, certainly not an important one.

A. The Meaning of Legislative Integrity

Before we can proceed to the main arguments, a few clarifications about the meaning of legislative integrity are necessary, and some assumptions must be rendered explicit.

1. Two Applications of Coherence to the Law

Legal theorists have applied the idea of coherence to the law in at least two distinct ways: As part of an explanation of what the law is, and as a value of political morality to which the law should strive to adhere. Dworkin has employed the idea of coherence in both of these ways,[2] but this should not confuse us into thinking that they are the same thing. In the former sense, coherence performs an explanatory function in a theory about the nature of law. In this sense, coherence constitutes part of the conditions for the legal validity of norms: A norm is legally valid if it forms part of, or is entailed by, the most coherent account of other norms that

1 Ronald Dworkin, *Law's Empire*, 176.

2 For a detailed account of Dworkin's use of coherence in legal theory, see my *Interpretation and Legal Theory*, Ch. 4.

we take to be part of the law.[3] This is not what Dworkin has in mind, however, when he discusses political integrity. The latter is not part of an explanation of what the law is, but a distinct value of political morality.

Coherence can be a value of political morality (either in the legislative or adjudicative context) even if coherence does not play a constitutive role in determining what the law is. In other words, you can reject a coherence theory of law (in its explanatory sense), but still maintain that coherence is a valuable objective that the law should strive to instantiate. And *vice versa*: A coherence theory of law does not entail that legislative integrity is a value or a moral-political ideal. Even if coherence forms part of the conditions of legal validity, it does not follow that coherence is a good thing or that we should want more of it rather than less. Thus, I will assume that we can discuss the value of integrity without taking a stance on the role coherence can play in a theory about the nature of law.[4]

2. Coherence and Truth

Another important clarification is in place here. Some people tend think that we should value coherence simply because an incoherent theory cannot be true. Whatever coherence is, at the very least it involves the avoidance of contradictions. Not every consistent set of propositions is necessarily coherent, but every inconsistent set is necessarily incoherent. If this is correct, one might conclude that the lack of coherence entails a contradiction, and since it cannot be the case that contradictory propositions are both true, it follows that an incoherent theory must be false. But this is a *non sequitur*. The lack of coherence does not necessarily entail a contradiction, although the opposite is true: an inconsistent set of propositions is, *ipso facto*, incoherent. The reason for this is very simple: coherence must mean something more than just the lack of consistency. When we talk about coherence we have in mind a set of propositions which are somehow mutually supportive; they somehow fit together in the overall scheme of things.[5]

---

3 For a possible distinction between an epistemic and a constitutive version of coherence theories of law, see Joseph Raz, "The Relevance of Coherence" in his *Ethics in the Public Domain*, 261–309.

4 I am quite confident that Dworkin would share this assumption. I do not think that Dworkin has sought to derive his conclusions about legislative integrity from his coherence theory of law.

5 An indefinite number of logically consistent but incoherent sets of propositions can be constructed. For example, consider the following set: "John is a law professor," "2+2=4," and "All swans are white." This set is logically consistent, but hardly coherent. Coherence requires some notion of connectedness and mutual support between the propositions which constitute the relevant set.

I'm not sure that I can explain what this means, precisely, but the point here does not require much more. It only requires the realization that a theory, or a set of propositions, can fail to be coherent even if it does not involve straightforward contradictions. Therefore, it does not follow that an incoherent set of propositions is necessarily false.[6]

3. The Scope of Integrity

Another clarification is appropriate here. Suppose that we espouse the ideal of legislative integrity. How far can it be carried? Whose obligation would it be to implement it? Should individual legislators actually be guided by it? Would legislators have a reason to vote for a law because it would be required by the principle of legislative integrity? Should it also extend to voters when they consider who to vote for, or when they participate in lawmaking through referenda and initiatives? I'm not sure how far Dworkin would take this principle, but it is quite clear that the main implication of legislative integrity Dworkin had in mind concerns the theory of adjudication. He has certainly maintained that judges should interpret statutory law following the principle of legislative integrity.[7] Judges should assume that laws are enacted with this ideal in mind, as it were, so that even if the legislature fails to achieve it, greater coherence can be imposed on legislation through judicial interpretation. Suffice it to say that none of these implications of the ideal of legislative integrity are logically entailed by it, though each one of them may be supported by other reasons. And *vice versa*; it should not be assumed that the rejection of legislative integrity as a distinct political ideal necessarily entails that judges need not be guided by a similar principle. The reasons for endorsing a coherence approach in adjudication might be different, independently justified on other grounds.

4. The Meaning of Legislative Integrity

Still, a crucial question remains unanswered: is there anything more to political integrity than the requirement that laws be made coherent? If I understand

6 I do not intend to imply that incoherence has no epistemic implications. Even a coherence theory of knowledge, however, is not committed to maintaining that any incoherent theory is, ipso facto, necessarily false.

7 R. Dworkin, *Law's Empire*, Ch. 7.

Dworkin correctly, then the answer actually is that there is less to political integrity than coherence, not more. Political integrity is the requirement that the law be made in a way which is *morally* coherent. The law can probably fail to be coherent in other ways which have nothing, or perhaps just very little, to do with morality. For instance, the law can be pragmatically incoherent, in that it actually creates incentives for behavior which are, from a certain pragmatic point of view (e.g. economic, environmental policy, etc.,) somehow incoherent. If this is a possibility, then it is possible for the law to be incoherent without violating the principle of political integrity. It may thus violate some other principle or ideal, but not necessarily the one of integrity.

Let us assume, then, that the law is morally incoherent if its various prescriptions and their underlying justifications cannot be subsumed under one coherent moral theory. Or, we could say that in such cases there isn't a conceivable single rational moral agent whose moral point of view could justify the entire set of prescriptions under consideration. I think that this is basically what Dworkin means by the value of integrity in law.

Unfortunately, however, Dworkin's famous example of what constitutes a violation of integrity in legislation does not actually support the meaning of "integrity" as he defines it. Dworkin asks us to envisage what he calls a "checkerboard" type of legislation which would prescribe, for instance, that abortions are legally permitted for women who were born on even days of the month, and forbidden for women who were born on uneven days. The reason we would find such checkerboard laws unacceptable, Dworkin claims, is because they would violate the integrity of the law.[8] No single moral agent, Dworkin claims, could justify such a checkerboard solution as a coherent compromise of conflicting considerations with respect to the permissibility of abortions. But this is a bad example. We do not need the requirement of integrity, or coherence, in order to explain what is wrong with such checkerboard laws. What is wrong with them is that they are not supported by a good reason. When the law makes a distinction, as it does here on the basis of women's birthdays, it must be a distinction which is somehow supported by reason. If there is no good reason for the different treatment, then the law is a bad one, simply because it is not supported by reason.[9]

---

8 *Ibid.*, 178–184.

9 *Ibid.*, 180. At some point, Dworkin admits that "this is in the right neighborhood," but then fails to acknowledge that it undermines the force of his example.

One may wonder, however, how we would distinguish such checkerboard laws from many other cases in which the law makes distinctions that seem to be rather arbitrary, but nevertheless are understandable and justified. For instance, the law can stipulate that only people who were born before a certain date are allowed to vote in the forthcoming elections. Surely, the particular date chosen is not supported by any particular reasons, it is just an arbitrary cutoff point. But this is precisely the point: in numerous cases, such as in solving coordination problems and other similar situations, we do have a good reason to use arbitrary cutoff points. In such cases, the cutoff point itself is arbitrary, that is, not supported by any particular reason, but there are good reasons to have it as an arbitrarily chosen cutoff point.[10] The problem with the abortion example is precisely that it is the kind of situation where there is no good reason to have an arbitrarily chosen cutoff point.

None of this means, however, that legislative integrity is a vacuous concept. Far from it. There are countless ways in which the legislature can enact laws that are morally incoherent. My point simply was that checkerboard legislation, as Dworkin describes it, is not one of them. Legislation which is not supported by a good reason is wrong just because it is not supported by a good reason. The law is morally incoherent, and thus violates the ideal of integrity, when the various norms or prescriptions it embodies are somehow morally contradictory. But here we have to be very cautious. Surely not every tension or potential conflict between moral principles amounts to an incoherence. Every comprehensive moral doctrine involves countless tensions and conflicts in the application of its principles and ideals. As we all know, the values of equality and freedom may often come into conflict. Liberalism endorses both ideals, but surely that does not render liberalism incoherent.

5. Conflict and Contradiction

It may be tempting to think that a moral theory is incoherent only when its principles are contradictory. There is, after all, a pretty clear distinction between a conflict of principles and a contradiction.[11] In a world of limited resources,

10 See, for example, D. Lewis, *On Convention: A Philosophical Study*. On the definition of arbitrariness, see also my "On Convention."

11 Dworkin makes this point drawing on the distinction between conflict and contradiction of principles in *Law's Empire*, 268–275.

a stringent protection of the environment may come into conflict with creating new jobs for the poorer segment of society. But surely these two types of concerns are not contradictory. A rational moral person can easily support both. On the other hand, maintaining that the state should guarantee equal rights to homosexuals and heterosexuals, but at the same time deny gays the right to get married, for instance, looks very much like a contradiction.[12] So there is a sense in which moral contradiction is quite distinct from conflict or tension between morally sound principles. It is also quite clear that a contradiction of principles does violate the requirement of coherence. The question remains whether moral principles or ideals can be incoherent even if they do not quite amount to a contradiction. Presumably, the answer is yes. As we have noted earlier, coherence must mean something more than mere logical consistency. So it must be the case that there are moral conceptions or worldviews that just cannot be subsumed under one coherent doctrine, even if it is the case that the overall set of propositions one believes in are not logically inconsistent.

6. The Background of Value Pluralism

Be this as it may, there are two types of moral incoherence that are relevant to the ideal of legislative integrity: one stems from the fragmentation of values within any given comprehensive moral doctrine; the other from the fact of reasonable pluralism (I use these Rawlsian terms advisedly). Let me call them *internal* and *external* incoherence, respectively. Internal incoherence stems from the complexity of the sources of moral thought. With the possible exception of a single-minded, monistic utilitarianism,[13] every comprehensive moral doctrine is bound to be incoherent, to some extent. Our moral and ethical concerns do not form a response to a single question; they reflect myriad human concerns, some of them private and individual, others public and social. As many moral philosophers have noted, it seems extremely unlikely that we can ever construct a

---

12 If you have doubts about this particular example, others can be easily thought of.

13 Arguably, however, monistic utilitarianism can only maintain its moral coherence at the expense of a huge simplification of morality. This lack of subtlety is partly what makes a monistic utilitarianism so suspect.

comprehensive moral and ethical worldview which would subsume all these divergent concerns under a coherent set of principles.[14]

The idea of external incoherence stems from a different fact about the moral complexity of our world: the fact of reasonable pluralism.[15] In most contemporary societies there is a whole range of comprehensive moral doctrines which are, on the one hand, mutually inconsistent, but on the other hand, also within the bounds of reasonable disagreement. It is important to keep in mind that there is a difference between a plurality of moral doctrines and value pluralism. Not every plurality of moral doctrines involves a deep form of conflict, even if the doctrines are mutually exclusive. There are many forms of life and moral worldviews which are mutually exclusive in the sense that a person cannot possibly entertain, or strive to instantiate, both. But this does not necessarily entail a deep conflict. It may simply reflect a choice between sets of incommensurable values or mixed goods.[16] On the other hand, when we talk about value pluralism, we refer to a deep moral or ethical conflict. There are many comprehensive moral doctrines or forms of life which are morally at odds with each other, in the simple sense that if the one is true, the other must be false, and vice versa.[17]

Pluralism, then, stems from the fact that comprehensive moral doctrines are potentially in deep conflict, entailing straightforward moral contradictions between different doctrines people adhere to and live by. Nevertheless, it has been the benchmark of liberalism for centuries that there is a sense in which value pluralism (and not just plurality) is reasonable. I cannot hope to explain the philosophical underpinning of the idea of reasonable pluralism here. But I will make two assumptions. First, that rational people can have reasonable disagreements

---

14 See, for example, Joseph Raz,"The Relevance of Coherence" in his *Ethics in the Public Domain*, 261–309. T. Nagel, "The Fragmentation of Value," in his *Mortal Questions*, 128–141.

See also, B. Williams, "Conflict of Values" in his *Moral Luck*, 71–82. It was probably Isaiah Berlin who most famously insisted on this fragmentation of values as being part of the foundation of liberalism. See his collected essays in his *Concepts and Categories*. I think it is fair to say that Rawls has also maintained such a position in *A Theory of Justice*.

15 Reasonable pluralism is a moral fact, not merely a social one. See Rawls, *Political Liberalism*.

16 By pointing to the fact that in such cases the various options are incommensurable I only mean that no ranking between the options is morally determinable.

17 Moral doctrines inevitably make certain claims to truth. Even a moral skeptic makes certain claims to truth—at the very least, to the truth of his metaethical stance and the practical implications following from it. Thus, it should not be surprising if many of these various claims to truth turn out to be mutually contradictory.

about fundamental moral and ethical values.[18] Second, I will assume that the idea of reasonable pluralism does not necessarily derive from, nor does it necessarily entail, moral skepticism. I may disagree with your moral views and believe them to be wrong or mistaken, but still acknowledge your right to live by your mistakes. In other words, reasonable pluralism may be as much a view about politics as it is about metaethics. Even if you are profoundly wrong, the assumption we make here is that the state should not be in the business of correcting your mistakes (up to a point, of course). So there are at least two possible grounds for acknowledging reasonable pluralism, and they are not mutually exclusive: reasonable pluralism may reflect a view about the nature of morality and the limits of moral knowledge, and it may be a political view about the limits on the coercive authority of the state. Either way, the argument about legislative integrity that I will now explore assumes that pluralism of comprehensive moral doctrines is reasonable and, as such, ought to be respected by a liberal state.[19]

B. The Argument from Pluralism

So now at long last we come to the main issue. There are two ways in which we can explore the value of legislative integrity. First, and this is probably the more important argument, I will try to show that the ideal of legislative integrity is directly at odds with the value of pluralism and the commitment of a liberal state to respect reasonable pluralism. Second, I will explore the main causes of the failure of legislative integrity in democratic legislatures, arguing that there is nothing regrettable about those causes and that often there is something to commend them.

Let me admit from the outset, however, that none of these arguments can be conclusive. It is generally very difficult to prove that something is not a value. I can only hope to show that there are important reasons to forgo legislative integrity. I cannot prove that legislative integrity is not valuable when those reasons are

---

18 This is certainly not tantamount to saying that *any* fundamental moral principle is subject to reasonable disagreement.

19 There is a very difficult question about the scope of this principle: does it apply to societies which are not, as a matter of fact, pluralistic? Is there anything inherently wrong in a political society which happens to be homogenous in terms of people's conception of the good, all, say, adhering to the same moral or religious comprehensive doctrine? At least in his later writings, Rawls certainly thought that the answer is yes; he called it the fact of oppression. See Rawls, *Political Liberalism*, 36–37. I do not take a stance on this complex issue here.

not present. I do hope to show, however, that we have no reason to maintain that *ideally*, the law should be morally coherent, or as coherent as possible.[20]

The main argument against the ideal of legislative integrity relies on two points: A moral-political ideal, very much inspired by John Rawls, and an observation, which actually rejects part of Rawls's stance on the matter. The moral-political ideal, which I can only assume here, is the requirement that in a well-ordered society the state should try to refrain, as far as possible, from enacting into laws comprehensive moral doctrines that are potentially contentious and subject to reasonable disagreement between various segments of the population. Note that this is not the ideal of neutrality that Rawls himself advocated, but a much more modest principle. I do not believe that the state can, by and large, remain neutral between conceptions of the good or comprehensive moralities. Partly because this is just not possible, practically speaking, and partly because often it is inherently unclear what neutrality would require, or that there is, indeed, any morally acceptable neutral stance with respect to the relevant conflict. (It is not part of my argument here to deny the plausibility of Rawls's conception of neutrality. I'm just pointing out the fact that I do not intend to rely on it.[21]) Nevertheless, Rawls's insight that there is something very objectionable to an attempt by the state to impose any particular comprehensive morality on its subjects is, I believe, a powerful insight that liberal conceptions of the state have in one way or another always endorsed.[22]

Rawls believed that the stronger principle of neutrality is possible partly because he thought that it is possible to delineate a sphere of public debate and state action—a sphere of *public reason*, as he called it—that can remain above the fray. As he put it, "a liberal view removes from the political agenda the most divisive issues."[23] This means that "in discussing constitutional essentials and matters of basic justice we are not to appeal to comprehensive religious and philosophical doctrine."[24]

---

20 I do not want to put too much weight on the distinction between a value and an ideal. However, there is a sense in which an ideal is something that we aspire to achieve as much of as possible or, at least (all other things being equal), something of which we would normally want to have more rather than less. This is not necessarily, or even typically, true of values in general.

21 For a comprehensive and powerful criticism of neutrality, see Raz, *The Morality of Freedom*, Ch. 5. For some of his replies, see Rawls, *Political Liberalism*, 190–200. See also my *Positive Law and Objective Values*, 147–152.

22 As Rawls himself suggests, and I think rightly so, this is a natural extension of the traditional principle of toleration. See Rawls, *Political Liberalism*, introduction.

23 *Ibid.*, 157.

24 *Ibid.*, 224.

Shortly thereafter, Rawls clarifies what he means by "constitutional essentials" and it becomes clear that he means quite a lot: "constitutional essentials" include "fundamental principles that specify the general structure of government and political process," as well as "basic rights and liberties."[25] Of course a lot depends here on what we would regard as "basic" and what as not so basic, but this is just one aspect of a deeper problem. Any attempt to draw a sharp line between constitutional essentials, which ought to be free from appeal to comprehensive doctrines, and other matters of law and legislation which need not be, is questionable, at best. First, it is often controversial just what is, and what is not, a matter of "constitutional essentials" and, moreover, such controversies often lie at the core of the relevant public debate.[26] Second, the law, as such, recognizes no inherent limits on its reach. The law cannot recognize such limits mostly because its quintessential function is to regulate and resolve conflicts, and there is no limit on which conflicts actually arise and need a resolution.

A brief illustration of the first point should suffice here. Consider, for example, the current controversy in American politics and jurisprudence about gay marriages. Those who advocate the right of gays and lesbians to marry do so on the grounds that the issue is one of basic constitutional rights, whereas those who oppose this social change may claim the exact opposite. Opponents may not see the issue as one of basic rights but as a matter of tradition that should be left out of the constitutional domain.[27] In other words, many of the legal/political controversies are partly, but crucially, about the very question of what is, and what is not, a matter of "constitutional essentials."

The second point is perhaps even clearer, and it is much more important: There is no practical way in which issues can be removed from the legal/political agenda just because they are divisive or deeply controversial. Even if we grant (generously, I would say) that certain aspects of constitutional law can be confined within the constraints of public reason, those constraints cannot possibly apply

---

25 *Ibid.*, 228. Another crucial sense in which it is notable that Rawls assumes quite a lot here concerns the fact that for him even Kantian morality or Utilitarianism are "comprehensive moralities" and therefore should be excluded from the realm of public reason. See C. Larmore, "Public Reason," in S. Freeman, (ed.) *The Cambridge Companion to Rawls*, 368–393.

26 Cf. Larmore, *ibid.*, 384–390.

27 I am not suggesting that these are the only two positions available. For example, many see the issue as one about state vs. federal jurisdiction, which is a different type of constitutional debate.

to legislation as a whole.[28] This should not be surprising. The law is essentially comprehensive in its reach because it must claim the authority to regulate any type of behavior in every sphere of life. Since the law must resolve conflicts that actually arise, it cannot abstain from judgment. Even when the law decides not to intervene in a given conflict, it is a decision that reflects judgment, namely, a judgment to refrain from taking a certain legal action or granting a certain remedy. Once again, we must keep in mind that an essential function of the law is to resolve conflicts in society, and there is no inherent limit on the kinds of conflict that may arise and need some sort of legal regulation. I think that in this respect, Dworkin's vision of the law as an all-encompassing "empire" that potentially reaches into every aspect of our lives is much more realistic than Rawls's ideal of a secluded sphere of public reason. Even if we can theoretically delineate such a sphere of public reason (and I actually doubt that we can), there is just no hope of enclosing the law within that realm.

But then, taken with the previous point about the need to respect reasonable pluralism, this is precisely the reason to refrain from espousing an ideal of legislative integrity. Any attempt to impose strict moral integrity on the law would undermine the essential and, we assumed, reasonable, moral fragmentation of a pluralist society. The more we wish to have moral integrity implemented by the law, the more we would have to expect it to implement a single comprehensive moral view. It is inconceivable that an entirely coherent legal regime could be endorsed by opposing (reasonable) comprehensive moralities. Therefore, integrity basically entails a "winner take all" strategy, which is directly at odds with respect for reasonable value pluralism. A certain moral fragmentation of values and incoherence is inescapable if we are to respect pluralism as such. The whole point of respect for value pluralism is that we do not want to have a legal-political system whereby the winner (be it the ruling majority or the Supreme Court, for that matter), imposes its comprehensive moral views on the rest of the population. Furthermore, as we have seen, even within a single comprehensive moral doctrine it is far from clear that coherence can be somehow imposed without a considerable loss to the subtlety and complexity of the relevant moral concerns.

---

28 This is not meant to be a direct criticism of Rawls, since Rawls himself believed that public reason should be confined to the basic constitutional domain and some other, limited, aspects of the "public political forum," as opposed to what he called the "background culture" or the media, and such. Whether any of these distinctions makes sense is questionable, but the argument in the text is more limited. It only purports to claim that even if public reason makes sense in some aspects of law and politics, it cannot be extended to encompass legislation as a whole.

(But my point here can be made even if we ignore the problem of internal incoherence, so I will not strive to defend this stronger claim.)

One interesting way in which Rawls expressed a very similar worry is by emphasizing that a well-ordered society governed by principles of justice "is neither a community nor . . . an association."[29] A democratic society does not have final ends or aims in the way that communities or associations do: "A well ordered democratic society is not an association, it is not a community either, if we mean by a community a society governed by shared comprehensive religious, philosophical, or moral doctrine."[30] Now, this is particularly interesting in light of Dworkin's argument in favor of political integrity that is premised on the duty of loyalty to one's community. Dworkin has argued that such a duty of loyalty entails an obligation to obey the law, and that the latter must be seen as the organized voice of the community, taken as a whole. From this Dworkin strove to derive the need to assume a personification of the law, as if it should be taken to speak with one voice, manifesting the community's collective decision.[31]

It is not my purpose here to offer a detailed critique of this complex argument. That has been done by others cogently enough.[32] My observation here is confined to one aspect of this argument, namely, its underlying assumption that a well-ordered democratic society can, and should be, seen as a community, and its laws perceived as the community's collective decision. I think that Rawls was right to argue that such a view of a political society, that is, of a liberal state, is quite straightforwardly at odds with the need to respect reasonable pluralism. A political society cannot speak with one moral voice because its moral voice is essentially fragmented and, taken as a whole, profoundly incoherent. An attempt to impose coherence on it can only mean that some comprehensive doctrines will win the day while others will be suppressed. This cannot be a liberal ideal.

Let me summarize the argument. I began with the Rawlsian insight that a well-ordered liberal society should respect value pluralism. One clear implication of this ideal is an aspiration to try to avoid, as far as possible, using the state and its legal coercive institutions to implement any particular comprehensive moral

---

29 Rawls, *Political Liberalism*, 40.

30 *Ibid.*, 42.

31 R. Dworkin, *Law's Empire*, 195–214.

32 In particular, see J. Raz, "The Relevance of Coherence" in his *Ethics in the Public Domain*, 291–298.

or religious doctrine. Contra Rawls, however, I do not think that such an ideal can (or should) be carried so far as to recommend a principle of neutrality. More importantly, I have argued that this principle cannot be implemented by designating a sphere of public reason that would enclose legislation within strict neutral boundaries. The law is inevitably comprehensive, and there is no hope of actually preventing the law from regulating aspects of our lives which are clearly, but reasonably, controversial morally, ethically, and otherwise. Therefore, I concluded, it would be wrong to insist on the ideal of legislative integrity. The law should not be expected to speak with one voice because there is no single voice that could possibly encompass the range of reasonable comprehensive moral doctrines held by various segments of the society.

There are two possible rejoinders to this argument. First, it can be argued that I have not quite proved what I promised: at best I have shown that the ideal of integrity just happens to conflict with the value of respect for pluralism, and thus may need to succumb to the latter, but I have not shown that integrity is not valuable at all. Secondly, it could be argued that integrity can incorporate the value of pluralism as one of the ingredients in a complex moral view that comprises a set of first order values, *and* the second order value of respect for value pluralism. When we expect the law to speak with one voice, as it were, it is a voice that already takes into account the need to respect the views of others who may disagree. Let me take up these two points in turn.

It is certainly possible that the conflict between integrity and pluralism is just that, a conflict between opposing (second order) moral principles. I have not shown that we have no reason to value integrity at all. But I am not sure that it is important to show that. The argument purported to show that there are important reasons to forgo legislative integrity, whether the latter is valuable or not. Furthermore, I am willing to assume that those reasons are not always present, partly because the value of pluralism has its own limits, of course, and partly because there may be cases in which pluralism is not at stake. As I have indicated from the start, it is generally very difficult to show that something is not a value under any circumstances. But again, such a proof is not really needed. We have seen that the need to respect value pluralism strongly counts against an ideal of legislative integrity, and this should be sufficient to show that even if integrity is valuable, we have no reason to regard legislative integrity as an ideal, that is, to expect the law to be as morally coherent as possible. Now it is true, of course, that if you feel that we should regret the need to respect pluralism, you may also regret the fact that we must forgo legislative integrity. Since I do not think that pluralism is regrettable, I would not share this sentiment, but a detailed argument about this would exceed the scope of this chapter.

Let us now consider the second counterargument. It suggests that even if we take into account the need to respect pluralism, we should still expect the law to speak with one voice, given that this "one voice" already incorporates the need to respect pluralism. This is a tricky argument, but its appeal dissipates as soon as we realize that it only adds a new label to the same package. It is like suggesting that the conflict between equality and utility can be solved by recognizing that there is some more complex value of equality that already contains a need to constrain equality when it stands in the way of greater utility. If there is a genuine conflict between the ideal of legislative integrity and the need to respect pluralism, the conflict cannot be resolved by relabeling integrity to incorporate respect for pluralism. In other words, I have argued for the need to respect value pluralism as an external constraint on the unqualified pursuit of any comprehensive morality. You do not gain anything of substance by incorporating this constraint into, say, a liberal comprehensive morality. The same constraint is there, it just has a different label now.

Finally, it can be argued that even if legislative integrity is not a distinct political ideal, the actual mechanisms which tend to engender moral incoherence in legislation are morally troubling or regrettable. In the next section I will try to show that the opposite is true. The main circumstances that bring about a failure in legislative integrity actually manifest morally commendable aspects of democratic practices and institutions.

C. The Causes of Legislative Incoherence

Since we want to focus on legislative, as opposed to judicial, integrity, let us stipulate a class of legal norms, call them *statutory law*, which would comprise all those legal norms that are enacted by legislative institutions, such as Congress, state legislatures, administrative agencies, and such. Now, if nothing else, at least the sheer number of such legislative institutions and their political diversity make it very unlikely that the entire body of statutory law at any given time would be morally coherent. Legislative integrity takes considerable effort to achieve and, often enough, it clearly fails. One of the ways in which we can examine the value of legislative integrity is by looking at the causes of its failure and asking ourselves whether those causes involve morally disturbing or regrettable aspects of our political institutions. Or, if we prefer to put it in a slightly different way: If legislative integrity is an ideal, what would it take to achieve it?

There are, presumably, many causes for the failure of legislative integrity. For example, the legislature can simply make a mistake. Needless to say, mistakes are always regrettable. Mostly, however, legislative integrity fails for much better reasons. Let me consider, in what follows, three of the main causes for the failure of legislative integrity.

1. Division of Legislative Power

First, as we have already mentioned, incoherence of statutory law often results from the great number of legislative institutions and the limited means by which their various legislative actions can be coordinated by a central authority. In fact, this results not just from the number of legislative agencies but also from their divergent social and political roles. For example, an administrative agency entrusted with the protection of the environment, like the EPA, is inherently biased in favor of certain social-political goals it is there to advance, and those objectives might be at odds with the social and political goals of a different legislative agency. Similarly, a state legislature is naturally expected to promote the welfare of the state's residents and their local interests, and such aims may be at odds with those of the federal government or some other state. So there is a division of legislative power here which is both numerical and substantive. A well-functioning democracy purposefully creates a complex division of legislative power by entrusting legislation to different institutions, some of them with relatively special and limited authority. There are, of course, very good reasons for creating such divisions of legislative power. First, any division of legal/political power is a safeguard against tyranny. Secondly, such division of power typically aims to achieve a deliberate diversity of legislative goals by establishing legislative institutions which would be inherently motivated to advance a certain type of political agenda. By the creation of relatively specialized legislative institutions, alongside general ones, we aim to promote a diversity of interests which we think of as worthy of special care or concern.

There is no reason to assume that division of legislative power is purposefully designed to undermine the integrity of legislation. But it is certainly the case that the more legislative power is divided between different, and often competing, legislative institutions, the less likely it is that integrity will prevail. However, to the extent that division of legislative power tends to undermine the integrity of legislation, it is, as we have seen, for good reasons. The failure of integrity here derives from aspects of our political institutions which are based on sound moral-political principles.

Needless to say, there is a certain level of legislative coordination and coherence which is essential for the efficient functioning of any legal system. Too much incoherence and confusion makes it very difficult for people to follow the law. But this means only that a certain *minimal* level of coherence is necessary for the functioning of a legal system. It does not come close to substantiating *an ideal* of legislative integrity. This is very much like the stability of law: a minimal level of stability over time is essential for the functioning of law, but again, this does not entail that stability is an ideal, or that ideally, the law should be as stable as possible.

2. Logrolling and Compromise

In the case of division of legislative power, as we have seen, the lack of integrity in legislation is a result of the multiplicity of legislative institutions and their diverse goals. However, even within a single legislative body, especially as politically diverse as a parliament or Congress, there are familiar legislative strategies which tend to undermine the integrity of legislation. Bargaining and compromise, which are so often necessary to achieve an act of legislation, may certainly result in laws that are morally incoherent. To be sure, not every legislative compromise undermines integrity. Roughly, there are two main types of compromise: either you have to retract some of what you wanted to achieve, or else you get it all, but then you also have to give the other party some of what he wants (which may, or may not, be related to what you get). In both of these cases, the question of whether the resulting compromise is morally coherent or not depends on many specific details which we need not explore here. Suffice it to say that compromise and logrolling *may* result in legislation that falls far short of the ideal of legislative integrity. Does it make the necessity of compromise a regrettable aspect of democratic decision procedures? Surely, that depends on the alternatives, and the relevant alternative is much worse. Political parties that do not have to compromise have too much power: They have the power to implement their comprehensive moral and political agenda without having to pay sufficient attention to the needs and interests of those who oppose their doctrines or whose interests are at odd with theirs. Once again, there is a delicate balance that needs to be maintained between too much and too little partisan political power. If the ruling majority is very flimsy and the government needs to compromise on every step it wants to take, governing itself might be seriously compromised. But this truism does not entail that the opposite is a political ideal: it does not follow that a good government is one which does not have to compromise with minority parties. In other words, in a pluralistic society compromise is not a regrettable necessity, but an important virtue of democratic decision procedures.[33]

3. Partisan Realignment and the Continuity of Law

In a well-functioning democracy, control of the government periodically changes hands among various political parties. Naturally, every government wants to implement its political and ideological agenda, *inter alia*, by enacting new laws that purport to implement its views or repealing old ones that stand in its way.[34] This is certainly not an anomaly; it is what elections are held for. On the other hand, no government or legislature can start from a clean slate. Previous governments have had their own moral and political agenda enacted into laws which are still in force, and those old laws can be at odds with the moral-political views of the new government. These are the circumstances of partisan realignment, and these circumstances are bound to engender legislative changes which are morally incoherent. New laws and policies may coexist rather uneasily with the laws and policies still in force from the previous regimes.[35]

The failure of legislative integrity here stems from both practical and principled reasons. Even if the new government wanted to wipe the slate clean and change or repeal all those laws and policies which are inconsistent with its new ones, it would normally fail. The vast amount and complexity of legislation make such a task dauntingly difficult to carry out. But it is noteworthy that governments do not even attempt the task, and for principled reasons. Two of those reasons are very important: First, there is a principle of legal stability and continuity. Legislation typically creates an expectation that it will be relatively durable. People

33 Cf. J. Waldron, "The Circumstances of Integrity," in his *Law and Disagreement*, 187–208.

34 Of course in the U.S. this is somewhat more complicated due to the separation between control of Congress and the presidency. For simplicity's sake, however, I will not dwell on this complexity and speak of "control of government" according to the parliamentary models in which the government is composed of the ruling majority in the legislature. Nothing in my substantive arguments should be affected by this difference.

35 See *supra* note 33, 188–189, and J. Raz, "The Relevance of Coherence" in his *Ethics in the Public Domain*, 280–281.

normally adjust their behavior and expectations to the legal regime currently in force. Changes in the normative environment often require an adaptation phase, which may be costly or otherwise disruptive. To be sure, none of this means that laws ought not to be changed or that any legal change is, *ipso facto*, costly or disruptive. But as we all know, some level of stability over time is essential for the law to achieve its purposes, whatever they are.

Second, and more important in the present context, a general recognition that partisan realignment should not involve an attempt to wipe the previous legislative slate clean also stems from a principle of respect for pluralism. If elections result in partisan realignment, it is because the minority party has become the majority, and *vice versa*. But the previous majority-turned-minority has not vanished; it is still there, often representing a considerable segment of the population. It is widely acknowledged in well-functioning democracies that it would be wrong for the new majority to eradicate all the legislative achievements of the previous majority, even if they were partisan and ideological, because such an attempt would manifest disrespect for the views and moral convictions of the majority-turned-minority segment of the population. There is a delicate balance that needs to be respected here. On the one hand, an electoral victory resulting in partisan realignment is certainly a mandate for change, but it is not normally conceived of as a license to ignore the moral-political convictions of those who lost, and this is as it should be.

To conclude, the circumstances of partisan realignment engender a considerable amount of legislative incoherence. The new government is typically forced to introduce legislative changes amidst a tight network of previous laws and policies that may conflict with the new ones. These circumstances are likely to produce a patchwork of statutory law which cannot possibly reflect the moral and ethical views of a single, morally coherent, legislature. But this is not a regrettable aspect of democracy. On the contrary. As we have seen, the resulting legislative incoherence reflects moral-political considerations which are supported by principled reasons. Those reasons derive both from the need to maintain a certain level of legal stability and from the need to respect value pluralism. Partisan realignment requires a delicate compromise between competing considerations. Not every compromise is regrettable. This is the kind of compromise that manifests respect for the moral complexity of our social and political realities. The best solution to social problems often consists in doing without the best.[36]

---

36 I am indebted to Scott Altman, David Dolinko, David Enoch, Elizabeth Garrett, Alon Harel, Joseph Raz, and Gideon Yaffe for very helpful comments on earlier drafts.

CHAPTER 3

Authority, Equality, and Democracy

Democratic regimes and democratic cultures instantiate many goods that we value, both intrinsically and instrumentally. Political participation may be intrinsically valuable for many people. A culture of free and open public deliberation is perhaps a good in itself, and it may also greatly facilitate a robust civil society. It seems to be the case that democratic regimes are conducive to economic prosperity. Thus, in different ways and to various degrees, democracies instantiate a large variety of goods that we value. The core idea of a democratic decision procedure, however, consists in the practice of reaching authoritative resolutions on matters of public concern by a majority vote. But this core aspect of democracy is famously puzzling: The relationship between the legitimacy of an authoritative resolution and its democratic credentials is far from clear. Few things become good or desirable only because most people want them. How can such accidental, almost arbitrary facts as the majority-minority divide determine the legitimacy of an authoritative resolution? Is democracy justified only because, and to the extent that, it leads to good government? Or is it also required by considerations of fairness?[1] My purpose in this essay is to argue that considerations of fairness play an essential (but not exclusive) role in the justification of democratic decision procedures. In the first part of this essay I will argue that considerations of fairness form part of a practical authority's legitimacy, and that in the political context, those considerations of fairness entail a principle of equal distribution of political power. Subsequently, I will elaborate on the kind of equality which is required in democratic procedures, arguing that different principles of equality should apply to the

1 This is an oversimplification. Voting in a democratic decision procedure may have expressive and cognitive values over and beyond its contribution to good governance or political fairness. Although I will largely ignore these aspects of democracy, I do not intend to underestimate their importance.

deliberation and the decision stages of democracy. Finally, I will conclude with a few remarks on the possible relations between considerations of fairness and soundness of democratic procedures.

A clarification is in order before we proceed. When I say that a majority decision procedure is the core aspect of democracy, I may have already taken sides in an important debate within democratic theory. Roughly put, contemporary theorizing about democracy is divided between those who emphasize the deliberative aspect of democracy, and those who regard democratic procedure as mainly an aggregative form of collective decision making. Deliberative democratic theory strives to articulate a fundamental political ideal centered around ideal deliberative procedures which aim at the common good. Such theories regard deliberation as an essential, not an instrumental, aspect of public reason.[2] Deliberation can be essential in two possible ways: either an ideal model of deliberation can be seen as yielding decisions which are *constitutive* of the common good, or they can be seen as models of deliberation aiming to discover truths about the common good.[3] In both cases, however, the focus of the theory is on models of ideal deliberation. On the other hand, aggregative models of democracy take voting, not deliberation, as essential to democracy. On this view of democracy, collective decision making is not an ideal in itself, but only a practical need forced on us by the necessities of our communal lives. Such theories take the need for authoritative decisions as basic, and seek to work out a theory of democracy as the best political process for legitimizing authoritative decisions.[4] Whether these two models of democratic theory are necessarily at odds is a difficult question I will not try to answer here. Nor will I have anything to say against the deliberative models of democracy. My main concern in this essay is how to justify the crucial role of majority rule in the political domain.

A. Authority, Autonomy, and Political Equality

One of the main puzzles about democracy begins with the general conditions for the legitimacy of a practical authority. Why should one ever have a reason to do

---

2 See, for example, Joshua Cohen, "Deliberation and Democratic Legitimacy."

3 The epistemic role of democratic deliberation is emphasized by Estlund; see, for example, his "Beyond Fairness and Deliberation: the Epistemic Dimension of Democratic Authority." Cf. H. Richardson, "Democratic Intentions."

4 This type of democratic theory is defended, for example, by Thomas Christiano in his *The Rule of the Many*, and by Jeremy Waldron in his *Law and Disagreement*.

something only because she has been told by an authority to do it? I will assume here that Joseph Raz suggested the most plausible answer: The role of authorities in our practical reasoning is to mediate between the putative subjects of the authority and *the right reasons* that apply to them in the relevant circumstances. An authority is legitimate if its putative subjects are likely better to comply with the relevant reasons which apply to them by following the authoritative directive than by trying to figure out or act on those reasons by themselves. This is, basically, what Raz called the *Normal Justification Thesis* for the legitimacy of an authority (henceforth, NJT).[5] Roughly, then, Raz's conception of practical authority maintains that the justification for compliance with a practical authority must rest on the likelihood that the person subject to the authority will do better by following its provisions than by attempting to rely on his or her own judgment. There are two main types of situation in which this may happen: either the authority knows better what ought to be done in the relevant circumstances, or else, it is just better situated to solve a collective action problem.[6] In both cases, however, the NJT would seem to render the legitimacy of democratic decision procedures purely instrumental. As Raz himself recognized, "it is the truth or soundness of the decisions which counts ultimately. Truth and soundness provide the argument for the legitimacy of the authority." Therefore, Raz concludes, democracy is justified only instrumentally, "only if it leads, by and large, to good government."[7]

I will suggest, however, that this view about the legitimacy of practical authorities is too narrow: the legitimacy of a practical authority, particularly in the public-political domain, rests on a combination of the soundness of its decision *and* the fairness of the process which has led to it. The NJT captures the essence of the former: an authoritative decision is sound when the authority's subjects are more likely to comply with the right reasons that apply to them by following the authoritative resolution, than by attempting to figure out or act on those reasons by themselves. But, as I will argue below, the fairness of the decision procedure is also an essential element of a public authority's legitimacy.[8]

---

5 See J. Raz, *The Morality of Freedom*, Chs. 2–4.

6 On the distinction between these two components of the NJT I have elaborated in my *Interpretation and Legal Theory*, Ch. 8.

7 J. Raz, "Liberalism, Skepticism, and Democracy," 778–779. Richard Arneson defends a very similar conclusion in his "Democracy is not Intrinsically Just."

8 An argument in this spirit has been advanced by S. Hershovitz, "Legitimacy, Democracy, and Razian Authority."

Let me answer an immediate objection before we proceed. Suppose that a putative authority renders a decision that is, under the circumstances, perfectly sound as required by the NJT, though it did not result from a fair procedure. Let us suppose that the decision actually violated the requirement of procedural fairness, whatever we take it to be, that should have applied in the circumstances. Still, would it not be irrational on the part of the authority's subjects to decline to follow the decision, sound as it is, only because the requirement of fairness has been violated? Under normal circumstances it would be irrational indeed, but this only means that not every aspect of the legitimacy of an authoritative decision bears on the subjects' reasons for following it. Raz is right to maintain that the subjects' main reasons for following an authoritative decision consist in the soundness of the decision. The concept of legitimacy, however, need not be exhausted by the reasons for following an authority's decree. The idea of the legitimacy of an authority may comprise elements which do not have a direct bearing on the reasons to follow the authority's decisions, though they may have an indirect and secondary role to play in such reasons for action.

Consider, for example, the analogy of parental authority. Suppose that George has a teenager daughter, Sarah, and they usually take an annual vacation together. George decided that they should go for a ski vacation, as he reasoned that Sarah would enjoy learning to ski, and that she would have the opportunity to acquire a new skill that will enable her many more enjoyable vacations in the future. Let us assume that under the circumstances, this decision was sound. But if George did not consult with his daughter on any of this, would she not have a legitimate reason to complain? Note that Sarah could not complain that the decision was made without regard to her interests. On the contrary—we have assumed that the decision is sound precisely because it adequately reflects the interests of Sarah. Nevertheless, it would seem quite understandable if Sarah complains that she should have been consulted on this issue. From her perspective, the soundness of the result is not all that matters, and understandably so.

We have not yet explained, of course, why the component of fairness is an essential part of the legitimacy of public authorities. Why would a sound but procedurally unfair authoritative decision be tainted with illegitimacy? As we have seen, the answer cannot be derived from the thesis that authoritative resolutions must be responsive, in the appropriate ways, to the interests of the subjects. Authorities can achieve this goal without following fair procedures.

Admittedly, the fairness requirement applied to a decision procedure is often grounded on epistemic considerations: Procedural justice is often designed to enhance the reliability of the relevant procedure in yielding correct outcomes.[9] Fairness may also have instrumental value which is not related to the reliability of the procedure. The fairness of a decision procedure may enhance such goals as communal solidarity, inclusion, and cooperative participation. Regardless of such instrumental considerations, however, it is sometimes the case that procedural fairness is intrinsically valuable.

One of the main values of procedural fairness derives from the value of respect for people. Consider, for example, the case of a group of friends who meet once a month in a book club. Normally, they would have different preferences about the book they would want to discuss in each session. Thus, they would need some decision procedure to settle these issues. A fair decision procedure amongst them would manifest their mutual commitment to respect for each other. The fairness of the decision procedure in such cases ensures that everyone is duly respected.[10] Note that in such cases, the value of fairness is intrinsic but not ultimate. Something is of ultimate intrinsic value if we value it for its own sake, regardless of anything else. Other intrinsic values, however, can be derived from ultimate values by practical reasoning. We justify their intrinsic value by non-instrumental derivation from other intrinsic values. The value of procedural fairness, as an instance of showing respect, belongs to this latter category; it is intrinsic but not ultimate.[11]

Thus, let me suggest that one line of thought which could justify the requirement of fairness with respect to authoritative political decisions is premised on the idea of fairness as *respect for people's right to personal autonomy*. The main value that we attach to personal autonomy is that people should create, as far as possible, their own lives through successive decisions and choices of their own. It is based on a vision of people controlling, to a considerable extent, their own destiny. As Raz put it, "[a]n autonomous person is part author of his life . . . . An autonomous person's well being consists in the successful pursuits of self-chosen goals and relationships."[12] Therefore, Raz argues, "to be autonomous a person must not

9 Criminal justice is a good example: Many of the requirements of fairness that we apply to the procedures of criminal justice, such as a right to fair police interrogation and to a fair trial, the right to counsel, etc., are there to ensure correct results of the criminal justice procedures, namely, that only the guilty be punished and not the innocent. In these cases the value of procedural fairness is purely instrumental.

10 See H. Brighouse, "Egalitarianism and Equal Availability of Political Influence," 123.

11 See J. Raz, *The Morality of Freedom*, 200. See also Ch. 12 in this volume.

12 J. Raz, The Morality of Freedom," 370.

only be given a choice but must be given an adequate range of choices."[13] Accordingly, the right to personal autonomy is the right to a social and political environment which enables people to lead an autonomous life. Now, assuming that political decisions potentially affect the lives of each and every individual in the community, one could claim that due respect for people's autonomy requires a fair decision procedure which would manifest respect for individuals' ability to make up their own minds about the right decision. We need not assume that everybody wants to participate in the political decision procedure. Surely, that would be a false assumption. But the value of respect for people's autonomy requires a political structure in which everybody has a fair chance to participate, and this is what a democratic decision procedure aims to achieve.[14]

Admittedly, however, this move from the value of respect for people's autonomy and the fairness of a democratic decision procedure is far from straightforward. In particular, the egalitarian aspect of this respect needs to be explained and justified. In fact, there are two separate questions here: Why does respect for people's autonomy require equal respect? And even if it does, why would equal respect entail anything like an equal right to political participation?

Respect for people is not necessarily an egalitarian concept. On the contrary, it is often a differentiating value: we typically assume that some people deserve more respect than others. Respect is normally a reaction to others' behavior, virtue, or ethical character. As these vary, respect owed to them may vary accordingly. For example, the conscientious, hard-working colleague would deserve more of our respect than the lazy and irresponsible one. Egalitarians have argued, however, that at some basic level, people, just by virtue of being humans, moral agents, or rational beings, deserve equal respect.[15] Needless to say, it has proved extremely difficult to articulate the grounds for this basic egalitarian concern, and I have no hopes of resolving this issue here. Even if we assume, however, that at some basic level people deserve equal respect as moral agents, it remains to be explained why respect for *their autonomy* should be equal. After all, some people are better at making decisions than others. People's deliberative rationality certainly varies a

13 *Ibid.*, 373.

14 See Brighouse, "Egalitarianism and Equal Availability of Political Influence."

15 But cf. Stephen Darwall, who argued that there are actually two separate concepts of respect involved here, which he named "recognition respect" and "appraisal respect." See his "Two Kinds of Respect." I tend to think that the former category is just an application of respect to special cases. In any case, the distinction does not affect my argument here.

great deal; why assume, then, that we should respect their autonomy to an equal degree?

I believe that the answer is comprised of two considerations. First, as the example of the respect for a colleague suggests, respect for people is always relative to a certain capacity in which we regard them. The hard-working, conscientious colleague deserves our respect *as a colleague*, but not necessarily as a friend or as a spouse. In fact, he may deserve our respect for his work even if, as it happens, he is otherwise a pretty contemptible person. Therefore, the question arises in what capacity people deserve respect for their autonomy in the political context. Plausibly, we may hold that in the political domain people deserve respect as the subjects of political authorities and as members of a body politic, namely, *as citizens.*[16] Citizenship I take to be a morally significant concept: From a moral perspective, citizens are bearers of rights and duties *vis a vis* the state and each other. Any liberal conception of citizenship should be committed to the view that citizens of a body politic should be regarded as having *equal rights.* Once we recognize a right that people should have *as citizens* of a body politic, we are committed to holding that at least in principle, they should have it equally.

Therefore, naturally, the second component of the reply resides in the idea of an individual's *right* to autonomy. As a matter of fact, it is of course true that people are bound to vary a great deal in the autonomy they actually achieve throughout their lives. Nor do people value their own autonomy to the same degree. Surely, for some people autonomy is much more important than for others. These variations notwithstanding, it is a plausible assumption that people, as citizens of a body politic, should have an *equal right* to personal autonomy. The right to personal autonomy is the right to a social, legal, and political environment that would *enable* people to have an adequate range of options to choose from, and that would enable them to decide for themselves what kind of life they want to lead, what kind of things they value in life, and how to implement those projects which they regard as valuable. For our present purposes, we should look at the idea of autonomy not from a perfectionist perspective, as a personal achievement, but as a right to the conditions which enable people to lead autonomous lives. Therefore, like any other individual right, the right to have one's autonomy respected is a right people should have to an equal degree. The fact that people differ in their abilities to make

16 I do not mean "citizenship" in its legal sense; from a moral point of view, it is far from clear that any distinction should be applied to legal citizens as opposed to other categories of residents in a given country.

use of a given right, or differ in their appreciation of its relative importance, does not normally entail that they do not have an equal right to it.

Thus, I suggest that from the perspective of individual rights, people are entitled to an equal respect for their autonomy. Does this entail a right to participate in political decisions to an equal degree? In other words, does equal respect for autonomy entail equal vote in political decisions? I think that the answer is yes, but only if some further assumptions are added. Surely it would be a violation of equal respect for a person's autonomy if that person is deliberately disenfranchised or otherwise denied the vote in a given decision procedure. But suppose that a decision procedure is inegalitarian in a more subtle way. Suppose that a decision procedure is devised which is responsive to the participants' differing capacities to reason. John Stuart Mill (in)famously suggested something along these lines when he claimed that votes should be allocated un-equally, depending on people's level of education.[17] Admittedly, this was a crude suggestion, assuming, very problematically, that education is a reliable proxy for political wisdom and deliberative rationality. Suppose, however, that a procedure along Mill's lines could be refined, so as to convince us of its reliability in differentiating people's deliberative capacities with respect to the relevant decision.[18] Would a scheme like this violate the principle of equal respect for people's autonomy?

The problem is that at least one plausible affirmative answer to this question might actually impose a severe limit on the desirable scope of democratic decision procedures. Why is that? Because when we think about the moral importance of personal autonomy, it would seem that the main value of personal autonomy is premised on the idea that in matters concerning people's *own lives*, it is more important for people to be able to choose for themselves than to choose correctly (that is, even if there is a correct answer). But if this is the underlying moral intuition behind the value of personal autonomy, then equal respect for autonomy need not go beyond those realms in which this underlying principle holds true. Namely, it need not extend to those issues in which it is more important to have the right decision than to let people decide for themselves. Put slightly differently,

---

17 J. S. Mill, *Considerations on Representative Government,* Ch. 8.

18 See, *e.g.*, David Estlund, who argues that strict political equality may be an unattractive ideal because it may damage the quality of political deliberation. See his "Political Quality."

the question is how an autonomy-based principle could give people the right to participate in decisions that affect the lives of *other* people.[19]

A very forceful, though somewhat stronger, version of this challenge has been advanced by Arneson. He claims that an equal right to political participation should not be acknowledged precisely because it entails a power to affect other people's lives. His position is "that there is no such basic moral right, because one does not have a basic moral right to exercise significant power over the lives of other people, to direct how they shall live their lives."[20] There are, it seems to me, two responses to Arneson. First, it should be noted that Arneson consistently addresses his argument against the claim that a right to equal political participation could be a *basic* moral right, arguing that in an inventory of our basic moral rights, one should not find any right which "confers on the right holder the power to direct how another shall live."[21] But I have not argued that a right to participate in political decisions, whether equally or not, is a basic right. It certainly isn't. To the extent that people should have a right to an equal distribution of the power to make political decisions, it would be a derivative right. It must be derived from the basic right to personal autonomy, combined, as we shall see, with certain assumptions about facts constituting our social lives.[22] Whether such a derivation is possible remains to be seen. But again, it is not my contention that a right to political participation, whether equal or not, is a *basic* moral right of anyone. Furthermore, it is not the case that the only alternative to a basic moral right is an instrumental conception of the relevant good or value. There are many things that we value intrinsically, without necessarily assuming that the good is basic or otherwise foundational.[23]

---

19 It may be worth keeping in mind that there is a whole tradition in political theory that would resist this formulation of the question since it views political participation as an essential ingredient of personal autonomy. (See, *e.g.*, Hannah Arendt, *The Human Condition*). As H. Brighouse rightly notes, however, this is a distinctly non-liberal conception of personal autonomy. See his "Egalitarianism and Equal Availability of Political Influence," 136.

20 Arneson, "Democracy is Not Intrinsically Just," 10.

21 *Ibid.*, 11.

22 Perhaps Brighouse's view can be seen as the main target of Arneson's argument, since Brighouse does seem to claim that the principle of equal availability of political influence is a basic moral principle. I do not share this view.

23 Consider, for example, the idea of friendship. Suppose we hold that friendship is intrinsically valuable. My particular friendship with John, for example, is therefore intrinsically valuable, as it instantiates, non-instrumentally, an intrinsic value. Similarly, there are many rights we hold that are not basic, but they instantiate non-instrumentally, other, more basic rights.

There is a second reply to Arneson. Putting aside the question of whether the right to political participation is basic or not, it remains to be asked whether *anyone* has a right to rule, that is, to make decisions which affect other people's lives. If the answer is yes, then it would be difficult to understand why some people might have such a right and others should not. If, on the other hand, Arneson wants to deny that such a right to rule is ever justified, his position would amount to straightforward anarchism, to which, I take it, he does not want to subscribe. (Nor is it consistent with his general position, which justifies political authorities on instrumental grounds.) In other words, once we acknowledge that there are legitimate political authorities, we must concede that some people have a right to make decisions about other people's lives. The only question that remains is whether or not such a right to rule should be subject to distributive concerns of fairness.

Perhaps Arneson would reply that since the only justification for the exercise of a political authority is an instrumental one, even if an authority is legitimate, it cannot claim *a right* to rule. I doubt, however, that so much can depend on the question of whether we associate the legitimacy of a political authority with a right to rule. Political authorities exercise power, and if the exercise of this power is deemed legitimate under the circumstances, the authority's subjects are under an obligation (albeit limited, of course) to follow its prescriptions. This is close enough to anything we might want to characterize as a right to direct how another shall live.

These replies to Arneson's argument, however, do not answer our general concern about the possible connections between the right to personal autonomy and the distribution of political power, namely, how to explain the rationale of democratic decision procedures in those realms in which we would normally hold that it is more important to have the right decision than to let people decide for themselves.

Some political philosophers have responded to this challenge by emphasizing the prevalence of value pluralism.[24] They point to the fact that we live in societies in which people are deeply divided over their conceptions of the good and the just. Furthermore, these divisions are unavoidable, they claim, in a deep sense: Even the most rational people can have *reasonable disagreements* on those matters

24 Most recently, for example, J. Waldron, *Law and Disagreement*.

which would admit of right and wrong, good or bad, just and unjust, etc. Note that the purpose of this move is *not* to doubt that there are sound political decisions, or that there are issues on which it is more important to have the correct decision than to let people decide for themselves. The argument from value pluralism is based on the premise that there is something wrong in imposing an authoritative ruling on people who may *reasonably disagree* with it.[25] Thus, in a way, the requirement of an equal vote as an application of equal respect for people's autonomy becomes something like a fallback position. Since we cannot rule out the possibility of rational disagreement about conceptions of justice and the good, we must assume that people should have an equal right to participate in the decision process, even if, objectively speaking, the instance in question may be one in which it is more important to have the correct decision than to let people choose for themselves.

I think that there is a lot to be said in favor of this argument from pluralism. However, there are two problems with it, and both of them concern its potential scope. First, the argument from value pluralism must be reconciled with the fact that even in the political domain, not everything is potentially subject to reasonable, principled disagreement. A great many functions of legal and political decisions in a modern society concern the resolution of such issues as collective action problems, cost-benefit analysis, the creation of public goods, and other tasks which have very little to do with principled disagreement. And if there is no principled disagreement lurking in the background of such political decisions, it is difficult to see how respect for people's autonomy entails a requirement of equal right to participate in the making of the decision.[26]

It is true that sometimes it is controversial whether an issue involves, say, only a solution of a collective action problem or disputed matters of principle. The boundaries between those issues about which people can reasonably disagree and those about which they cannot are sometimes blurred, and may well be subject to reasonable disagreement. Perhaps this would extend the scope of the argument, but not enough. We should be careful not to generalize from some cases to all.

Secondly, the argument from value pluralism entails the problematic conclusion that the more homogeneous a society is, the less democracy it requires. Pluralism is a

---

25 Cf. D. Estlund, "Jeremy Waldron on Law and Disagreement."

26 See my book review of *Law and Disagreement*.

fact in certain societies, but not in all of them. Those "circumstances of politics," as Waldron called them,[27] whereby different segments of the population are deeply divided over conceptions of the good and the just, simply do not obtain in all contemporary societies. Would we want to say that in homogeneous societies, where people share a conception of the good and evaluative schemes, there is no need for democracy? (That is, at least not from the vantage point of fairness.) Perhaps some political theorists who endorse the argument from pluralism would be willing to bite the bullet at this point, simply admitting that democracy is not universally valuable; it may not be required in all contemporary societies. Others have argued that the lack of pluralism in a given society is in itself something wrong that needs to be changed.[28] Both of these views raise many difficult questions that I cannot deal with here. Instead, I will argue that it is not only the background of pluralism that explains the need for equal participation in politics, but, perhaps more importantly, the background of scarcity and competition over those social resources which, ultimately, constitutes *the conditions* of autonomy. As Thomas Christiano aptly put it, it is mainly conflicts of interest and not conflicts of judgment that ground the need for democracy.[29] It is true that the distinction between these two is not very sharp: Conflicts of interest tend to translate into conflicts of judgment, and often conflicts of judgment lead to conflicts of interest. Nevertheless, the distinction is a very important one, for two reasons. First, a conflict of interest is present even if the parties to the conflict do not grasp it as such. A conflict of interest does not necessarily depend on its self-awareness. More importantly, by focusing on conflicts of interest, we can show that the need for democracy is not confined to pluralistic societies, since conflicts of interest can be pervasive even in homogeneous societies where people share, more or less, the same conception of the good and the just.

It may be objected, however, that conflicts of interest, in themselves, are irrelevant to the justification of democracy because the latter must show that it is important to take people's judgments into account in making decisions. Otherwise, why consult them at all? This is true, of course. The importance of focusing on conflicts of interest, however, rests on the idea that we should take conflicts of judgment seriously precisely because they tend to manifest genuine conflicts of interest.

---

27 Waldron defines the "circumstances of politics" as a combination of two facts: Value pluralism and the practical need to have authoritative decisions. See his *Law and Disagreement*, 102, 144, 159–60.

28 See, for example, J. Rawls, *Political Liberalism*, 35–38.

29 See T. Christiano, *The Rule of the Many*, 53. Generally speaking, the argument that follows reaches conclusions similar to Christiano's.

In other words, the question is which type of conflict we regard as basic. The view advanced by Christiano, I take it, is that we have reason to take conflicts of judgment seriously mainly because, and to the extent that, they manifest conflicts of interest. Let me try to explain, in some detail, why I think that he is right about this.

One crucially important aspect of political authorities concerns the fact that they deal with problems of scarcity and competition over resources. Scarcity is not confined to material resources; it pervades all those social factors which affect the *conditions* of personal autonomy. In a complex society, individuals have very limited abilities to control their lives and shape the environment in which they live. Most of the options we can choose from, and our actual ability to make those choices which constitute our autonomy, are determined by forces outside our control. Some of these limits are determined by natural causes, but many others are determined by economic and social factors. In one way or another, all political decisions affect these conditions and continuously reset the boundaries of social opportunities. Even decisions which have nothing to do with material resources would normally affect people's condition of autonomy: They would make certain forms of life relatively more easy or difficult to pursue. In other words, an individual's conditions of autonomy are determined by a very complex set of factors prevailing in the society in which she lives. Some of these factors consist of material resources, but many others do not. One's ability to choose and pursue a certain form of life is also determined by such factors as social confirmation, self esteem, political opportunities, means of expression, culture, religion, and so on.

Generally speaking, the kinds of values, rights, and ideals that are affected by legal-political decisions, and the extent of their protection, greatly affect people's conditions of autonomy; they determine the forms of life which could be pursued in that community, and how easy or difficult would it be to pursue them. This essentially competitive feature of political decisions lends considerable support to the claim that political power, that is, the power to make authoritative political decisions, could be regarded as a kind of "primary good" which should be subject to concerns of fairness and distributive justice.[30] Thus, assuming, as we did, that the ideal of equal citizenship carries with it the ideal of an equal right to have one's

30 I do not intend to put too much weight on the idea that political power is a "primary good," partly because the latter lends itself to several possible interpretations, and I cannot go into this here. For my purposes it is sufficient to maintain that political power is the kind of good which should be subject to fair distribution.

autonomy respected, it would be natural to conclude that the fair distribution of political power should be, at least *prima facie*, an egalitarian one.

To be sure, it is not assumed here that the value of personal autonomy increases indefinitely in direct proportion to the number of choices available. The availability of an adequate number and diversity of choices is sufficient in order to fulfill the ideal of personal autonomy. However, the argument does assume that for most people living in a complex society, conditions of autonomy present a problem of scarcity and competition over economic and social resources. In a world of limited resources, the political affirmation of one form of life normally comes at the expense of another. Furthermore, it should be kept in mind that scarcity of resources creates competition even when the relevant parties share the same conception of the good or the just. The present argument need not assume that there must be any principled disagreement in the background of such competition over the limited resources which constitute people's conditions of autonomy.

It may be argued, however, that the scope of this argument is more limited than suggested above, since there are many types of societal goods created or modified by legal-political decisions which are not essentially competitive. The creation of *public* goods, so this argument runs, is not subject to competition since those are the kinds of goods which people can enjoy without subtracting from the potential enjoyment of others. Public goods, once created, can be enjoyed by all in a non-exclusive and non-excludable manner.[31] Therefore, this argument concludes, even if there are conflicts of interest and competition over resources at the background of many political decisions, this cannot be generalized to all cases; the creation of public goods, which forms a major part of the role of political authorities, should be excluded from the argument from scarcity.

There is a grain of truth in this objection, but much less than meets the eye. A closer look at the nature of public goods would reveal that it is much more competitive than one might have thought. To begin with, the *production* of many types of public goods requires collective action, and solution to collective action problems is often a matter of competition and conflict of interests. Second, we should keep in mind that the production of any type of good, including public goods, involves opportunity costs which can be very significant. This is yet another way in which

---

[31] For a detailed account of the distinctions between public, collective, and common goods, see Ch. 10 in this volume.

the production of public goods is potentially competitive. But I think that even at the consumption end, public goods tend to be more competitive than is generally assumed. To begin with, the non-excludability of public goods is a matter of degree. A beautiful public park may be enjoyed by many without the enjoyment of one subtracting from the enjoyment of another. But only up to a point, of course; once too many people begin to use the park it may well become less enjoyable. There are very few goods which are perfectly non-excludable in their consumption. Perhaps the beauty of a work of art, or the achievement of an artistic genius, may be an example of near-prefect non-excludability, although the possibility of exclusion can never be ruled out even in such innocuous examples. More important examples of public goods, however, are definitely more competitive than this. Consider, for instance, the suggestion that freedom of speech is a public good. A society which protects free speech, it is often argued, creates a public good that can be enjoyed by all, without thus subtracting from the consumption of this good by others. But this is actually false. An extensive protection of freedom of speech might protect such expressions which make speech itself much more difficult for some than for others. If freedom of speech protects the continuous hate-speech of one group against another, people who belong to the target group, which could be a vulnerable minority, may find the effectiveness or perhaps even the possibility of their free speech seriously impeded. Similar considerations also pertain to many other public goods. It is true that their consumption is not necessarily exclusive, but in practice, they do tend to involve many competitive elements. The number of public goods which are perfectly non-exclusive and non-excludable, involving no conflict of interest between persons who might be affected, would shrink under closer scrutiny to a very insignificant number.

I believe that this admittedly contingent element of socioeconomic scarcity which lurks in the background of political decisions may help us to bridge the gap between the ideal of equal respect for people's autonomy and the principle of equal participation in the political decision process. The competitive aspect of politics lends considerable support to the conclusion that an equal respect for people's right to personal autonomy should be implemented by a right to an equal participation in the political decision process. To be sure, this is not a conceptual link; but then, few arguments in political theory should be expected to be a priori. In a very different, much less competitive world, people might need different principles of fairness and different political institutions. That should come as no surprise.

Arguably, however, there is still a missing link in the chain. It can be objected that the argument from autonomy merely supports the conclusion that the conditions of autonomy ought to be distributed fairly, but it does not follow that the political power to make decisions about such matters must also be distributed fairly. This is a forceful objection, and it has two possible aspects. First, it might be an issue of institutional design: Can we think of any alternative political structure that could guarantee a fair distribution of people's conditions of autonomy, without also providing them an equal opportunity to shape the outcomes of such political decisions? I do not think so, but of course, I cannot be sure. If there is such an alternative political structure, then we would have to admit that at least from the vantage point of fairness, there is a great deal to be said in its favor.

Secondly, and more importantly, however, there is a question of principle here. Suppose that I am wrong about the institutional issue, and a nondemocratic political structure could be envisaged so that it would achieve a fair or equal distribution of people's conditions of autonomy. Could it also manifest *respect* for people's autonomy? Respect for a person's right to personal autonomy is (among other things) a respect we owe to her freedom of choice. How can we demonstrate such respect if we do not ask the person to express her choice in any meaningful way? To be sure, there are many goods which can be distributed fairly without the need to have the subjects of the distributive principle express their views about the proper distribution or influence its outcomes. But this cannot be the case when the relevant distributive concern is essentially tied to people's right to choose the kinds of goods they would want to have in the first place. Only an equal right to participate in the decision process can instantiate to a full extent the need to respect people's choices, and enable them to have a fair chance to shape the underlying conditions that would enable them to exercise their choices.[32] Needless to say, the nature of the equal right to participate in political decisions is problematic, and the question of what kind of equality it would entail needs careful elaboration. The following sections take up some of these difficulties.

B. Political Deliberation and Equality of Opportunity

So far, we have seen that equal respect for people's autonomy needs to be implemented by acknowledging a right to equal participation in the decision process. Therefore, from now on, I will assume that in the political domain people have a

32 See Brighouse, "Egalitarianism and Equal Availability of Political Influence," 125.

right to an egalitarian distribution of political power,[33] and I will try to suggest a few clarifications about what kind of a right to equality it is. First, however, we need to mention a familiar but important distinction. A political process that results in an authoritative resolution comprises two main stages, deliberation and decision. Political power is measured by one's ability to influence both of these stages of the political process. Deliberation begins with setting the agenda. For any authoritative result, it matters a great deal what the agenda for decision is, how it is determined and defined. People's ability to influence the setting of the agenda is a first and crucial step in the exercise of political power. Once the agenda is set, a process of deliberation begins, whereby people attempt to influence the result in various ways, by proposing rational (or irrational) arguments, bargains, enticements, etc. A considerable aspect of political power is determined by people's ability to influence this process of deliberation.[34] At some point, however, deliberation has to come to an end and an authoritative decision must be reached. Needless to say, it matters a great deal who makes the decision and what kind of decision procedure is followed.

Now suppose that democracy is a commitment to a principle of fairness which should apply at both of these stages of the political process,[35] and suppose that this is some principle of equality. It often goes unnoticed that such a principle of equality need not be the same kind of equality with respect to these two main stages of the political process, namely, deliberation and decision. An equal distribution of political power with respect to the deliberation process is basically a

---

33 The notion of "political power" should be understood here simply to mean the power to make authoritative public decisions. It should be noted, however, that the argument of the previous section is limited to politics at the basic structure of society, so to speak; it is not intended to apply, without qualifications, to many "micro" levels of decision making, such as a faculty meeting or a condo association.

34 One could claim that agenda-setting and deliberation are two separate stages in the political process. In many respects surely that is correct, but for the purposes of the argument under consideration, it makes no difference. I will regard both as aspects of the deliberation stage of democratic procedures.

35 It may be objected that the very need for deliberation cannot be explained on grounds of fairness. Only the objective of reaching sound political decisions can rationalize the importance of the deliberation stage of democratic decision procedures. I think that D. Estlund makes this objection in "Jeremy Waldron on Law and Disagreement," 111. See also, H. Richardson, "Democratic Intentions," 359. This is not quite true, however. Once we assume that people should have an equal opportunity to influence political results, the deliberation stage of democracy cannot be exempt from requirements of fairness; after all, part of what it means to have political power is determined by one's ability to influence deliberation. Furthermore, it should be kept in mind that alternative ways of addressing a political problem, and different structures of decision making, are almost always biased in favor of particular outcomes. Perhaps Estlund would be right in this objection if one assumed that fairness is the *only* consideration supporting democracy; but we have made no such claim.

principle of *equal opportunity*, whereas the kind of equality which would be required to implement fairness at the stage of the authoritative decision is a principle of an *equal share* of the power to make the decision, namely, majority vote.

Dworkin's distinction between "impact" and "influence" may be helpful in explaining the first point. According to Dworkin, the distinction between political impact and influence is as follows: "Someone's impact in politics is the difference he can make, just on his own, by voting for or choosing one decision rather than another. Someone's influence, on the other hand, is the difference he can make not just on his own but also by leading or inducing others to believe or vote or choose as he does."[36] Dworkin is right to conclude that at least with respect to the democratic deliberation process, if equality matters, it is equality of influence, and not impact, that should count. After all, the whole point of the exercise of political power at the stage of deliberation is to have the maximum influence on the emerging decision, and that surely means one's ability to lead or induce others to vote or choose as he does. But, Dworkin argues, equality of influence is not an attractive political ideal. Basically, his argument is as follows: There is a substantial variety of factors which determine people's differing abilities to influence political decisions, such as money, social status, natural skills, willingness to devote time and resources, and so on. Even on the face of it, it would seem to be morally groundless to strive to eliminate the differences between people on all these different dimensions. Perhaps the influence of money should be eliminated because wealth is not the kind of difference that should affect people's relative political influence. But other differences are not illegitimate: Presumably, a person who is willing to devote more time, energy, and personal resources to political participation is entitled to reap the benefit of her effort by having greater influence on the result. In other words, Dworkin claims that people cannot complain about inequality of influence unless they can trace the relative lack of influence to a source that is *itself illegitimate*.[37] From this Dworkin concludes that "equality of influence is incompatible, even in principle, with other attractive aspects of an egalitarian society."[38]

Even if we accept the premises of this argument, as I think we should, it does not follow that equality of influence is not the principle of fairness which is required at the deliberation stage of the political process. The natural conclusion that follows is that the relevant principle should be the principle of equality *of opportunity* of

---

36 R. Dworkin, *Sovereign Virtue*, 191.

37 *Ibid.*, 199.

38 *Ibid.*, 198.

political influence.[39] That is so, because equality of opportunity is *always* relative to a set of factors which we consider as independently illegitimate in determining social outcomes. The distinction between potentially relevant and irrelevant differentiating factors is one which is presupposed by *any* principle of equality of opportunity. Suppose, for example, that we hold an egalitarian conception with respect to the opportunity of school children to receive adequate education. Surely, such an ideal must be driven by the assumption that among the factors which can affect children's educational prospects, there are some which ought to be eliminated because they are illegitimate sources of differentiation. However, there must also be factors, such as, perhaps, natural intelligence or talent, that we regard as legitimate sources of influence on the educational outcome. Otherwise, if nothing can legitimately differentiate the outcomes, equality of opportunity necessarily collapses into equality of outcome. Dworkin's argument, therefore, cannot be regarded as an objection to the principle of *equality of opportunity of political influence* at the deliberation stage. Roughly, the idea is that people should have an equal opportunity to influence the setting of the political agenda and once the agenda is set, they should have an equal opportunity to influence the results of the deliberation.

Now, this is an essential part of what democracy is all about. The commitment of democratic regimes to equality of opportunity of political influence is manifest in a wide range of principles and institutions which we normally regard as essential to the proper functioning of a democracy. These principles and institutions include freedom of association; equality of access to political institutions; an extensive protection of freedom of speech; regulation of political parties, lobbying groups, etc.; campaign finance restrictions, and so on. All these, and doubtless many other principles and institutions, aim to guarantee equality of opportunity of political influence at the stage of deliberation. Needless to say, the details of these principles are controversial. For example, people differ in their views about political campaign finance restrictions, some seeking more, and others less, regulation. Some of these differences of opinion are about matters of fact (e.g. what kind of restrictions are feasible, more effective, and so on), but others are about matters of principle and fairness. This is natural: as with any other principle of equality of opportunity, people tend to have different views about the distinction between legitimate and illegitimate differentiating factors. Although we tend to agree, for example, that people's willingness to devote time and energy to political

---

39 Cf. D. Estlund, "Political Quality," 176, and Brighouse, "Egalitarianism and Equal Availability of Political Influence."

participation is a legitimate factor that may be allowed to affect political deliberation, we tend to disagree about the legitimacy of the factor of wealth. But again, once we regard the relevant consideration of fairness at the stage of political deliberation as one of a principle of equality of opportunity, these controversies are precisely those which are to be expected.

C. Equality and the Decision Stage

Equality at the stage of the decision procedure is a different matter altogether. Here we need a principle of a fair distribution of the actual power to make the decision. An equal distribution of the power to make a decision would seem to entail the familiar principle of one vote to one person, that is, a straightforward majority decision procedure. This is not so simple, however, for a number of reasons. First, the idea of an equal distribution of political power does not necessarily *entail* a system of majority vote. If the whole point of a majority vote is to provide each one of the participants with an equal share of the power to determine the result, then any fair lottery system would seem to be an adequate way of implementing this egalitarian principle.[40] Maybe so. But we have good reasons, based on the considerations we have mentioned so far, to reject the lottery system. A lottery decision procedure would undermine the rationality of the *deliberation* stage of democracy. Let us recall that the considerations of fairness at the deliberation stage were premised on the idea that people should have an equal opportunity *to influence* the political decision. It makes no sense to maintain that people should have a meaningful opportunity to influence a political result when the result is entirely determined by chance. The rationality of the principles of fairness at the stage of deliberation requires that people's input into the deliberation process have a potential influence on the output. This can be achieved only if there is some causal connection between the deliberation and the decision. Any type of a lottery system severs such a causal connection, and thus renders the deliberation process entirely superfluous. In other words, democratic theory assumes that deliberation is, at least potentially, a rational process that can lead to changes in people's views which will culminate in the final vote.

The idea that an equal distribution of political power at the decision stage requires the "one person, one vote" model is obviously a simplification. Let me consider

40 See, for example, J. Waldron, *The Dignity of Legislation*, 160–161, and D. Estlund, "Jeremy Waldron on Law and Disagreement," 119–120.

several complications, beginning with the question of the appropriate "majority." It is natural to assume that an equal distribution of political power requires the 1/n formula for determining the voting procedure, where n simply represents the number of voters. This would seem to entail that anything which deviates from a simple majority model amounts to a non-egalitarian distribution of power and is therefore, at least *prima facie*, unfair. In most familiar democracies, however, supermajority requirements are not uncommon. Are these procedures undemocratic? Is it always wrong to deviate from the simple majority model?

One rationale that is often suggested for supermajorities ties its justification to the relative importance of the decision. Many people find it intuitively problematic, almost frightful, that crucial political decisions, profoundly important to the future of their nation, can be decided by simple majorities. There is a strong temptation to believe that the more important a decision is, and the more far-reaching its long-term effects, the larger the majority which should be required for its adoption. The intuition here is clear enough; it relies on the assumption that there is a strong element of contingency, almost arbitrariness, in the particular majority which happens to prevail at any given set of circumstances, and people feel that such arbitrary factors should not determine crucial political decisions. Given how easily political processes are subject to manipulation, there is certainly a grain of truth in this kind of concern. But as a matter of principle, it is not warranted. If anything, the contrary is true. From the perspective of fairness, the more important a decision is, the more scrupulous we should be with respect to the equal distribution of the power to make that decision. A supermajority requirement always disrupts the equal distribution of political power because it is necessarily biased in favor of the *status quo ante*; it always reduces the relative political power of those who favor a social change. As a matter of principle, then, the relative importance of the decision, by itself, cannot justify a supermajority decision procedure.

It may well be argued, of course, that there are certain decisions in the public domain which *should* be immune from change. Perhaps there are certain rights or principles which should be protected from the vagaries of political decisions and removed from the ordinary democratic decision process. This is the main idea behind the constitutional protection of rights, principles, and certain political structures.[41]

---

41 Constitutional entrenchment is always a form of supermajority decision procedure. Constitutions vary a great deal in the details of the procedures and in the degree of entrenchment. Basically, the more rigid a constitution is, the greater the supermajority which is required to introduce a constitutional change.

The question of whether there are, indeed, matters of political morality which should be protected from standard democratic decision procedures will be discussed in the next chapter.

Other cases of a supermajority requirement, however, are not necessarily at odds with the equal distribution of political power. Consider, for example, the case of a relatively large persistent minority. Suppose that country A is comprised of two main social groups; let us call them the greens and the reds. The greens form about 55% of the population, and the reds 45%. Now suppose that these two social groups are in a deep and longstanding conflict with each other, whereby the greens and the reds tend to vote on most issues according to their group interests which are typically at odds with the interests of the other group. Under these circumstances the reds are extremely unlikely to have their interests protected by a simple majority. In a very simplified way we can say that instead of having their political objectives materialized in about 45% of the cases, the reds are actually going to lose in 100% of the cases. Under these circumstances, it seems that a supermajority decision procedure may actually facilitate a much more egalitarian distribution of political power, thereby giving the reds a fair chance of having their votes affect the political outcomes.[42] In other words, we sometimes need a supermajority decision procedure as a corrective measure when certain social forces make it very unlikely that a simple majority voting rule will implement an equal distribution of political power.[43]

To be sure, a supermajority requirement is not the only potential deviation from a strict majoritarian principle. Many other familiar political procedures and institutions raise similar worries. For example, it is probably impossible to defend the American system of senatorial representation among the states (namely, an equal number of representatives regardless of the population size) as a proper implementation of a majority-rule principle. Similar concerns apply to various forms of

---

42 To be sure, I do not want to suggest that a supermajority decision procedure is always the best way to handle the problems of persistent minorities. Particularly when the minority forms a smaller proportion of the population, other means might be required. Some of these issues will be taken up again in the next chapter.

43 There are other cases in which supermajority can be justified. For example, sometimes the rationale of a supermajority requirement stems from a concern about very low voter turnout. In particular, constituencies which face relatively frequent initiatives and referenda tend to have very low turnout at these elections, which makes it problematic to leave crucially important decisions turn on a fraction of the votes. In such cases the requirement of a supermajority seems justified. See E. Garrett, "Issues in Implementing Referendums in Israel: A Comparative Study in Direct Democracy." For a rationale of supermajority requirements in legislative bodies, see S. Levmore, "Bicameralism: When Are Two Decisions Better Than One?"

non-proportional representation systems, various "creative" designs of voting districts, and many other familiar features of contemporary democracies. I do not intend to argue that any democratic institution which deviates from the majority rule principle is therefore unjustified or illegitimate. Democratic regimes strive to implement many values and moral-political concerns, some of which are bound to conflict with each other. It would be naïve to presume that any single principle can justify such complex institutions. Each case must be judged on its particular merits.

Another familiar worry about majority vote concerns the fact that such a decision procedure is not designed to take into account the voters' *intensity* of preferences. This is usually understood to be troublesome for those theories that strive to justify democracy on utilitarian grounds. This understanding of democracy is premised on the idea that the good government is the one which maximizes the overall satisfaction of preferences. Within the utilitarian model, however, the issue of the intensity of preferences becomes a serious problem: if each voter gets to cast one vote that is meant to express her preference, the intensity of such preferences cannot be taken into account, and this would seriously corrupt the utilitarian calculus.[44] But even if we reject the utilitarian model, the question of whether the intensity of preferences should be taken into account remains, though from a different angle. Majority decision procedures are agnostic about the reasons for which people cast their vote. Intensity of preferences is typically determined by reasons; one's reasons for a given vote determine, among other things, how much one *should* care about the issue, and how important it actually is for that person to have the result come out as he would have it. Doesn't fairness require that such considerations be taken into account?

The answer is both yes and no. From the perspective of the egalitarian distribution of political power, intensity of preferences should not matter. In a way, the whole point of a majority decision procedure is to ensure that at the end of the day, when a decision has to be reached and votes cast, each person should have an equal share of the power to make the decision. This simply requires counting the votes. However, we should keep in mind that this egalitarian principle is premised on the value of personal autonomy. Although the right to personal autonomy should be

44 This should not be confused with the problems created by the *ranking* of preferences that lead to the famous cycling problems extensively discussed in the Public Choice literature. See K. Arrow, *Social Choice and Individual Values*, and D. Mueller, *Public Choice*, 384–99.

distributed equally, any fair political decision procedure must take account of the fact that political decisions affect people's lives and social opportunities differently; therefore, some people may have good reasons to care more about the decision than others. A certain increase in the tax rate, for instance, might be much more burdensome for some people who happen to be in the minority than it is advantageous to those who happen to form the majority. Thus it would seem to be unfair if we disregard the reasons for voting preferences altogether. But democracies can actually cope with this problem by facilitating means of reasoning and bargaining. First, intensities of preferences can make some difference at the deliberation stage of the political process, which allows certain, though limited, mechanisms for reasoning, bargaining, and compromise. Much more importantly, however, an essential part of the rationale of *representative* democracies is to facilitate this bargaining aspect of the decision procedures and allow for intensities of preferences to count. Political parties will find it much easier, at the parliamentary level, to engage in bargaining, compromise, and logrolling which would give effect to the intensities of the preferences they represent.[45]

In other words, considerations of fairness about the distribution of political power must be mixed. On the one hand, we must give each person an equal share of the power to make the decision, and this is, basically, a matter of counting votes. On the other hand, considerations of fairness also require that due weight be given to the fact that political decisions matter differently to different groups of people. This means that any fair decision procedure should make room for fair bargaining and compromise. Representative democracy is particularly well suited for accommodating both of these concerns.[46]

Acknowledging the need for bargaining raises another puzzle: Why don't we take one further step and allow vote trading? If a particular decision is much more important for some people than others, why do we not allow those who would be willing to pay for the votes of others to purchase them? From the vantage point of fairness, it is not obvious that the right to vote should be regarded as inalienable, as it is in all contemporary democracies. The principle of fairness, in itself, would not explain the inalienability of the right to vote: The principle of an equal

---

45 See J. M. Buchanan & G. Tullock, *The Calculus of Consent: Logical Foundations of Constitutional Democracy*, and R. Cooter, *The Strategic Constitution*.

46 This is not meant to be a general argument against direct democracy. The latter involves many complicated issues that cannot be explored here. The point in the text does suggest, however, that even from the limited perspective of fairness, it should not be assumed that the more direct a democracy is, the better.

distribution of political power requires that each person be given *a right* to vote. It does not explain why people cannot trade those rights under any circumstances. Let me consider a tempting, but wrong answer first. It might be tempting to think that the right to vote is inalienable because voting expresses one's consent to be governed. This argument is premised on the idea that the legitimacy of a government resides in the consent of the governed, and without the subjects' consent, the authority is illegitimate. The exercise of the right to vote is then taken to embody this element of consent, and its inalienability is regarded as essential for maintaining the legitimacy of the government *vis-à-vis* each and every one of its putative subjects.[47]

This line of thought, however, is doubly flawed. First, it relies on the mistaken assumption that the legitimacy of an authority depends on the consent of its putative subjects. Nothing in the conditions for the legitimacy of a practical authority warrants such a thesis. Neither the soundness of the authoritative decision, that is, the NJT, nor the considerations of fairness we have mentioned above, rely on the idea of consent.[48] But suppose that I am wrong about this, and that consent is rightly regarded as a condition of legitimacy. Would it render the right to vote inalienable in the requisite sense? It is very difficult to see how. Theorists who tend to regard voting as the expression of the consent to be governed immediately acknowledge that those who deliberately abstain from voting must also be taken to have expressed their consent to be governed, that is, they are taken to have acquiesced in whatever result turns out at the relevant ballot. But this makes it impossible to explain why selling one's vote voluntarily and under fair bargaining conditions would violate the consent element of the vote. If deliberate abstention amounts to acquiescence, why not voluntary transfer as well? Contractual rights, like property rights, are transferable.[49]

Perhaps we should look for the rationale of the prohibition on vote trading in more mundane places. A familiar problem with vote trading consists in the fact that it is particularly vulnerable to exploitation. The temptation to trade a non-tangible asset like the vote for immediate material benefits would be extremely strong among poor people: After all, they know that the marginal impact of their personal

---

47 Perhaps this is the sentiment which is manifest in those democracies which make it legally obligatory for their citizens to vote in elections (*e.g.* Australia, Brazil).

48 See, *e.g.*, Raz, "Authority and Consent."

49 It is worth keeping in mind that only the trade of vote for money (or other tangible goods) is prohibited; political vote trades, in various forms, are part and parcel of political bargaining.

vote amongst millions of others is almost nil. Since only the rich, or the very rich, would be able to afford buying votes in sufficient quantities to make a political difference, a vote-trading system would dramatically increase the effect of wealth on politics, entrenching, *de facto*, a very unequal distribution of political power. Thus the prohibition on vote trading is basically a safeguard against the slide from democracy to wealth-aristocracy.[50] Admittedly, this is basically a "slippery slope" argument. But it is worth keeping in mind that the slope is very steep here.

Finally, we should bear in mind that the fairness of majority decision procedures crucially depends on the demarcation of the constituency. When we say that power must be distributed equally, the question always arises: equally amongst whom? In the complex world we live in, constituencies cannot be regarded as some kind of natural political entities, established in advance of political interests and decision procedures. When democratic decision procedures pervade such an enormous range of public decision levels, from condo associations through town meetings to national and even international levels, the demarcation of constituencies becomes a ubiquitous problem, and there is little hope for generalizations and abstract answers.[51] There is, however, one important point that should be stressed here. The argument for an equal distribution of political power was grounded on the idea of equal respect for people's personal autonomy. I have argued that in the context of political authority, this principle entails a majoritarian decision procedure. But the argument is limited to the basic structure of the political domain. In many other, let us say "micro," contexts, such as faculty meetings or condo associations, the rationale of a majority decision procedure might be quite different. I would venture to suggest that in most of these contexts, the requirement of a majority vote is grounded on some principle of equal respect, but not necessarily respect for the participants' autonomy. In the context of a faculty meeting, for instance, it is presumably the equal respect for the participants' professional judgment that we should appeal to if we want to justify a majority decision procedure. At other times, it may be a principle of equal respect for people's

50 One may be tempted to think that while a system of vote trading increases the inequality of political power, it may increase the equality of material resources, transferring money from the rich to the poor. This is just unrealistic since votes are ludicrously cheap to buy. I have been told that in the happy days of former Mayor Daley in Chicago, votes were bought for a few cans of beer. Vote trading does not seem to be a good system for the redistribution of wealth. See R. L. Hasen, "Vote Buying." Furthermore, as Levmore argues, a system of vote trading would be plagued with problems of collective action. See S. Levmore, "Voting with Intensity."

51 For some discussions of the constituency demarcation problem, see, for example, Raz & Margalit, "The Right to Self Determination," Ch. 6.

stake in the outcome of the decision which could warrant an egalitarian distribution of power. In any case, it should not be assumed that the justification of democracy and the principles of fairness it instantiates necessarily apply, without modifications, to all levels of decision making, even if those decisions ought to be conducted according to some majority-rule principle.

D. Fairness and Soundness of Democratic Procedures

So far we have regarded the fairness of an authoritative decision procedure and the soundness of its result as separate issues. Sometimes, however, soundness and fairness are closely entangled, and at other times they may turn out to be in conflict. For the rest of this chapter I would like to explore some of these relations between fairness and soundness of democratic procedures.

Perhaps the closest link between the fairness of a democratic decision procedure and the soundness of the result obtains in those relatively rare cases in which the democratic decision procedure instantiates a form of *pure procedural justice*. As Rawls defined it, "pure procedural justice obtains when there is no independent criterion for the right result; instead, there is a correct or fair procedure such that the outcome is likewise correct or fair, whatever it is, provided that the procedure has been properly followed."[52] Now it is true that public authoritative decisions are rarely of this nature. Normally, we should be able to know what the criteria for the right decision are, regardless of the decision procedure. However, there are some cases in which something like pure procedural justice obtains. Consider, for example, a case where we have to choose a certain public official and there are several equally competent candidates (or candidates who are incommensurably on par with each other). Assuming that those candidates do not represent different ideological constituencies, and that the election is purely a question of personal competence, this may well be a case in which any decision which is reached by a fair procedure is rendered correct and fair, and only because it results from such a fair decision procedure. Note, however, that in such cases a democratic decision procedure is only one option; any other fair procedure, like a fair lottery, would instantiate pure procedural justice and render the result equally acceptable. But again, such cases are relatively rare, and I do not want to argue that pure procedural justice plays a major role in democratic decision procedures. Nevertheless, the model is important, as I will explain in a moment.

52 J. Rawls, *A Theory of Justice*, 86.

Second, we should consider those cases in which a public decision is good only because most people actually want it. These are the cases that Dworkin labeled "choice-sensitive" issues: "Choice-sensitive issues are those whose correct solution . . . depends essentially on the character and distribution of preferences within the political community."[53] Roughly, then, choice-sensitive public decisions are those which become the correct decisions just by virtue of being supported by the majority. Consider, for example, a need to choose between allocating certain public funds to the construction of a swimming pool or a football stadium. Presumably, the right and fair decision would be the one which is supported by the majority. But why? There are two possible explanations for this intuitive stance. One would rely on the utilitarian conception which favors the maximization of the overall satisfaction of preferences. Assuming that we leave the intensity of preferences constant (or that we just ignore this complication), it would be natural to conclude that a majority decision procedure is likely to lead to the best results: If more people prefer the swimming pool over the football stadium, building the former would satisfy more preferences than the alternative.

But there is a better, nonutilitarian explanation for the rationale of choice-sensitive decisions. Some choices are basically a matter of taste, either because they are not supported by any particular reasons, or else, because the reasons which support them are entirely agent-relative. The essential nature of a choice which reflects taste, as opposed to other evaluative choices, consists in the *self-regarding* nature of its underlying reasons. Such choices are not based on reasons which ought to apply to others. Perhaps I prefer to have a swimming pool in my neighborhood, but this is not a preference that I can rationally regard as one that others *should* have as well. If they prefer something else, so be it. When decisions have to be reached on matters concerning preferences of taste, nobody can claim to have a better other-regarding reason than anyone else supporting any particular decision. Therefore, fairness of the decision procedure and soundness of the result are very closely linked here: If we cannot have all our taste-preferences satisfied, and none is better supported by reasons than any other, at least we should have the result which gets most people what they want.[54]

---

53 *Sovereign Virtue*, 204. The missing part of this quote includes the words "as a matter of justice." I omitted these words advisedly, since it implies an unnecessary restriction. See also Raz, "Liberalism, Skepticism, and Democracy," 778.

54 See Raz, "Liberalism, Skepticism, and Democracy," 778. It is arguable that in such cases, when a decision has to be reached on matters of taste, a lottery decision procedure would be just as fair as voting. I think that this is basically correct. As a practical matter, however, there would often be a problem in isolating choice-sensitive decisions from others. Often such decisions are closely entangled with other decisions which ought to be reason-based and open for rational deliberation.

The scope of choice-sensitive decisions in politics, understood as concerning matters of taste, is very limited. Political decisions are far more complex, and even if some choices are based on preferences of taste, they are often inextricably entangled with other, substantive issues of justice, culture, efficiency, and so on. Thus in most political contexts, the fairness of the decision procedure, and the soundness of the result, are separate issues, quite independent of each other. This brings us back to the question of legitimacy, and the reasons for following democratic authorities. As we have noted earlier, the primary reasons for following an authoritative decision consist in the NJT, that is, in the assumption that the subjects are more likely to comply with the reasons which apply to them by following the authoritative decision, than by trying to figure out, or act on, those reasons by themselves. Now, the relation between the fairness of the decision procedure and the NJT raises two important questions: First, are there reasons to believe that democratic decision procedures are likely to yield sound results? Second, would we have reasons to follow democratic decisions only because they are fair, even if the decisions do not comply with the NJT? An attempt to answer the first question would need to rely on a great deal of empirical evidence, and I cannot hope to answer such a question here.[55] I would like to conclude, however, with a few sketchy comments on the second question.

Thus, the question is this: Would people have reasons to follow democratic decisions even if they are not sound, that is, even if the decision does not comply with the NJT? This is a very wide and complicated issue, so let me try to narrow it down since I do not want to discuss the entire range of arguments which have been offered to justify political obligation in democratic regimes. I will assume here, following Joseph Raz's conception of authority, that people's primary reasons for following an authoritative decision consist in the NJT. As we have noted from the outset, however, the fairness

---

55 For example, many of those who are inclined to justify democracy on utilitarian grounds think that the famous Condorcet "jury theorem" provides a very promising line of thought: Roughly, this theorem holds that if the following two conditions obtain, the probability of getting the correct result increases with the number of voters. The conditions are, first, that each and every voter is more likely than not to have the decision right, and second, that votes are cast independently of each other. The main problem with the application of the Condorcet theorem to democratic decision procedures is that these two conditions rarely obtain. Generally, even under ideal conditions of deliberation, we have no assurance that all voters, or even that most of them, have a greater than 0.5 probability of reaching the right decision when they cast their vote. Nor is it generally true that in a democratic process, voters cast their votes independently of each other: Voters often tend to follow those whom they regard as more knowledgeable than they are; then we have bargaining, strategic behavior, and other familiar factors, all which undermine the second condition of the Condorcet theorem. See, for example, Dahl, *Democracy and Its Critics*, 141–142; Waldron, *Law and Disagreement*, 140; Levmore, "Voting Paradoxes and Interest Groups."

of the decision procedure does not seem to form any part of the reasons for following an authoritative directive. But this is not quite accurate, and it is time now to qualify this statement. I will consider two such qualifications.

First, in addition to the primary reasons for obeying an authority, captured by the NJT, people often have secondary or auxiliary reasons as well. The main example of such auxiliary reasons obtains where obedience to a mistaken decision is instrumentally conducive to supporting an otherwise legitimate and well-functioning authority.[56] The question remains whether the fairness of the authoritative decision procedure is sufficient to ground such auxiliary reasons for obedience. It is not difficult to see that under certain circumstances, the answer would be affirmative.

When we have a reasonably fair and well-functioning democracy, the duty to obey mistaken decisions can be derived from the duty to support just institutions.[57] When the democratic institutions operate in a fair and just manner, people would normally have good reasons to support the democratic institutions, even if such a support occasionally involves the need to obey mistaken decisions. Note, however, that this is a very limited conclusion, based on instrumental considerations, and therefore it does not entail a *general* obligation to obey the law. Not every act of obedience to the law is instrumentally valuable for supporting the democratic regime.[58] For instance, the publicity element is a crucial factor: If the authority's decision is mistaken, and one can disobey the decision without anyone else knowing about it, it is difficult to see how the duty to support just institutions would tell against such an act of disobedience. So this line of thought entails a very modest conclusion: The subjects of a democratic authority would have a reason, or maybe an obligation, to obey a mistaken authoritative decision only if such an obedience is, as matter of fact, instrumentally valuable as a means of support for the proper functioning of the democratic regime, assuming that the regime is by and large legitimate.

Second, in addition to such auxiliary reasons for political obligation, there may also be cases in which it is *initially* more important for the subjects of an authority to have a fair decision procedure than a sound result. In fact, there is one very limited type of cases in which this is evidently so: When the authoritative decision instantiates a form of pure procedural justice, it is clearly the case that the fairness of the procedure is more important than the soundness of the result, simply because,

---

56 See my *Positive Law and Objective Values*, 102–103.

57 See Rawls, *A Theory of Justice*, 354.

58 See Raz, *The Authority of Law*, 241.

ex hypothesis, we do not have a procedure-independent criterion for the soundness of the result. Now, despite the fact that pure procedural justice has very limited application to politics, it does suggest a more general point. The fairness of the decision procedure in cases of pure procedural justice is decisive of the legitimacy of the result because we just do not have any independent criterion for the desired result. But the question of whether we do or do not have a procedure-independent criterion for the soundness of the result is not necessarily a dichotomous issue; even if there are such criteria sometimes they are not knowable, or are extremely difficult to ascertain, or are not supported by enough available evidence. In other words, we can regard pure procedural justice as a limiting case, with some other cases closer or farther removed from it to various degrees. This would suggest that if the criteria for the soundness of an authoritative result are in serious doubt, it may become more important to have a fair decision procedure than a sound result.

A note of caution might be appropriate here. I am not suggesting that *the fact* of controversy, or pluralism, renders certain aspects of democratic politics close enough to the model of pure procedural justice. The fact that people disagree on the criteria for the sound political result does not necessarily render the existence and content of such criteria in serious doubt. Controversy, by itself, does not entail warranted skepticism. However, to the extent that skepticism about criteria for sound political results *is objectively warranted* in particular cases, the fairness of the decision procedure may become decisive in determining the reasons for following an authoritative decision.

Let me sum up: We have seen two types of cases in which the reasons for following an authority's decision are primarily determined by the fairness of the decision procedure rather than the soundness of the result. One type concerns cases in which the duty to obey the authority's decision derives from the duty to support just institutions. Another type is cases in which the democratic decision procedure comes very close to a model of pure procedural justice. Admittedly, both of these cases are rather limited in scope. Ultimately, the justification of democratic authority must also rest on the soundness of the results. No political authority can be regarded as legitimate unless it meets the condition of the normal justification thesis. Fairness, I have tried to argue here, is very important. But fairness is not enough. If we are to be content with democracy, we must also assume that, by and large, democratic decision procedures are likely to result in sound decisions.[59]

59 I am grateful to Scott Altman, David Enoch, David Estlund, Elizabeth Garrett, Chaim Gans, Alon Harel, Gregory Keating, Charles Larmore, and Joseph Raz for very helpful comments on drafts of this essay.

CHAPTER 4

Are Constitutions Legitimate?

Liberalism may not have won the global victory that some commentators predicted, but constitutionalism certainly has. The vast majority of countries in the world, democratic and nondemocratic alike, have written constitutions that are designed to entrench the basic legal structure of their regime. Most constitutions also enumerate a list of rights and general principles that purport to have a higher legal standing than ordinary law, and most countries entrust the interpretation of their constitution to a court of law. I will not try to speculate here about why this is the case. My aim is to scrutinize the idea of constitutionalism from a moral point of view, arguing that constitutionalism does not quite deserve the celebration that it has occasioned.

The argument proceeds as follows: after a preliminary outline of the main features of constitutionalism, I will present what I take to be the main moral concerns about its legitimacy. I will then consider a number of arguments that have been offered to answer those concerns, arguing that the arguments fail to meet the challenge. I will conclude with a few words about the moral implications of this failure and some suggestions for reform.[1]

A. The Constitutional Package

Constitutionalism comes in different packages, varying along an important dimension that I will call "robustness." The main elements of robustness are comprised

---

1 Allow me an apologetic note on bibliography: the literature on the critique of constitutionalism is vast, particularly in the U.S. Dozens of books and hundreds of articles cover many, if not all, of the issues I discuss here. I couldn't possibly do justice to all this literature, and I am sure that most of the arguments I raise here have been alluded to by somebody somewhere. My purpose here is to present a systematic, but not an encyclopedic, treatment of the debate on the moral legitimacy of constitutionalism. I have tried to incorporate the relevant references, but the notes are not meant to be comprehensive.

of the degree of the constitution's "rigidity," the relative power of the courts in determining the constitution's content, and their power to prevail over the democratic legislature. I will explain all this in a moment. First, a terminological clarification.

The word "constitution" is ambiguous. When we talk about the constitution of a legal order, or its constitutional law, we may refer to the basic structure of the legal system in question. Every legal system, as such, must have some rules or conventions that determine who makes the law in that system, and how; who gets to interpret and apply it to particular cases; what are the main organs of government and what their authority is; and so forth. In this sense of "constitution," each and every legal system, as such, necessarily has a constitution. Most countries, however, have more than this; they have a *written constitution*, namely, a document (or, sometimes, a limited number of documents) that contains the canonical formulation of the country's constitution. In theory, the existence of a document that is referred to as "The Constitution" shouldn't necessarily make a difference. In practice, however, it typically does. The essential rationale of written constitutions is to remove certain important moral/political decisions from the ordinary business of lawmaking. In democratic regimes—and for the rest of this essay I will confine myself to a discussion of constitutionalism in democracies[2]—the essential point of written constitutions, accompanied by the legal power of judicial review, is to remove certain decisions from the ordinary democratic decision-making processes; basically, to shield them from the majority rule. To be sure, this is not a necessary feature of written constitutions. In practice, however, almost all of them have this essential feature, to some extent.[3] Thus, from now on, I will refer to the idea of a constitution, or constitutionalism, in this second sense.

There are six main features of constitutions that are characteristic and morally significant. Let me list them here briefly.

---

2 And I will confine myself to constitutions of countries, not sub-federal states or regions. Those raise very different moral/political issues.

3 The main reason why the existence of a constitutional document makes such a difference consists in the fact that without such a canonical document, courts would find it very difficult to exercise their power of judicial review. Typically, this power is granted to the courts by the constitutional document. But even if it is not, the document makes it much easier for the courts to hold the legislature under their review power.

1. Normative Supremacy

Constitutions purport to establish and to regulate the basic structure of the legal system, and thus they are deemed normatively superior to all other forms of legislation. The constitution, as we say, is *the supreme law of the land*.[4] Generally it is assumed that unless the constitutional provisions prevail over ordinary legislation, there is no point in having a constitutional document at all. I will therefore assume that this is an essential feature of written constitutions.

2. Judicial Review

In order to implement the constitution's supremacy, legal systems typically entrust the application and interpretation of the constitutional document to the hands of the judiciary. Some constitutions establish a special constitutional court for this purpose; others leave it in the hands of the regular court system.[5] The essential point here is, however, that it is the judiciary that determines what the constitution means, and such decisions are taken to prevail over the decisions of the democratic law-making institutions.[6]

3. Longevity

Constitutions, by their very nature, purport to be in force for a very long time, setting out the basic structure of the legal system for future generations. Ordinary statutes may happen to be in force for a very long time as well. But this is not an essential aspect of ordinary legislation. It is, however, an essential aspect of constitutions that they are meant to be lasting, that they are intended to apply to generations well beyond the generation in which they had been created.

---

4 The constitution's normative supremacy should not be confused with the idea that all law derives its legal validity from the constitution. This latter thesis, famously propounded by Hans Kelsen, is probably false in most legal systems. (See H. Kelsen, *Introduction to the Problems of Legal Theory*, Section 31.)

5 Typically, this would mean, *de facto*, that the highest court of appeal in the country is basically its constitutional court. Whether this is the case, and to what extent, mainly depends on how easy it is to appeal constitutional cases to the country's highest court.

6 A very interesting and suggestive exception is Article 33 of the *Canadian Charter of Rights and Freedoms*, which allows the legislature to overrule constitutional decisions of the supreme court (both preemptively or *ex post*), as long as it is done so very explicitly and renewed every five years. More on this in the last section.

4. Rigidity

The main technique by which constitutions can be guaranteed to be lasting for generations is their rigidity: Constitutions typically provide for their own methods of change or amendment, making them relatively much more difficult to amend than ordinary democratic legislation. The more difficult it is to amend the constitution, the more "rigid" it is. Constitutions vary considerably on this dimension, but it is an essential aspect of constitutions that they are relatively secure from formal change by the ordinary democratic processes. Without such relative rigidity, constitutions could not achieve their longevity.[7]

5. Two-Pronged Content

Most constitutions regulate two main domains: the basic structure of government with its divisions of political power, and the area of human and civil rights. In the first domain we normally find such issues as the establishment of the main legislative, executive, and judicial branches of government and their respective legal powers; the division of power between the federal and local authorities, if there is such a division; the establishment and control of the armed forces; and so on. In the second domain, constitutions typically define a list of individual and sometimes group rights which are meant to be secure from encroachment by governmental authorities, including the legislature. There is nothing essential or necessary in this two-pronged constitutional content, and the reasons for it are historical. The moral content and moral importance of a bill of rights is obvious. It is worth keeping in mind, however, that many aspects of the other, structural, prong of constitutions involve moral issues as well. Determining the structure of government, rules for enacting legislation, etc. is perhaps partly a matter of efficiency and coordination, but many aspects of it are not without moral significance. After all, we are not morally indifferent to the question of who makes the law and how it is done. It is, however, mostly the bill of rights that I will focus on in this essay, simply because its moral content and moral importance is much more salient.[8]

---

7 As I have argued elsewhere, the content of the constitution is bound to change according to its interpretation by the courts. See *Interpretation and Legal Theory,* revised 2nd ed, Ch. 9. Some implications of this will be discussed below.

8 To be sure, I am not claiming that important moral content is unique to constitutions. A great deal of statutory law also regulates matters of great moral importance.

6. Generality and Abstraction

Many constitutional provisions, particularly in the domain of the bill of rights and similar matters of principle, purport to have very general application. They are meant to apply to all spheres of public life. This is one of the main reasons for the high level of abstraction in which constitutional provisions tend to be formulated.[9] The aspiration for longevity may be another reason for abstractly formulated principles. And of course, sometimes an abstract formulation is simply a result of compromise between competing conceptions of the relevant principle held by opposing groups of framers. Be this as it may, we should keep in mind that important constitutional provisions are often formulated in very abstract and general terms.

Constitutions vary considerably with respect to all of these six features, and many others, of course. Let me suggest, however, that from a moral point of view, there is dimension of *robustness* that is particularly significant. I will call a constitution robust if it is relatively rigid and allows for substantial power of judicial review. So the more rigid the constitution is, and the more power it entrusts to the judiciary, the more robust it is. Robustness is morally significant because it basically determines the extent to which constitutional decisions actually remove moral-political issues from the ordinary democratic processes: The more robust the constitution, the more it shields its relevant content from the regular democratic/majoritarian decision-making procedures. Robustness is basically a legal feature of a constitutional regime. As such, it has both a formal and a practical aspect. A constitution which is formally, that is, legally, robust, may not be so robust in practice, and *vice versa*. The practice is partly determined by political and social realities.

Both of these elements of robustness are somewhat complex. Rigidity is closely tied to the element of longevity. It is partly because constitutions purport to be long lasting that they are designed to make it relatively difficult to amend them. Rigidity is also linked to the idea of supremacy. The easier it is to amend the constitution by the regular democratic process, the less practically significant its supremacy is. Similarly, when we consider the power of judicial review, we must consider it in the relevant context that takes into account the other features of the constitutional regime. For example, the more abstractly formulated the

9 Once again, constitutions vary considerably in this respect as well. Many constitutions contain very specific provisions even in the realm of rights and principles.

constitutional provisions are, and the more numerous the rights and principles it enlists, the more power judges would typically have in determining the actual content of the constitution. And of course, the extent of the power of judicial review is considerably determined by the constitution's rigidity. The more difficult it is to amend the constitution, the more lasting the power of the judges in determining its content. Another important factor that determines the power of judicial review concerns the political independence of judges, mainly from the other branches of government, the executive and the legislative. The more independent the judges are, the more power they would normally have. However, it is not my assumption here that judges are the only actors in this play. Many other legal officials are also engaged in constitutional interpretation, and their actions and decisions may determine, to some extent, what the constitution actually is. (For simplicity's sake, however, I will largely ignore this complication.)

To sum up, the relative robustness of constitutions is a package deal. Only by looking at the whole package can we determine whether, and to what extent, a given constitutional regime is robust. I will assume here, however, that this is not a practically difficult judgment to make. By examining the main features of a constitutional regime, we should be able to determine, quite easily, whether it is a relatively robust package or not. For instance, I take it that the U.S. Constitution is one of the most robust constitutional regimes in the world. The U.S. Constitution is very difficult to amend, its supremacy over all other sources of law is absolute, and the U.S. Supreme Court has considerable power (legal and political) to determine the content of the constitution, partly due to the fact that many of its provisions are highly abstract and allow for a very wide range of interpretative results.[10] Many constitutional regimes come close to this level of robustness, and some are much farther removed from it, sometimes so much so that they hardly deserve the title of a constitutional regime at all. Needless to say, from the vantage point of moral legitimacy, the more robust the constitutional regime, the more pressing the moral concerns it poses. Therefore, in the subsequent discussion, I will assume that we are dealing with a relatively robust constitution, more or less along the lines of the U.S. model.

---

10 Another aspect of the U.S. constitutional regime that makes it relatively robust has to do with the fact that in the U.S. there is no separate constitutional court. The highest court of appeal in the country is also the main constitutional court. Many countries have separated these two legal functions. There is something to be said in favor of such a separation, but I have no evidence to support my intuitions here.

B. The Moral Concerns

In order to understand the main concerns about the moral legitimacy of constitutions, we need to understand their basic moral-political rationales. And we also need to clarify a distinction between questions of legitimacy and other aspects of the potential value of legal-political institutions. Let me take up these two points in reverse order.

Institutions may have all sorts of valuable aspects, and they may instantiate those values to various degrees. Not all of the evaluative aspects of an institution bear on the question of its moral legitimacy. John Rawls may have had such a thought in mind when he stated at the beginning of *A Theory of Justice*: "Justice is the first virtue of institutions, as truth is of systems of thought."[11] I am not sure that we need to subscribe to Rawls's idea here about the absolute primacy of justice. But his analogy with the relations of truth to systems of thought is telling. Theories may have all sorts of valuable aspects, such as practical usefulness, simplicity, or theoretical elegance. But of course, Rawls is quite right to claim that those values are crucially parasitic on the truth of the theory; if the theory happens to be false, then in spite of any other value it may have, we should discard the theory. Similarly, Rawls suggests, institutions may instantiate a wide variety of values. However, if the institution is unjust, it is illegitimate, and therefore, in spite of other values it may instantiate, we should abolish it. I do not purport to suggest here that the legitimacy of an institution is an all-or-nothing matter. Presumably, institutions can be more or less legitimate. I do want to suggest, however, that there is a certain primacy to questions about the legitimacy of institutions even if, as is often the case, there are other values the institution may have.

So what is it that determines the legitimacy of an institution? Rawls seems to suggest that it is justice; an institution is legitimate if it is just, and illegitimate if it is not. We can be less committed here by saying that an institution is legitimate if its main purpose, or rationale, is morally justified, and the justification is not defeated by countervailing moral considerations.[12] Since moral justification can come in degrees (something can be more or less justified), I am happy to assume that an institution can be more or less legitimate. However, the crucial point is

---

11 J. Rawls, *A Theory of Justice*, 3.

12 I am using purpose or rationale in the singular only for the sake of simplicity. Constitutions may have several rationales.

that legitimacy is a primary moral criterion for appraising an institution, while there may be other values the institution instantiates that are only secondary and parasitic on its legitimacy. Let me give an example that is relevant to our concerns: Presumably, constitutions have certain educational values. The constitution is something that can be taught to the young, its moral content recited and celebrated in various educational contexts, etc. This is a potentially valuable aspect of written constitutions. But of course it is not something that can make a written constitution legitimate. The educational value of a constitution is entirely parasitic on the constitution's moral legitimacy. That is so because the educational value of a constitution, important as it may be, is not one of the main purposes of a constitution, and cannot possibly *justify it as the kind of institution that it is*. If the constitution is legitimate then, of course, it is even better that it has this additional educational value. If it is illegitimate, then we should not have a constitution at all, and the educational value of it is something that we will just have to forgo, regrettable as it may be.[13]

One conclusion that follows is this: In order to be able to determine the legitimacy of an institution like a constitutional regime, we must first have a clear idea about its main point or purpose, its alleged rationale. And then we must ask ourselves whether that rationale is morally justified. So what is the main rationale of a written constitution? At a superficial level, the answer is clear enough: the main point of constitutions is to shield certain principles of government and moral-political rights from the ordinary democratic decision-making processes, that is, by basically removing them from that ordinary decision-making process. But what is the point of this? Why would we want to do that in the first place?

The basic answer must reside in the assumption that we have reasons *not to trust* the ordinary democratic process in those areas in which we seek constitutional entrenchment. We want to make sure that things don't go wrong in those areas, and the assumption must be that by following the regular democratic process,

13 Let me add two clarifications. First, there is another sense in which the educational value of a constitution is parasitic on its legitimacy: for something to have such value, it must be morally sound. There is no reason to celebrate and teach something that is actually wrong. But this is not the main point I want to make in the text. Second, it may be suggested that if an institution is not quite, but almost legitimate, its additional values may tilt the balance, as it were, and then these values may turn something that would otherwise not be legitimate into a legitimate institution. Perhaps so. But this would be an odd chance, and I think we may dismiss it.

they may go terribly wrong. This is the basic idea of precommitment, often drawn from the famous Ulysses myth.[14] Ulysses had good reasons not to trust his judgment once his ship approached the sirens. Thus he commanded that he be tied to the ship's mast, and, crucially, commanded his subordinates to *disregard his commands in the future*, when the sirens' influence might curtail his judgment, knowing in advance that his judgment at that future time, under the influence of the sirens, was not to be trusted. The Ulysses strategy is basically the rationale of constitutionalism. Ulysses is the framer of the constitution, and democratic procedures are the potential victims of the sirens. Their singing is delightful, but their influence deadly. Thus we decide, in advance, to tie ourselves to the mast and disregard our orders in the future. Constitutionalism is a precommitment to remove certain issues from the ordinary democratic procedures, precisely because we know in advance that the democratic procedure is not to be trusted when the sirens sing.

Furthermore, this rationale goes some way in explaining the special role of the courts in a constitutional regime. The constitutional entrenchment of rights and principles is required, according to this reasoning, because on such issues democratic procedure is not to be trusted. We want to protect some rights and principles from the vagaries of momentary, shortsighted, political temptations and pressures. The assumption is that precisely because courts are not democratic institutions, they would be relatively free from such shortsighted political temptations. Therefore, it makes a lot of sense to assign the implementation of the constitution to the courts.

There are two main moral problems with this rationale of constitutionalism. To follow the Ulysses analogy, the problems are these: first, what we have in the constitutional case is not Ulysses tying *himself* to the mast, but a Ulysses who ties others, his political successors, to the mast with him. Second, unlike Ulysses, who knows that the sirens' singing is a deadly temptation, we may not quite know this in the constitutional case and we certainly do not agree about it. Even if we suspect that there are sirens out there, we tend to have serious and reasonable disagreements about who those sirens are and when their singing is deadly. The first is the intergenerational problem; the second is the problem of pluralism.

---

14 See J. Elster, *Ulysses Unbound*, Ch. 2.

The intergenerational issue is central to the question of the legitimacy of constitutions. The enactment of a constitution purports to bind the current and future generations by imposing significant constraints on their ability to make laws and govern their lives according to the ordinary democratic decision-making processes. Thus, the question arises: Why should the political leaders of one generation have the power to bind future generations to their conceptions of the good and the right? It is crucial to note that the moral significance of this question is not confined to old constitutions. Even if the constitution is new, it purports to bind future generations. It is this intention, or rationale of constitutions, to impose constitutional constraints for the distant future that is problematic, and thus it doesn't really matter how old the constitution is.

It may be objected that this formulation underestimates the significance of "We the people," that it ignores the fact that constitutions tend to embody widely shared principles and ideals, representing, as it were, the nation's *raison d'état*. But this would make very little difference. Even if at the time of the constitution's enactment its principles and ideals are really shared across the board, the intergenerational issue remains: perhaps no one, even an entire generation, should have the power to make important moral decisions for future generations, at least not deliberately. It is true, of course, that a great number of our current practices and collective decisions are bound to affect, for better and worse, the fortunes of future generations.[15] But these collective actions and decisions do not purport to have *authority* over future generations. They are not deliberately designed to legally bind future generations to our conceptions of the good and the just. Constitutions purport to do just that: bind future generations to certain conceptions of good government and just laws. Therefore, supporters of constitutionalism have to explain what makes it legitimate to make authoritatively binding decisions on important matters of morality and politics that are guaranteed to be lasting for generations and difficult to change by ordinary democratic processes.

One might think that this challenge is not difficult to meet. Constitutional documents typically allow a considerable interpretative flexibility. They can be interpreted and applied by the courts in ways that meet the specific needs and

---

[15] And, of course, some of them are morally very disturbing (*e.g.* huge national debt, irreparable damage to the environment, etc.).

moral conceptions of the society at the time of application. Thus, even if constitutions purport to bind future generations, this binding is not very strong; it allows enough flexibility in adjusting constitutional interpretation to the specific needs and conceptions of each generation.

In response, let me mention two points. First, flexibility has its limits. The flexibility of interpretation always takes place against the background of the constitutional text and some general understandings about what the constitution means and the rights and principles it embodies. Constitutions inevitably create a culture of discourse, and determine certain permissible and impermissible moves that constrain, to a significant extent, the kind of moral and political decisions that would be deemed legitimate interpretations of the constitution at any given time. In other words, in spite of the considerable freedom judges may have in the interpretation of a constitutional text, it is often a very limited freedom, constrained both by the meaning of the constitutional text and, perhaps even more so, by previous precedents and an entire culture of constitutional interpretation.

Second, the more flexible the culture of constitutional interpretation is taken to be, the more power it grants to the courts in determining its content. In a clear sense, then, the more flexible the culture of constitutional interpretation, the more antidemocratic it is. Thus, the less you have reason to worry about the intergenerational constraints, the more reason you have to worry about the antidemocratic role of the courts in determining matters of moral-political importance in the constitutional domain. And this brings us to the second main worry about constitutional precommitment, the worry about pluralism.

The problem of pluralism is different, though related. The essential point is this: In order to justify constitutional entrenchment of some rights and principles, it is just not enough to know that ordinary democratic procedures are not to be trusted to yield correct results on these issues. It is also necessary to assume that (1) we can tell in advance *what those rights and principles are* and (2) we can be sufficiently confident that a judicial determination of the content of those rights and principles is going to yield *better results* than its democratic alternative. Both of these assumptions are problematic, to say the least. Mostly, however, as Jeremy Waldron points out, it is far from clear that we have a warranted conception of what "better results" on such issues are.[16] Does it mean that we know what rights

16 J. Waldron, *Law and Disagreement*, 243–249, 268.

people should have and to what extent, and then we just expect the courts to figure it out better than the legislature would? The problem here is not necessarily, or primarily, an epistemic one. It is a moral concern about the need to respect value pluralism. In pluralistic societies, different segments of the population are deeply divided about matters of rights and moral principles; they are deeply divided over their conceptions of the good and the just. Crucially, respect for pluralism is premised on the idea that at least some significant portion of such deep disagreements is *reasonable*. Reasonable people can have genuine and deep disagreements about conceptions of the good and the just.[17] In other words, it is not so much that we don't know who the sirens are and when their singing is deadly, but that we have reasonable, and often quite deep, moral disagreements about all of this. Constitutional entrenchment of values, or of conceptions of the right and the good, necessarily favors certain conceptions over others by essentially shielding some favored moral-political conceptions from the democratic decision-making process. It is very difficult to see how this shielding is compatible with respect for pluralism.

Or perhaps not? It seems possible to reply that constitutions can entrench those values that are conducive to pluralism and purport to secure it. According to this argument, then, far from threatening value pluralism, constitutions can actually secure it by entrenching those principles of government and moral values that are necessary for pluralism to flourish. This seems like a powerful argument; its strength comes from the realization that the protection of certain rights and principles is indeed very conducive, perhaps essential, to the possibility of pluralism flourishing. After all, how can we maintain a pluralist society without a protection of freedom of speech, freedom of conscience and religion, a right to privacy, etc.?

The argument, however, is deceptive. The objection to constitutionalism need not deny that pluralism requires the protection of certain rights and principles of government. In fact, it is an explicit, though I hope not controversial, assumption of this essay that pluralism can flourish only in a well-functioning liberal democratic regime. The question here is why it would require anything more. Reasonable disagreements pertain to questions about the scope of the rights

---

17 This is one of the well-known themes in Rawls's *Political Liberalism*; I tend to agree with Waldron, however, that reasonable disagreement extends to conceptions of the rights as well, not just conceptions of the good, as Rawls seems to have maintained (at least in *A Theory of Justice*, though less clearly later, in *Political Liberalism*).

people should have, and also to countless moral dilemmas about conflicts between rights, and between rights and other moral-political concerns.[18] The dispute about constitutionalism is an institutional one: It is about *who* gets to determine what those rights and principles are, and according to what kind of procedure. The objection from pluralism maintains that we tend to have deep and reasonable disagreements about the rights people should have and about the scope of those rights, and that by removing those decisions from the ordinary democratic processes, we undermine the respect that is due to such reasonable disagreements. There are two concerns here. First, we must keep in mind that however abstract the rights and principles entrenched in a constitution, the entrenchment necessarily favors certain conceptions of the good and the just in ways that simply make it much more difficult for those who favor a different conception to change it. Constitutions necessarily favor a certain status quo, thus making certain social changes more difficult to achieve for some than for others. That is, at least relative to the baseline of a regular democratic process. Second, we must keep in mind that the debate about constitutionalism is basically a debate about institutions and procedures: it is common ground that pluralism requires, for example, the protection of free speech. The question is *who* gets to determine what free speech is, and how to delineate its limits. The objection to constitutionalism maintains that given deep and pervasive disagreements about such issues, there is no justification for removing them from the democratic processes.[19]

But now you may wonder why the democratic process should be privileged at all. Why is it the appropriate baseline? Needless to say, a comprehensive answer to this question would far exceed the scope of this essay. One essential point, however, should be made. At least from the vantage point of respect for value pluralism, a regular democratic process, that is, basically a majority vote, has this moral advantage: It is importantly egalitarian.[20] A majority vote expresses equal concern and respect for the views of all those concerned. Ideally, each and every member of the democratic decision-making process is accorded an equal right to participate in the decision, and his or her vote is counted equally with the votes of all the others in the process. This is the main sense in which we may assume that respect for pluralism is instantiated by a democratic process: it treats everybody equally.

18 See Ch. 9 in this volume.

19 I take it that this is Jeremy Waldron's view. See *supra* note 16.

20 I have defended this position in my "Authority, Equality, and Democracy," Ch. 3 in this volume.

C. The Main Arguments

None of this was meant to be conclusive. In this section I consider several arguments that purport to justify the legitimacy of written constitutions. I begin with arguments that are relatively easy to answer, and proceed to the more promising ones.

1. The Argument from Stability

We need a constitutional regime, some people say, because it ensures the long-lasting stability and predictability of the regime and the basic principles of its legal system. Note that this argument does not rely on the precommitment rationale of constitutions. The argument is premised on two main assumptions. First, it relies on the great importance and value of the stability and predictability of a legal system. Second, the argument assumes that constitutions are instrumentally essential for achieving adequate stability and predictability of the regime and its legal order. A nice aspect of this argument is that it goes some way in meeting the intergenerational objection. The more we should value the long-lasting stability of a legal order, the better case we have for the longevity of constitutions and their intergenerational application. After all, this argument would hold, it is precisely because we value stability across generations that we would want to have a constitution in the first place. So why worry about its intergenerational application?

Rebuttal: First, though the argument from stability would seem to make some sense with respect to the structural prong of constitutional entrenchment, it would have very limited application to the domain of rights and moral principles. There are some good reasons to value stability in such areas as who makes the law and how it is done, how legal authority is structured and what is the governmental division of labor, and similar aspects of an orderly regime. But these concerns hardly apply to matters of principle and moral issues. In such matters, it is mostly truth that we value, not stability. People ought to have the rights that they ought to have, not those that they have had for a long time. Stability is just not a very important value in the realm of basic rights and moral principles.

Secondly, the argument from stability crucially relies on an empirical assumption that is very questionable: it is far from clear that constitutions actually guarantee a greater level of stability than nonconstitutional regimes. There does not seem to be any evidence that would support such a conclusion.[21]

2. The Argument from Opportunity

This argument assumes that constitutions entrench values and principles that are widely held anyway. The explanation for their constitutional entrenchment is historical: in the history of a nation, there are sometimes unique opportunities to enshrine in a constitutional document moral principles of great importance. Such historical opportunities should be seized, this argument contends, since the values they entrench are fundamental and reflect a deep level of consensus. If an opportunity to legalize such important matters of principle arises, it is justified to make use of the opportunity.

Rebuttal: This argument trades on a crucial ambiguity. Either the constitutional entrenchment makes little practical difference, or it does make a significant difference. If the argument assumes that the constitutional entrenchment makes little practical difference because the nation widely shares those evaluative judgments anyway, then it becomes very unclear what is the point of their constitutional entrenchment.[22] If, on the other hand, constitutional entrenchment makes a practical difference with respect to the rights and principles that it entrenches, then the justification for such a difference cannot reside in the fact that there was an opportunity to make it. Generally speaking, pointing to a historical opportunity can only answer a question about why *now*, but not a question about why *at all*.

---

21 England has had a pretty stable regime for the last few centuries without a written constitution. New Zealand does not seem to be in any danger of instability because it does not have a written constitutional regime. At the same time, we know that there are countless instances of political instability in countries that have admirable constitutions.

22 Perhaps one can point to the familiar idea of the role of constitutions as a "civic religion." The idea is that constitutions tend to provide a focal point of civic identity and social cohesion. A trite saying has it that constitutionalism is our civic religion with the constitution as its holy scripture. The problem is not with the sociological insight here, which may well be more true and more interesting than it sounds, but with its normative significance; it is difficult to extract a moral-political argument from this piece of folk sociology. Perhaps we should stick to constitutional atheism: It is far from clear that healthy democracies ought to have a civic religion. (Nor is it clear that constitutions have a significant role to play in actually creating the conditions for its emergence.) In any case, to the extent that constitutions are conducive to the maintenance of some social cohesion and civic identity, that might be an added benefit of constitutionalism (akin to its potential educational value), but not a moral justification of its legitimacy.

Sometimes the argument from opportunity is compounded by the further claim that in those unique historical moments, the framers of the constitution are rightly held to have possessed superior moral knowledge, and thus we should defer to their relative moral-political wisdom and expertise. As I have argued elsewhere in greater detail, this type or reasoning rests on two mistakes: First, it relies on the mystification of great moments in history, a mystification that is very unlikely to meet any critical scrutiny. Secondly, and more importantly, the argument is mistaken because it assumes the possibility of expertise in matters of basic moral judgments. It is very doubtful that there is any possibility of expertise on such matters.[23]

3. The Argument from Practice

A great many aspects of a legal system are conventional. Social conventions determine, to a great extent, what the law is, what counts as law in a given community, how it is to be enacted or modified, etc. Law is, profoundly, a conventional practice. Conventions, by themselves, do not vindicate a practice of following them. Some conventions may be wrong and ought not to be followed. However, if the conventional practice is within the bounds of moral permissibility, it would seem that people have reasons to follow the conventions just because they are the conventions that are being followed by others in their community. Similarly, Raz claims,

> *As long as they remain within the boundaries set by moral principles,* constitutions are self-validating in that their validity derives from nothing more than the fact that they are there.
>
> [P]ractice-based law is self-vindicating. The constitution of a country is a legitimate constitution because it is the constitution it has.[24]

Rebuttal: The argument from practice is valid in a very limited sense. In fact, there are two important limits here. First, like the argument from stability, this argument makes some sense with regard to the structural aspects of a constitution, but not its bill of rights. The kind of issues that are determined within the structural prong of constitutions are typically determined by social conventions

---

23 See my *Interpretation and Legal Theory,* 137–138, 146.

24 J. Raz, "On the Authority and Interpretation of Constitutions," 173.

in those legal systems that don't have a written constitution. In such matters as what counts as law and how law is to be made or changed, I tend to agree with Raz that practices can be self-vindicating, that "their validity derives from nothing more than the fact that they are there." But this kind of reasoning cannot vindicate the constitutional entrenchment of important matters of moral rights and principles unless, of course, one assumes that such entrenchment is "within the boundaries set by moral principles." But then one has just assumed the very point that needs to be proved. We cannot simply assume that Ulysses was morally justified in tying us to his mast; whether he was justified or not is precisely the moral question that we raised here.

Furthermore, I indicated that I *tend* to agree with Raz that conventional practices can be self-validating, because this needs to be qualified. True, conventions create reasons for action because they are practiced, and as long as the convention is not morally impermissible, the reasons for action it creates are valid reasons. The fact that we could have had a different, perhaps even better convention under the circumstances does not normally entail that there is anything wrong with following the convention that we do have. Similarly, I presume that Raz wishes to claim that, as long as the constitution we have is not immoral, the fact that we happen to have it is a good reason to abide by it. But we have to be more careful here. Our reasons for following a social convention are not entirely derivable from the fact that the convention is practiced, though they certainly depend on it. Conventions evolve either in order to solve a preexisting social problem—as responses to some antecedent social need—or else they partly constitute their own values by creating a conventional practice that is worth engaging in.[25] Either way, there must be something valuable in the practice of following the convention for it to give rise to reasons for action, beyond the fact that the convention is there and just happens to be followed. Similarly, the fact that the constitution is there and happens to be followed cannot be the complete reason for following it. It must serve some values, either by solving some problems which were there to be solved, or by creating valuable practices worth engaging in, or both. To conclude, the argument from practice has some merit, and it can justify some, limited aspects of constitutionalism, but it leaves the main moral questions about constitutionalism unanswered. Whether those answers can be provided by other arguments remains to be seen.

---

25 For a much more detailed account of the nature of social conventions see my "On Convention" and *Positive Law & Objective Values*, Chs. 1–2.

4. The Argument from the Inherent Limits of Majority Rule

Here (at long last you may think) we reached an argument for constitutionalism that purports to justify directly its main rationale as pre-commitment device. Constitutionalism, as we have seen, is deliberately designed to be anti-majoritarian; the whole idea of a written constitution is to remove certain issues from the ordinary democratic decision-making processes. A natural move here would be to justify this by pointing to the inherent moral limits of a regular democratic decision-making process. As far as I can see, there are two main lines of thought here. One is the familiar point that regular democratic processes cannot adequately protect vulnerable minorities. The second point is more subtle, maintaining that a democratic process has its inherent moral limits that go all the way down to the very justification of democracy itself. Let me answer the first point, and then move on to develop the second.

i. Protection of minorities

The protection of potentially vulnerable and persistent minorities is certainly an important concern, but it is not clear that robust constitutionalism is a particularly good way to deal with it. Basically, there are two ways to try to secure the protection of minorities, and the question boils down to an empirical one about which system is likely to yield better results (in terms of fairness, I presume).[26] One way of protecting minorities is by entrusting their protection to a constitutional court, on the basis of a bill of rights that the court is expected to apply. Another way to deal with it is by designing the regular democratic processes in such a way as to maximize the relative bargaining power of minorities, thus making it difficult for the dominant majority to reach decisions without at least partly heeding the interests of the minority.[27] Which structure works better is basically an empirical issue.

---

26 Note that we are talking here about *persistent* and *vulnerable* minorities. Anyone can find himself in the minority on some issue or other, but this is not particularly problematic. Our moral concerns pertain to minorities that are particularly weak or vulnerable and tend to persist as minorities for a considerable period of time.

27 One clear example is the election system: Proportional representation tends to protect minorities much better than non-proportional representation. Other examples concern districting, the role and structure of political parties in the political landscape, etc. See, for example, A. Lijphart, *Patterns of Democracy, Government Forms and Performance in 36 Countries*, and D. Horowitz, *Ethnic Groups in Conflict*.

So far as we can speculate about this, however, I think that reason (or, is this experience?) sides with the nonconstitutional option. Judges have no particular incentive to go out of their way to protect vulnerable (often very unpopular) minorities. True, judges are less vulnerable than politicians to pressures of popular sentiment, but that does not give them any particular incentive to shift the other way. It all depends on their good will, or moral conscience, if you like. (It may be worth keeping in mind that judges tend to come from the ranks of the successful elite, not from the social circles of disempowered minorities.) Relying on the good will and moral wisdom of a few individuals is not necessarily a stable mechanism for the protection of vulnerable minorities.[28] Sometimes it works, and many times it doesn't. Structural constraints, built into the regular democratic process, on the ability of the dominant majority to ignore the interests of the minority would seem to work much better.

But now you may wonder how can such structural constraints be implemented without constitutional entrenchment? There are two related questions here: How can we move to a system of representation that is more conducive to minorities' rights, and what would make that system stable in the long run? After all, the majority would not seem to have any incentive to shift to a system that constrains its power, and if it did, the new system might not be stable enough. The majority would always have the incentive to strengthen, rather than weaken, its own power.

I think that there are two replies to these concerns. First, it should be kept in mind that the problem of how to move, initially, to a system that is more conducive to minorities' rights also applies, and for the very same reasons, to the question of how constitutions get to be adopted. In both cases the majority gives up part of its power in order to secure a better democratic regime. In both cases, those who have the power must be convinced to give up part of it. There are, presumably, two main reasons for the powerful majority to concede part of its power. Sometimes the concession is simply a *bona fide* attempt to construct a fair system of government; other times, it resides in the fact that political actors operate under a partial veil of ignorance: those who form the majority today know that they may find themselves in the minority in the future. Political actors would

---

28 This formulation is admittedly too strong. Of course there are some constraints on judicial decision-making in constitutional cases, mostly those that derive from precedents and constitutional tradition. But it should be kept in mind that those precedents and traditions are created by the judiciary, that is, by the same institution that is supposed to be constrained by it.

normally have an interest in securing a system of fair play when they cannot be sure in advance what is the role that they may play in that game in the future.[29] And then, once you have a system in play that makes it difficult for the majority to ignore the interests of the minority, the system is likely to maintain its stability, just because it is difficult to change without the minority's consent.

Second, even if I am wrong about this and these concerns justify constitutional entrenchment, they would justify it only in the very limited domain of the structure of the democratic process, not the realm of substantive rights and moral principles.[30]

Let me explore the second line of thought. In fact, there are two very different arguments here, so let me deal with them separately.

ii. The Instrumental argument

This argument starts with the premise that there is nothing *intrinsically just* in a democratic decision-making process. Democracy is justified only to the extent that it leads to good government, to good decisions; its value is basically instrumental. Therefore, there is nothing inherently, or intrinsically, wrong with an authoritative decision that is nondemocratic. If a nondemocratic system works better, that is, in terms of the likelihood of yielding just results, then we cannot have a moral objection to that system. Why prefer a system that is less just (in its end-results) to one that is more?[31] Now, assuming that this is a sound argument, proponents of constitutionalism can add the requisite moves to complete the defense of constitutionalism: All we need is to substantiate the assumption that democracy works well in certain contexts, but that it is likely to fail when the sirens sing. And then, of course, we have to add the assumption that when the sirens sing, it is better to leave the decisions to a constitutional court. Courts are more likely to reach the just decisions in such cases than the legislature. Ergo, constitutionalism can be justified on instrumental grounds.

---

29 See, *e.g.*, E. Garrett, "The Purposes of Framework Legislation."

30 This is basically the main intuition, I think, that drives J.H. Ely's "procedural" conception of judicial review. What he sees as legitimate in the U.S. constitutional review is the protection of the democratic process, not "substantive" rights. See his *Democracy and Distrust*. It is a difficult question, that I need not address here, whether Ely's position is a feasible constitutional interpretative strategy. Many have raised doubts about this, and I suspect rightly so.

31 See, for example, R. Arneson, "Democracy is not Intrinsically Just," 40–58.

Rebuttal: The main problem with the instrumental argument is that it is likely to fail on its own terms, and for two main reasons. First, the argument must assume that in the ordinary business of lawmaking, democracy basically works, that it is instrumentally justified. Otherwise, everything should be removed from the democratic process, not just constitutionally entrenched matters. So there must be some explanation of why democracy is likely to yield adequate results in the ordinary (viz, nonconstitutional) context. For example, one might rely on the epistemic value of democratic procedures, maintaining that such procedures are relatively reliable in generating the kind of knowledge that is needed for just decisions, more reliable than some other procedure.[32] Or one can maintain that democracy is relatively reliable in aggregating overall preferences, or such. Either way, the assumption has to be that in the ordinary business of lawmaking, democracy works. The challenge for the instrumental argument, then, is to justify the difference: What makes it the case that democracy works in some cases and not others? Let us assume that on some instrumental grounds, this question can be answered. The problem is that there is no guarantee that the differences in the *reliability* of democratic procedures would match the distinction between constitutional and nonconstitutional matters. In fact, some familiar examples would seem to point to the opposite conclusion. For instance, we know that democratic procedures tend to be very unreliable in times of national emergency, when the country feels seriously threatened by outside forces. It is precisely in those moments of national emergency that constitutional protections tend to be set aside, and the executive branch gets most of the say in political decisions. Or, more generally, consider the reliability of democratic procedures in those areas that require considerable expertise on matters of fact. Democracy is not particularly well equipped to yield correct results in such matters. But those are typically not constitutional cases either. To be sure, I am not assuming that there is some natural distinction between constitutional and nonconstitutional issues. The claim here is that constitutions tend to entrench matters of moral-political principle, not a decision-making process that is designed to be more reliable in domains that require expertise.

Furthermore, we should keep in mind that the reliability of a democratic procedure is profoundly context-dependent, and the context is fluid, varying according to specific circumstances and across time and place. How can we know so far in advance, often decades if not centuries in advance, what would be the

---

32 See D. Estlund, "Beyond Fairness and Deliberation: the Epistemic Dimension of Democratic Authority," 173–204.

circumstances that are likely to undermine the reliability of a democratic procedure? Note that instrumentalism initially rules out a principled answer to this question; perhaps, as a matter of moral principle, one could come up with an answer about why certain issues ought not to be decided democratically. But this is not the instrumentalist's line; instrumentalism has confined itself to an empirical approach here. It must base the unreliability of democratic procedures on their likelihood of yielding just results. But then again, it is just difficult to see how we can determine well in advance what types of cases would make democratic decisions unreliable. Surely that depends on specific circumstances.

The second reason for the failure of the instrumental argument consists in reasons that have to do with relative institutional competence. Instrumentalists must assume that courts are more likely than the legislature to reach better decisions on important moral issues. But this assumption is not quite warranted. It is true, of course, that courts have certain advantages in this respect. For example, they must listen to arguments put forward to them by the parties concerned; courts have to justify their decisions, publicly, by reasoned arguments, and so forth. So there are some institutional elements in the way courts reach their decisions that are conducive to sound moral deliberation. On the other hand, there are some serious problems as well. To begin with, courts are typically under serious political pressure to cast their arguments in legal terms, justifying their decisions by legalistic means, even if it is the case, as in most constitutional issues, that the decision is, actually, straightforwardly a moral or political one. This legalistic pretense that courts would find very difficult to avoid is not particularly conducive to sound moral deliberation. Second, courts typically operate in an adversary fashion, whereby parties to a specific dispute argue their case in front of the court. Moral and political issues of great importance, however, ought to take into account a much wider range of issues and interests that may not be adequately represented in an adversary procedure. Finally, it should be kept in mind that judges are no experts in moral deliberation. Constitutional judges may be kings, but they are not philosopher kings. Nothing in the legal education and legal expertise that judges acquire prepares them better to conduct sound moral deliberation than legislators or other (reasonably educated) members of the community.

One has to admit that such issues about institutional competence are not likely to be conclusive either way. But at least we should be cautious. Legislation often looks like a messy business, and then people tend to look up to the courts, admiring their civility and deliberative procedures. It is too easy and very misleading to jump to the conclusion that courts are therefore more likely to reach better moral decisions than the legislature. We should keep in mind that judges in constitutional cases are often just as divided about the conclusion as the general public.[33] At the very least, we should suspect the instrumental argument in this respect, and assume that it is inconclusive.

iii. The Intrinsic value argument

This second argument begins with the opposite assumption. It is premised on the intrinsic value of a democratic decision-making process, but it also points to the inherent moral limits of this value. Assume, for example, that the justification of democracy is premised on the value of equal distribution of political power. But now the question arises: What should count as *political* power that ought to be distributed equally? Surely not just about any decision people can make; not even any decision that would affect the lives of many others.[34] For something like the argument from equality to work (or any similar argument based on fairness, for that matter), we need to articulate a certain conception of what counts as a political decision, one in the making of which people ought to have an equal share. But this only entails that the value of democracy must have its inherent limits in the scope of its application; it can only apply to certain areas and not others. And this, the argument contends, is precisely what we do when we remove certain decisions from the ordinary democratic process; we just delineate, as we must, the sphere in which the value of equal distribution of political power applies.

Rebuttal: Constitutions do not alleviate the need to make authoritative decisions on matters of public controversy. They just shift the decision-making authority from the many to the few; i.e. to those few individuals who make up the constitutional or the supreme court. In order to justify constitutionalism, it is just not enough to justify the *exclusion* of certain matters from the democratic process. One must also justify their *inclusion* in the decision-making authority of the courts. It is very difficult to see how such a justification would be forthcoming on the basis of considerations of fairness. What principle of fairness could possibly justify the unique authority of the courts to make those public decisions that

---

33 This point is often stressed by J. Waldron; see *supra* note 16.

34 As an example, consider this: J. K. Rowling's decision whether to write another episode in her *Harry Potter* series affects the lives of millions. Surely, that is not the kind of decision that ought to be subject to democratic process.

should be removed from the democratic process? Fairness, to be sure, has a great deal to suggest about the authority of courts to decide private disputes and resolution of conflicts between individuals. Fairness may also support the legitimacy of courts' decisions on matters of applying the law to particular cases, resolving issues of legal interpretation, and so forth. But this is not what is at stake here. What we seek is an argument to show that there are matters of general public concern, potentially controversial and morally important, that the courts, and not the legislature, should resolve, because such issues should not be subject to democratic authority. I am not aware of any considerations of fairness that could possibly support such a conclusion.

5. The Argument from Deep-Consensus

This argument maintains that constitutions purport to entrench matters of moral and political principles that reflect a deep level of consensus in the community. The whole point of constitutional entrenchment, as we have noted from the start, is to protect deeply held values from the vagaries of momentary, shortsighted, political temptations. Therefore, the argument contends, it is quite justified to remove the protection of these deeply held values from the regular democratic process and entrust them to the court. Now, a crucial aspect of this argument from consensus is the distinction it draws between matters of moral opinion that are superficial and potentially controversial, and some deeper level of moral commitment that is widely shared in the community. As Wil Waluchow has recently put it: "the role of judges is not to bow to the inauthentic wishes of the majority and enforce their misguided moral opinions and evaluative dissonance . . . . Their job is to respect and enforce the true commitments of the community's constitutional morality in reflective equilibrium."[35]

The need for this distinction between moral opinions and deep moral commitments is pretty clear. In pluralistic societies, people do not seem to agree on many of their moral judgments about the conception of the good and the just. Moral disagreements are copious. But, this argument contends, there is a deeper level of moral commitments, widely shared in the community, and it is this deeper level of consensus that we must bring to the forefront in constitutional cases. In fact, the point is more subtle than this. As Waluchow emphasizes, there is no need to

---

[35] W. Waluchow, *A Common Law Theory of Judicial Review: The Living Tree.*

assume that at this deeper level moral consensus is in any way explicit. And there is certainly no consensus on details. The assumption is that there is enough shared moral commitment at the deep level to generate a more articulate constitutional morality by some process of reasoning or "reflective equilibrium."

The argument from consensus needs to establish a further point. Even if there is such a deep level of consensus about the constitutional morality of the community, it must also be shown that the judiciary is more likely than the democratic legislature to apply those values correctly. If there is a distinction between authentic values and inauthentic, often misguided, moral opinion, the thesis must be that judges are more likely to reach their constitutional decisions on the basis of the correct authentic values than is the legislature or any other democratic institution. Are there any reasons to support that assumption? Presumably, the reason is this: Democratic legislation is a representative and bargaining process. Legislators represent the (self-perceived) interests of their constituencies. Those interests are often at odds with the interests of other constituencies, and the process of legislation is basically one of bargaining and compromise. Legislation is a deal between parties that have some interests in common and many others that are at odds. Such a bargaining process is very unlikely to be based on the underlying, authentic, moral values of the community as a whole. More likely, it will reflect a tentative and often skewed compromise between superficial interests and opinions. Judicial decisions, on the other hand, are not based on representation and are not reached by a process of bargaining.[36] Judges have no constituencies to represent, and no bargains to make. They are free to base their decisions on the moral values that are deeply shared by the community as whole. Furthermore, as Waluchow emphasizes, judicial decisions in constitutional cases have this crucial advantage, which he calls the "bottom-up" approach: Constitutional interpretation proceeds on a case-by-case basis. Constitutional law develops in a common-law fashion, from concrete decisions on particular issues to gradually greater generality, and not the other way around, from general, and thus potentially controversial principles, to concrete rules and decisions.

As Waluchow sees it, the idea about the deep level of consensus on which constitutionalism rests basically answers concerns about pluralism; and the

36 Those who know something about the workings of the U.S. Supreme Court may raise their eyebrows here; at least in the U.S., a great deal of decision making in the Supreme Court is certainly based on subtle bargaining among the nine justices.

common-law approach that is characteristic of constitutional law answers the concern about the inter-generational problem. As Waluchow puts it:

> Far from being based on the unwarranted assumption that we can have, in advance, all the right answers to the controversial issues of political morality which might arise under Charter challenges to government action, and that we are warranted in imposing these answers on those by whom we are succeeded, the common-law conception stems . . . from the *exact opposite* sentiment: from a recognition that we do not have all the answers, and that we are well advised to design our political and legal institutions deliberately in ways which are sensitive to this feature of our predicament.

This is a complex argument, so let me summarize it.

i. Beneath the surface of disagreement in moral opinion, there is a deep level of consensus on fundamental moral values or, at least, sufficient consensus to generate some principles that would reflect such a deep consensus. Constitutions purport to entrench those deep values.

ii. The constitutional entrenchment of these deep values is needed in order to protect them from the vagaries of momentary populist sentiments and potentially inauthentic or misguided opinions.

iii. At least compared with the legislature, the judiciary is better equipped to discover[37] what those deep values are, and apply them to concrete moral dilemmas in constitutional cases.

iv. This discovery and application of deep values is a "bottom-up," case-by-case process, and one which need not presuppose that we know all the truths about values in advance, as it were. On such a case-by-case basis, constitutional decisions are adapted to the particular circumstances

37 I do not wish to put any weight on the term "discovery" here. Waluchow advocates something like a Rawlsian Reflective Equilibrium method, Dworkin relies on his theory of "constructive interpretation," and yet others may have different ideas in mind. Whatever method one has in mind, it should not affect the arguments in the text with one notable exception. The so-called "originalism" in constitutional interpretation would not be compatible with Waluchow's argument. But on this we are in complete agreement. On the question of why originalism makes no sense in constitutional interpretation I have elaborated in my "Constitutional Interpretation."

and the relevant social needs that are present at the time of the relevant decision.

v. Therefore, constitutionalism (a) does not undermine respect for pluralism, and (b) does not involve the kind of intergenerational binding mechanism that the precommitment argument assumes.

Rebuttal: Every step in this argument is questionable. However, I will focus on two main myths that the argument relies on: Something like Rousseau's myth about the "general will," and the Blackstone myth about the wisdom of common law. Waluchow does not cite Rousseau in his book, but his spirit is all over the argument. Beneath the superficial level of individuals' particular will, there is a deeper, more authentic, communal moral self that addresses itself to the common good. This common good, or "general will," abstracts from the concrete moral opinion, from the self-interested superficial self, and can be revealed only collectively, by a process that is deliberately designed to be non-aggregative. It is a process that must be oriented towards the common good, towards the underlying authentic communal self. Rousseau thought that democracy, properly constrained, is the appropriate process to generate the general will. Constitutionalists like Waluchow and Dworkin (at least as Waluchow understands him[38]) believe that it is exactly the other way around: democracy is inevitably and hopelessly skewed towards the particular and the inauthentic. Only a nondemocratic process, a process that is not designed to aggregate particular wills or moral opinions, can possibly allow the "general will," or the underlying "constitutional morality," to triumph.

Needless to say, this is not the place to offer a critique of Rousseau's conception of the "general will" or of similar theories about the common good.[39] My purpose in pointing this out is much more limited. First, that one should realize what it would take, philosophically speaking, to subscribe to the argument from deep-consensus: Nothing short of a comprehensive philosophical defence of the "general will," or some similar conception of the common good. Second, and more importantly,

---

38 Not without good reasons. Dworkin's arguments in *Law's Empire* (about the value of integrity and the importance of seeing political decisions as if the community speaks with one voice), certainly support Waluchow's interpretation of Dworkin. More generally, their constitutional theories are very similar.

39 Notably, contemporary theories that espouse such an emphasis on the common good, the so-called "deliberative democracy" theories, hold the opposite view: They rely on the value of broad, inclusive, and egalitarian public deliberation as the kind of process that is likely to yield decisions that constitute, or are in line with, the common good. See, for example, J. Cohen, "Deliberation and Democratic Legitimacy."

one should realize that Waluchow's argument does not really address the argument from pluralism, it simply assumes it away, as it were. Those who object to constitutionalism on grounds of respect for pluralism, like Waldron (and myself, in this case) rely on the observation that in pluralistic societies, people are deeply divided over their conception of the just and the good. And, crucially, that these deep moral controversies are, within certain limits, reasonable and therefore worthy of respect. The argument from deep-consensus contends that this is not really the case. There are two ways to understand this claim. One is basically a factual matter; it is simply the contention that pluralism is based on a false premise. Moral disagreements, according to this claim, just do not run as deep as pluralism would have it. Alternatively, the claim could be that even if moral disagreements are deep, they are not worthy of the kind of respect pluralism assumes since they are not sufficiently authentic; they do not manifest the true moral values that people living in a political society ought to share.

I will not try to defend pluralism here. Suffice it to point out one relevant aspect of it: pluralism does not maintain that every moral issue is deeply and reasonably controversial. Even in the face of deep and pervasive disagreement, there are many moral values that we all share or, at least, it would be unreasonable not to share. The objection to constitutionalism is based on the idea that these shared values are just too general and abstract to settle particular moral and political controversies that tend to arise in constitutional cases. Consider, for instance, the controversy over the permissibility of abortions. To put the point in a very simplified form: Some people claim that abortion is (or is like) murder and thus ought to be prohibited. Others vehemently deny this. Admittedly, those who deny that abortion is like murder would concede that *if* abortion is like murder, it should be prohibited. So there is something that both camps agree upon; we all share the view that murder is a serious wrong and ought to be prohibited. But this general agreement cannot possibly settle the controversy over the permissibility of abortions. Those who believe that abortion is just like the murder of an adult human being base their belief on a religious, or some other worldview, that is deeply opposed to the worldview of "pro-choice" liberals. It is not just some superficial disagreement that can be brushed aside as inauthentic. For devout Catholics, for example, there is little else that is as authentic and profound as their religious beliefs. And for some atheists there is little else that is more authentic than their opposition to such beliefs. So the problem is not that there is nothing about values that we can really agree upon. The problem is that there are many issues of deep moral conviction that we do disagree about, that many of those disagreements are reasonable and ought to be respected, and that most controversies that tend to reach the constitutional courts are about the values and moral views that we are deeply divided over, not about those that we all share.

The argument from consensus, at least as Waluchow develops it, relies on another myth, the myth about the wisdom of common law. Let us assume, for the sake of the argument, that there is a deep level of consensus, call it the constitutional morality of the community, that should sometimes prevail over results of democratic procedures. Why should we think that a constitutional or supreme court is the appropriate institution to work out the content of the constitutional morality of the community and apply its principles correctly? Even if we grant that the democratic legislatures are ill equipped, institutionally, to apply our constitutional morality correctly, that does not entail that judges would necessarily do a better job in this respect. We need some positive argument to convince us that this is the case. Now it is here that the wisdom of common law comes to our aid: As opposed to the legislature that must typically enact general rules, courts develop the law on a case-by-case basis. Hence, courts can focus on the particular moral subtleties of the case at hand, and develop the constitutional law piecemeal, more humbly, as Waluchow claims, and thus more truthfully.

One interesting implication of this common-law approach to constitutionalism is that it renders the constitutional *text* much less important than it is usually assumed to be. In part, this is a matter of constitutional tradition that may vary from place to place. I will not press this issue here further. I do want to put some pressure, however, on the main assumption that common law is generally progressive and morally reliable. I think that it is neither.

My point is not going to be that common law is, overall, a bad system. Far from it. The argument I want to make is that common law has some inherent problems, and that those problems are considerably augmented in the constitutional context. Let me mention, briefly, three familiar problems with common-law adjudication. It is typically insular, self-perpetuating, and lacks adequate feedback mechanisms. Common law tends to be relatively insular precisely because it is locked into a decision-making process that focuses on particular cases, in an adversary procedure that does not necessarily allow the courts to see the entire social or moral problem in its full range of complexities. In deciding particular cases, judges are forced to focus on the particular features of the case at hand (at least to some extent), and they are constrained by the arguments and the factual evidence that parties to the litigation bring forth. Sometimes this is quite enough to enable a good decision to emerge, but often it isn't. Secondly, common-law adjudication is based on the binding force of precedent. Judges rely on their previous decisions, typically extending their scope piecemeal. This is basically a self-perpetuating mechanism. Its danger consists in the fact that just as it enables the expansion of truthful insights, it is equally bound to expand the effect of errors.[40]

Finally, and most importantly, a closed common-law system has very few opportunities to correct itself by relying on feedback mechanisms. The main feedback judges have is in the form of additional cases that are brought before them. But then they are already locked into their previous set of precedents, so typically this is not much of a feedback. (In fact, it is even worse: Precedents in an area of law tend to channel the kind of cases that would initially reach higher courts. Potential litigants usually don't have the money to waste on hopeless litigation.) In contrast, legislatures have a much more developed feedback mechanism at their disposal. Interest groups, grassroots organizations, governmental agencies, election results, and the courts of course, are there to provide the legislature with input about the potential or actual effects of their legislation. The great advantage of nonconstitutional common law is that it is not a closed system: at any point in time, the legislature can intervene and correct the course, sometimes shift it entirely, by statutory law. But in constitutional cases, this option is not quite available. The only way to shift course is by constitutional amendment. And that is often much too costly and difficult to achieve.

In nonconstitutional cases, common law and statutory law complement each other. The law develops in an ongoing process of negotiation between the judiciary and the legislature, where each institution can correct the other. The problem of constitutional common law in a robust constitutional system is precisely the lack of this mutual adjustment process. It is a closed system whereby the courts get the final say in constitutional matters and their decisions are very difficult to change by an amendment process. Furthermore, because amendments are relatively difficult to make, constitutional decisions tend to be very long lasting. I see nothing particularly humble in this process, and nothing much to reassure us that constitutional common law is sufficiently sensitive to the recognition of our moral fallibility, as Waluchow maintains. For all its familiar shortcomings, democratic legislation has this considerable advantage: the decisions reached by a democratic process can be changed by the same democratic process. And if the decision is particularly controversial, it is not likely to last for too long. Those who

40 See J. Raz, *Ethics in the Public Domain*, Ch. 12.

lost today may gain the upper hand tomorrow. In a pluralistic society, this is as it should be.

You may think that all of this is just speculation. After all, we have a long history of constitutional judicial review, and this history can show us . . . well, what exactly? That the constitutional courts tend to be more progressive than the legislatures? That courts have generally done an admirable job in protecting the rights we should have? Or perhaps that the courts tend to hold firm against public opinion and protect vulnerable and unpopular minorities? Such lessons from long and complex history are very difficult to learn. The image of history is in the eye of the beholder. And our sight is blurred anyway, since it is very difficult to know what the relevant counterfactuals would be. Perhaps without judicial review, legislatures would have erred even more; or perhaps it is the other way around, and bearing full responsibility for their actions, legislatures would have done (even) better. It is very difficult to know.

D. Some Conclusions

If my arguments are correct, robust constitutionalism faces some serious problems of legitimacy. What are the moral, political implications of this? There are two main domains to which this question is pertinent: The domain of constitutional interpretation, and the domain of constitutional design. I would like to conclude with a few words on each.

This is not the place to articulate a conception of constitutional interpretation. I have done some of that elsewhere.[41] The question I would like to address here is whether the legitimacy problem should have any particular bearing on the question of how judges ought to interpret the constitutional document. In fact, I would only like to answer one tempting line of thought. It might be tempting to think that if the very legitimacy of a robust constitution is in doubt, judges should exercise considerable restraint in their constitutional interpretation. In other words, one might think that the doubts cast on the legitimacy of constitutions implies an argument against judicial activism in the constitutional domain. I don't think that it does.

41 See my "Constitutional Interpretation."

Constitutional issues are mostly (or, at least, very often) moral issues. A sound constitutional decision has to be morally sound. In constitutional cases, judges have the power to make a significant moral difference. The doubts we raised about constitutionalism entail that judges should not have that kind of power. But they do *not* entail that if judges do have the power, then they should refrain from making the moral decision that is warranted under the circumstances. Consider the following example: Suppose that decisions about hiring new faculty ought to be done in a deliberative, inclusive, quasi-democratic process that includes the entire faculty. As it happens, however, in school X, such decisions are made only by the dean. (Assume that this is given, that there is no way in which the dean or anybody else can change this.) Now consider the following dilemma that the dean faces: There are two candidates for one hiring slot; one of the candidates is academically (and in all other relevant respects) better than the other. Or so the dean has good reasons to believe. She also has good reasons to believe that the faculty would have chosen the other, inferior, candidate. How should the dean decide?[42] The argument under consideration would have us conclude that since the dean's authority to make such decisions is morally questionable, she should bow to the presumed wishes of the faculty and reach a decision that is, on the merits of the case, inferior. But I can see no good reason to substantiate such a conclusion. If it is given that the dean is the only one who has the authority to make the decision, doubtful as this authority may be, the right conclusion is that the dean should reach the best possible decision on the merits of the case. Otherwise, we just compile one error on top of the other: We will have a bad process and bad results. If the bad process cannot be changed, at least we should aspire to get the best possible results. Admittedly, the analogy with judicial review is not entirely accurate. In some constitutional cases judges have the option of actually rolling the decision back into the democratic playfield. If that is an option, I see no argument against it.[43]

Let me now conclude with a few words about constitutional design. Here the conclusion is more straightforward: If there is a serious concern about the legitimacy of robust constitutionalism, we should aspire to make constitutional regimes

---

42 For the purposes of the example, we should ignore practical or institutional constraints that may be involved in such decisions.

43 I need to qualify this: I do not wish to claim that this argument applies without qualifications to federal systems, where the court's decision amounts to allowing the states (or regions) to make the decision democratically within their jurisdiction. This is a much more complicated matter, involving difficult questions about the appropriate division of democratic processes between federal and local authorities.

less robust. To be sure, I am not suggesting that we ought to have written constitutions. But if we do have them, then at least we should have them in a less robust package. There are various ways of doing this; some may be better than others. Something like the "notwithstanding clause" of Article 33 in Canadian Charter seems to be a particularly attractive way of softening the robustness of constitutions. Basically, Article 33 enables the legislature to override constitutional decisions of the courts, but it only enables them to do that with a political price attached: The legislature must make it very explicit that it is doing just that, overriding a constitutional decision of the court, and it must renew the decision periodically.[44] This legal arrangement goes a considerable way in responding to the kinds of concerns about the legitimacy of constitutions that we raised here. First, it certainly mitigates, quite substantially, the intergenerational concerns. As long as the final say in constitutional matters is kept with the democratically elected legislature, the binding effect of the constitution is substantially reduced; Ulysses is tied to the mast, but he can be untied by the democratic process at any given time. True, there is a price attached to untying Ulysses, but the price does not substantially undermine democratic authority. For similar reasons, though perhaps to a lesser extent, the "notwithstanding clause" also mitigates our concerns about pluralism. To what extent? I am afraid that this is a very difficult question to answer. Partly, it depends on the specific circumstances of the society in question, its political culture, and particular aspects of the regime that we cannot speculate about in the abstract.[45]

---

44 The specific formulation of Article 33 raises interpretative issues, mostly about its scope, that we need not discuss here. I am not suggesting that the particular formulation of Article 33 is ideal. To this date, Article 33 has not been invoked by the Canadian legislature at the federal level. I would not find this particularly discouraging. Legal sanctions don't always have to be applied in order to change the behavior of the relevant agents.

45 I am indebted to Scott Altman, Richard Bronaugh, Marshall Cohen, Chaim Gans, Elizabeth Garrett, Alon Harel, and Wil Waluchow for helpful comments on earlier drafts.

PART II

Legal Theory, Law, and Morality

CHAPTER 5

Legal Positivism: Still Descriptive and Morally Neutral

It has become increasingly popular, amongst friends and foes alike, to advance the claim that legal positivism is actually a normative theory, and not (or not mainly, or exclusively) a descriptive one about the nature of law. Some philosophers suggest that a plausible version of normative legal positivism can be developed, while others claim that legal positivism has always been a normative theory, or that it can be defended only as such.[1] It is mostly this second type of claim that I want to address here. I will argue that legal positivism is best understood as a descriptive, morally neutral, theory about the nature of law, along the lines suggested by H.L.A. Hart. By "descriptive" I mean that such an account does not purport to justify or legitimize any aspect of its subject matter. By "morally neutral," I mean that the theory need not take a stance on any particular moral or political issues, nor is it committed to any moral or political evaluations.

Needless to say, both of these characterizations are too rough, and we shall have to refine them as we go along. Furthermore, the terms "normative" and "descriptive," though widely used, are not particularly well suited to characterize the debate, partly because "normative" and "descriptive" are not necessarily opposed or mutually exclusive, and partly because "normativity" can mean many things, some of which are not relevant to the debate, and others which are confusing.

---

1 Often the same philosophers make both types of claims. Prominent examples of the first type of normative positivism were suggested by Ronald Dworkin, Jeremy Waldron, Tom Campbell, and Neil MacCormick; the second type of claim has been put forward by Dworkin, Waldron, Michael Moore, Stephen Perry, Gerald Postema, and others. References to these works will be mentioned in appropriate places below.

Roughly, when people use the term "normative" in this context, they mean to refer to the realm of judgments that reflect moral evaluations, or evaluations like moral judgments. I will continue to use these terms, bearing in mind that the terminology is confusing, and hoping that the arguments can clarify things that these terms obscure.

The term "normative legal positivism" does not uniquely apply to a particular view. There are at least five possible views about the relations between normative claims and legal positivism. Not all of them are necessarily opposed to the thesis that I wish to defend here. In order to give a basic account of these five views, let me assume that there is some core descriptive content of legal positivism, and let us stipulate that P stands for this core descriptive content, whatever it is. Accordingly, here are the five positions I have in mind:

1. It ought to be that P (or something roughly coextensive with P)

To the extent that "ought" implies "can," such a view would also be committed to the thesis that P is a real possibility, that it can actually be materialized, at least to some significant extent. But the main focus of this version of normative positivism is on the moral-political domain: it argues that legal positivism is a good thing, that it ought to be materialized in a free and democratic society, for instance, because it is a practice of law that best promotes the goods favored by such a theory. I take it that this is basically the view propounded by Tom Campbell[2] and, following Campbell, I will call it Ethical Positivism.

2. It is the case that P, and it is morally-politically good if it is generally recognized that P

I believe that this is the position held by H.L.A. Hart. He thought that legal positivism, as a general theory about the nature of law, is basically descriptive and morally neutral. However, Hart also believed that a general, public recognition of the truth of P would free us from romanticizing myths, and thus enable a

2 See T. Campbell, *The Legal Theory of Ethical Positivism*.

more critical attitude to law that is not just theoretically correct but also morally-politically beneficial.[3]

3. It is the case that P, and it is a good thing too

Perhaps at some point Hart may have held such a view as well. Hart seems to have indicated not only that a general recognition of P is morally good, but also certain aspects of P itself (though this is not quite accurate, as we shall see below).

4. The law ought to be a morally legitimate institution; for law to meet conditions of moral legitimacy, it should be the case that F; F entails P, therefore it is the case that P

Dworkin's account of what he calls "legal conventionalism" is a prominent example of such a view. In *Law's Empire*, Dworkin understands legal conventionalism to be a partly normative theory with descriptive conclusions, a theory that purports to reach conclusions about the nature of law on the basis of some normative moral-political ideals. I will call this view Substantive Normative Positivism.[4]

5. Determining whether it is the case that P or not-P necessarily relies on some normative, moral-political claims

This is basically a methodological view about the nature of jurisprudence. As such, it purports to refute Hart's claim that general jurisprudence *can* be purely descriptive and morally neutral. According to this view, then, part of the debate between positivism and its opponents necessarily boils down to a normative one, and if legal positivism can be defended, it must rest, *inter alia*, on some normative claims.

---

3 See H.L.A. Hart, *The Concept of Law*, 205–206. If I understand MacCormick correctly, this is one of the main arguments he also makes in "A Moralistic Case for A-Moralistic Law." However, at points MacCormick seems also to endorse a version of the argument of type 3.

4 One may wonder how this view differs from Ethical Legal Positivism. I will try to explain this in Section C.

My aim here is to show that the first two versions of normative positivism do not threaten Hart's claim that legal positivism is basically a descriptive and morally neutral theory about the nature of law. The third view is crucially ambiguous: in one sense it may be problematic; in another, and the one that Hart actually maintained, it is not. Mostly, however, I will focus on the latter two versions of normative positivism, the substantive and the methodological, arguing that they are wrong, both as expositions of legal positivism and as critiques of it. First, however, we need to have a clearer sense of legal positivism's descriptive content.

A. What Legal Positivism Is, and What It Is Not

Legal positivism is not, of course, a single theory about the nature of law. It is a whole tradition of thought, spanning over two centuries, comprised of numerous contributions that often diverge, sometimes even conflict, on key issues. Nevertheless, there are a few core insights that legal positivists share, and I believe that the following three theses capture the core commitments of legal positivism. The first, and probably the least controversial insight, consists of the idea that the law is essentially a means. Law is an "instrument of social control," as Kelsen put it,[5] and like any instrument, the law can be put to good or bad uses; it can be used for good or bad purposes.[6] And like any instrument, the law can be more or less suitable for its tasks, more or less efficient. Whether this insight is controversial at all is not clear.[7] In any case, the insight certainly does not imply that law has no moral value, or even that the law is not necessarily good. (I will say more on this in a moment.)

The second main insight of legal positivism has been labeled the *social thesis*. According to the social thesis, law is a social phenomenon, it is a social institution,

5 Hans Kelsen, *General Theory of Law and State*, 20–21.

6 Arguably, there are single-purpose instruments that can be used only for one particular purpose, that may be either good or bad, or perhaps neither. No pure example comes to my mind, however, and in any case, it is clear that the law is not such a case. And of course we should also bear in mind that instruments can be used for purposes other than those for which they were created.

7 One way to understand Thomist Natural Law is that it claims that the law essentially promotes the common good, and therefore the law is essentially good. (See Aquinas, *Summa Theologica*, Article 2, concl.) Still, there is ambiguity here about what this "essential" predicate denotes. As I explain below, something can be necessarily valuable instrumentally. *If* this is a plausible interpretation of Aquinas's thesis, it is not at odds with legal positivism.

and therefore what the law is is basically a matter of social facts. What kind of social facts? To begin with, "social" is used here somewhat stipulatively to exclude moral and other evaluative-normative facts. Early legal positivists, like Hobbes, Bentham, and Austin, thought that the relevant kinds of social facts that determine what law is are general social facts about political sovereignty (coupled with particular facts about communicative-acts of the political sovereign). Later, twentieth-century legal positivists have repudiated this focus on political sovereignty, and replaced it with an emphasis on social rules. In every society there are certain social rules that determine what the law is, how it is to be identified, created, and modified, and those social rules basically determine what the law in that society is.[8] An account of the precise nature of these social rules has become rather controversial amongst legal positivists themselves. Some legal positivists claim that these rules are social conventions (and they still disagree about what kind of conventions they are), while others maintain that the conventional nature of these social rules is somewhat doubtful.[9] Contemporary legal positivists would generally agree, however, that what the law is basically depends on the social rules that prevail in the relevant society.

The third, and most problematic, insight of legal positivism is the thesis that has been called *the separation thesis*. There is a great deal of confusion about the precise meaning of the separation thesis, and we have to proceed with caution here. There is a minimal version of the separation thesis that all legal positivists, as such, maintain. And then there is a dispute about its more extended reach. The minimal content of the separation thesis consists in the claim that *determining what the law is does not necessarily, or conceptually, depend on moral or other evaluative considerations about what the law ought to be in the relevant circumstances*. The main controversy is about an additional, extended version of the separation thesis: Inclusive legal positivism maintains that moral and other evaluative considerations

---

8 It may be thought that Kelsen is a notable exception. The Basic Norm is not a social rule, Kelsen claimed, but a theoretical presupposition. But this is not quite accurate, since Kelsen acknowledges that what the Basic Norm in any given society is, depends on actual practice, or its "efficacy," as Kelsen calls it. (*e.g. General Theory of Law and State*, 118). Thus even if the idea of the Basic Norm is a presupposition, what the Basic Norm in any given society at any given time is, is a matter of social practice. (I have elaborated on this in my entry on Pure Theory of law, *The Stanford Encyclopedia of Philosophy*). Also, it is not entirely clear whether Joseph Raz subscribes to this idea about social rules. As far as I know, he has not explicitly endorsed it anywhere. His *sources thesis*, however, is certainly compatible with it. See, for example, Raz, *Ethics in the Public Domain*, 195.

9 See A. Marmor, *Positive Law and Objective Values*, Chs. 1–2, and cf. J. Coleman, *The Practice of Principle*. For a criticism of understanding the rules of recognition as conventions, see, *e.g.*, L. Green, "The Concept of Law Revisited."

may determine, under certain circumstances, what the law is, but this is a contingent matter, depending on the particular social rules of recognition of particular legal systems, at particular times (and, perhaps, depending on the law itself in certain cases). The so-called exclusive legal positivism denies this possible dependence of law on moral considerations. It maintains that moral and other evaluative considerations about what the law ought to be in the relevant circumstances cannot, as a conceptual matter, determine what the law is. This debate between the two main versions of contemporary legal positivism is very intricate, but it will not form part of my arguments here, and I will largely ignore it.[10] For our present purposes, the minimal content of the separation thesis, as formulated above, will do.

Before we proceed, it is important to clarify what the separation thesis does *not* amount to, what is not in dispute or, at least, should not be. First, as many contemporary legal positivists have repeatedly emphasized, legal positivism has no theoretical reasons to deny that the law is a good thing, that we have good reasons to have law and have flourishing legal systems.[11] Whether the law, as such, has any intrinsic value may well be controversial. But positivism certainly concedes that the law has considerable instrumental value, and therefore, whenever the reasons to use law are present, law would be instrumentally valuable or instrumentally good. Furthermore, legal positivism can concede that the law is necessarily good, if it is true that human nature, or the nature of human society, is such that it is necessary to have law. If E is an end we necessarily have, and L is a necessary instrument to achieve E, then L is necessarily good, even though L is still valuable only instrumentally. I am not claiming that this is the case, only that legal positivism has no theoretical reason to oppose it.

Second, legal positivism has no reason to deny that law's *content* necessarily overlaps with morality. It may well be the case that every legal system, immoral or wicked as it may be, would necessarily have some morally acceptable content, or that it would necessarily promote some moral goods.[12]

---

10 For my own defense of the exclusive version of legal positivism, see *Positive Law & Objective Values*, Ch. 3.

11 See, for example, J. Gardner, "Legal Positivism: 5½ Myths."

12 Why necessarily? The idea would have to be that a form of regime or de facto authority that is completely wicked and promotes absolutely nothing of value, could not be recognized as a legal order, would simply not function as law, so to speak. I am not sure about this argument, and I certainly do not wish to defend it here. I tend to think that this is contingently true as a rough generalization, but not necessarily.

Finally, consider this quotation (from Campbell): "In legal theory, Legal Positivism is generally taken to be the view that the concept of law can be elucidated without reference to morality, and that it is the duty of judges to determine the content of and apply the law without recourse to moral judgments."[13] Both parts of this claim are misleading and it is important to see why. First, I doubt that legal positivists have ever held the view that the concept of law can be elucidated "without reference to morality." Legal positivism is a view about the nature of law. It purports to understand and explain what the law is, what makes it a special instrument of social control, how it figures in our practical reasoning, and what makes it the kind of social institution that it is. None of this can be understood without a great deal of knowledge about the numerous functions and purposes the law serves in our culture. Generally speaking, you cannot even begin to understand a social practice without knowing what it is there for, what it is supposed to do. Without an understanding of the essential functions, or rationale, of a social practice or institution, it would be hopeless to attempt a theoretical understanding of it. Now, it is not difficult to see that law has moral and political functions in our society. It is there to solve, among other things, moral and political problems. Therefore, it would be futile, if not meaningless, to try to elucidate the nature of law in terms that do not employ moral concepts and do not involve an understanding of the kind of moral and political problems that the law is there to solve. For example, if the law is essentially an authoritative institution, we cannot understand the law without an understanding of what authorities are, what their rationales are, and how authorities function in our practical deliberation. No theory about the nature of authority can do without "reference to morality." And the same applies to the question of whether the law (or what part of it) is essentially a coercive institution, whether its sanctions are an essential aspect of it, and the question of whether law addresses itself mostly to its officials or to the public at large. All these are important questions about the nature of law, and none of them can be understood without understanding morality, the moral and political needs of a society, and practical reasoning generally.

The question of whether such reliance on understanding moral issues necessarily implicates a philosophy of law with normative-evaluative claims is a separate one, and I will consider it in some detail below. But it would be a mistake to begin with the assumption that legal positivism purports to be an account of the concept of law (that I take to stand for an account of the nature of law) that could be reduced

---

13 Tom Campbell, *Legal Theory of Ethical Positivism*, 69.

to a language which contains no moral terms and has no reference to morality. That just cannot be done, and I am very doubtful that any legal positivist thought otherwise.[14] Once again, to clarify, I do want to deny that an understanding of the moral and political concepts that are essential for an understanding the nature of law necessarily implicates jurisprudence with any particular moral-political stance, or moral-political evaluations. But this is a far cry from the folly that legal positivism purports to account for the nature of law "without reference to morality".[15] I will say much more about this crucial distinction in Section D.

The second part of the quotation from Campbell is also misguided. Legal positivism is not a theory about the moral duty of judges. Whether judges have a moral duty to apply the law in any given case is a moral question that can be answered only on moral grounds. Furthermore, no legal positivist of whom I am aware has ever suggested that judges need to set aside morality, so to speak, in their official judicial roles. Perhaps this is the source of the confusion: Hart, and other legal positivists, have repeatedly emphasized that the law often runs out, and then judges have basically no other option but to rely on their best (sometimes moral) judgment in order to determine the case at hand, or in order to determine how to change the law and modify it. But from this it in no way follows that when the law *is* clear, judges have a *moral* duty to apply it. They may trivially have a legal duty,[16] but the question of whether there is a moral duty to follow a legal obligation is always open, and should normally be determined on moral grounds. There is, however, a grain of truth in this quotation from Campbell, but it is not about the *duty* of judges in figuring out what the law is or how to apply it. It is true that according to legal positivism (or, at least, its "exclusive" version), the law has to be such that it can be *identified* without having to rely on the relevant moral considerations about what the law ought to be in the circumstances. But again, this has nothing to do with the question of what judges ought to do, or how they should decide particular cases.

At this point one may wonder: If the famous separation thesis is so minimal in its content, if it only maintains that determining what the law is does not necessarily or conceptually depend on moral considerations, then what is all the excitement

14 With the exception, perhaps, of John Austin.

15 Unless, of course, by "reference to morality" one means a reliance on moral judgments and evaluations.

16 Not necessarily, though. Even when the law is clear, it may be the case that judges are not under a legal duty to apply it to the particular case at hand; they may still have the legal power to change the law.

about? Have we not reduced the separation thesis to such a modest claim that nobody could object to it? Perhaps one could have hoped so, but as a matter of fact, the answer is no. Basically, the dispute is about the conditions of legal validity. Non-positivists assert, while positivists deny, that moral considerations form an essential part of the conditions of legal validity, and conceptually so. There are three main versions of this anti-positivist stance:

1. According to (what we call) traditional natural law doctrine, the separation thesis is false because moral considerations form a *necessary condition* of legal validity. Unjust law (or grossly unjust law) is not law, not legally valid.[17]

2. According to (early) Dworkin,[18] though morality is not a necessary condition of legal validity, it is sometimes a *sufficient* condition. A norm can be a legal norm because it derives from the best moral justification of other norms ("legal principles"). Thus, at least in some cases, there is a conceptual connection between legal validity and morality.[19]

3. According to *Law's Empire* Dworkin, legal validity is *always partly* a matter of moral judgment—because it is always a matter of interpretation what the law is, and interpretation is always partly a matter of moral/-evaluative judgments.[20]

I will not attempt to answer any of these anti-positivist theses. I have only mentioned them in order to clarify what the debate over the separation thesis is about.

B. Ethical Positivism and the Ethics of Positivism

Assuming, then, that the three main insights of legal positivism that I have mentioned in the previous section basically constitute the core descriptive content of

17 John Finnis, in *Natural Law and Natural Rights*, denies that it is accurate to ascribe this view to Thomist Natural Law. But the position is not unfamiliar, and adherents persist. Robert Alexy, for instance, purports to defend such a view. See his *The Argument from Injustice: A Reply to Legal Positivism*.

18 R. Dworkin, *Taking Rights Seriously*, Ch. 2.

19 For a more detailed account of how Dworkin sees the essential moral element in determining the legal validity of principles, see my *Positive Law & Objective Values*, 81–88.

20 See R. Dworkin, *Law's Empire*.

legal positivism, let us now turn to the question of whether they can be viewed from a normative perspective, or indeed, whether they are, somehow, partly normative by necessity. I will have very little to say here about Campbell's Ethical Positivism or any such similar view. Quite explicitly, Campbell does not purport to argue for the truth of legal positivism as a theory about the nature of law. He argues for a moral-political stance that would require a certain vision of law and legal practice that accords with what he takes legal positivism to be. In short, Ethical Positivism is a political theory, not a theory about the nature of law. In one respect, however, it does implicate a theory about the nature of law. Ethical Positivism is committed to the view that legal positivism is at least a possible form of legal practice. In particular, if anti-positivism is right about the falsehood of the separation thesis, Ethical Positivism prescribes the impossible. If it is really the case that determining what the law is *necessarily* relies on moral considerations about what it ought to be, then there is no room for a prescription that, say, judges should apply the law without consideration about what it ought to be. It would be something that they could not possibly do. Admittedly, the extent of this worry for Ethical Positivism partly depends on the extent to which it is true that "ought" implies "can." But this is not something for me to worry about here.

The only relevant point about Ethical Positivism that we have to notice is that it is not at odds with the view I want to defend here, namely, that legal positivism, as a theory about the nature of law, is basically descriptive and morally neutral. Ethical Positivism does not deny this claim because it does not compete with it. "It ought to be that P" is perfectly consistent with the proposition that "It is the case that P" or that "It is a fact that P." True, the more obvious it is that P, the less interesting it may become to insist that it ought to be that P. But again, this is not something for me to worry about here. Generally speaking, the truth of a descriptive proposition is not affected by interest in its moral, normative, endorsement.

H.L.A. Hart's normative endorsement of legal positivism's descriptive content is quite different. Hart occasionally mentioned the following type of normative claim: "It is the case that P, and we are all better off recognizing it as such."[21] Hart clearly

---

21 See, for example, H.L.A. Hart's *The Concept of Law*, 205–206, and, *Essays in Jurisprudence and Philosophy*, 72–78.

thought that P is a social fact, though in some respects, a sobering one at that. Basically, Hart believed that the more we can come to realize that legal validity and morality are not necessarily or conceptually linked, the easier it is to subject the law to critical appraisal. It is crucial to note, however, that Hart has never thought that the descriptive content of his claims about the nature of law somehow derive from the fact that it is morally or politically beneficial to believe in those facts and to recognize their importance. And rightly so, since it is all too clearly a *non sequitur*. From the fact that "It is morally good that everybody believes that P" it does not follow that P.[22]

Perhaps there is a more general suspicion that looms large here: Looking at the various legal theories on offer, one would quickly observe that almost every theory about the nature of law is accompanied by its normative endorsement by its author. They all seem to claim that it is the case that Q, and in some sense, this is a good thing too. One might then suspect that the theory's claim that Q is actually motivated by the presumed moral-political appeal of Q, or the moral advantage of recognizing Q's truth. Now, it would be difficult, and in any case, pointless, to deny that descriptive theories, particularly about such a normative domain as law, are often motivated by the normative assumptions of their authors. But there are two points to remember here. First, that in a sense this is more generally so, that is, not only with respect to normative preconceptions. It is often the case that we first have a sense of a philosophical conclusion before we can articulate the arguments that support it. Rational deliberation is always an ongoing negotiation between conclusions that seem right to us and the arguments or evidence that would support them. The essence of dogmatism is the refusal to revise one's conclusion in light of contrary evidence. One essential purpose of criticism and philosophical scrutiny is to resist dogmatism. And that is the best we can hope for. We cannot eschew our theoretical or moral preconceptions; but we should always try to subject them to scrutiny, and we should always be willing to revise our initial conclusions in light of contrary evidence.

Secondly, and more to the point, it is, again, undeniable that legal theories emerge from a particular intellectual and political background, and are often motivated,

22 Note that we assume that P is a set of descriptive propositions. At points, one may get the impression that MacCormick, in "A Moralistic Case for A-Moralistic Law," actually makes this mistake of inferring that P from the thesis that it is morally good if everybody believes that P. But it is not always clear that he takes P to consist of descriptive propositions. In other words, one can interpret MacCormick as advancing a form of Ethical Positivism.

more or less explicitly, by a moral-political vision. For example, as Gerald Postema has convincingly demonstrated, Bentham's legal positivism formed part of his moral-political agenda, and was considerably motivated by Bentham's utilitarianism and his aspiration for legal reform.[23] Similarly, it is probably the case that Hart's concerns about the relations between law and morality, and the debates about his views at the time, were partly shaped by the intellectual concerns of the post–World War II era. Crudely put, the manifest legalism of the Nazi regime, and the practical need to judge its perpetrators *ex post facto*, evoked a dilemma that has never been so stark before: Either to admit that law can be so utterly wicked, or to deny that such morally heinous law can be law at all. For those who sought a legalistic justification of the Nuremberg trials, the latter option seemed to offer a neat solution: The Nazi perpetrators could not seek to shelter themselves under the law that they had allegedly complied with at the time, if such wicked law is not law at all.[24]

Hart clearly thought that this solution is wrong, and that we would better learn the lessons of the Nazi regime by coming to realize that law is not necessarily just, that the law can be morally heinous and still be law. Hart thought that this is an important and sobering political lesson we should learn from jurisprudence, and that we would be on safer grounds, morally and politically, to be alert to the fact that legality is never a guarantee of justice or moral soundness.[25] That such views partly motivated Hart's legal positivism I have no doubt. And that I actually share these views I have no qualms to admit. But this neither shows that legal positivism is, in any interesting sense, a normative theory, nor that the truth of its descriptive content depends on the truth of its normative motivation, to the extent that there is one.

Put in simple terms: A descriptive theory about the nature of law makes a claim to truth. The only philosophically relevant question about a philosophical description is whether its claim to truth is warranted or not; whether it is, actually, true. The intellectual and historical background of such a theory, whether moral,

---

23 See Postema, *Bentham and the Common Law Tradition*. Furthermore, Postema argues that it is not entirely clear that Bentham was sufficiently aware of the distinction between an account of law *as it is* and his arguments about how to make law more useful or beneficial. *Ibid.*, 331.

24 These kinds of concerns have resurfaced recently with the collapse of the Berlin Wall and the decision to prosecute former East German guards who had "shot to kill" escapees to the West, allegedly following the legal orders of the regime at the time.

25 See *supra* n. 21.

political, or other, may help us to a better sense of the content of the theory, but it does not bear on its truth. The motivation for claiming that P is one thing, and the truth of P is another. The former is the business of intellectual historians. Philosophy should be interested in truth.

There is another normative aspect in Hart's theory that may seem more problematic, and this is the third version of normative positivism I have mentioned. At points it seems that Hart claimed not only that a general recognition of P's truth is morally good, but also that certain aspects of P are good as well. Of particular concern is chapter 5 of *The Concept of Law*. One of Hart's most important claims about the nature of law is that any developed legal system is a union of primary and secondary rules. In chapter 5, where he presents this thesis, Hart seems to be making the additional claim that this is a good thing too, as the addition of secondary rules remedies certain defects of a rudimentary legal system that would be comprised only of primary rules. Thus, the addition of secondary rules makes the law more developed and better in serving its social functions. Jeremy Waldron and Stephen Perry understand this argument as a normative one. It "gives the lie to Hart's claim to be engaged in purely descriptive jurisprudence," Waldron says.[26]

It is easy to misunderstand Hart's claim because it is ambiguous. Consider the difference between the following two propositions:

1. L is x, and this makes L good.

2. L is x, and this makes it good L.

If Hart had made a claim of type 1, perhaps we should have been worried about his mixing a description of law with its normative appraisal.[27] But Hart clearly makes a claim of type 2. His claim is not that the development of secondary rules makes the law a better institution, morally more legitimate, so to speak. Hart simply claims that the development of secondary rules enables the law to better serve its functions; it makes it more efficient, *qua* law. This is perfectly consistent

---

26 See J. Waldron, "Normative (or Ethical) Positivism," 429. See also S. Perry "Hart's Methodological Positivism," *ibid.*, at 323ff.

27 Even in this case, however, much would depend on the exact content of the claim. As I have earlier indicated, legal positivism is compatible with the thesis that law is necessarily good.

with the claim that the law just is whatever it is, regardless of its moral merit, or that it is not necessarily good to have more, rather then less, efficiency in law's functioning. In other words, this is not a normative claim in the relevant sense. That a knife is sharp, for example, does not make the knife good in any normative-moral sense of "good." It just makes it a good knife; better suited for its putative function.[28]

Some philosophers claim that any view about law's essential functions, or purposes, renders it normative; and since, as we have already admitted, no plausible theory about the nature of law can avoid such claims about law's functions in society, they conclude that any theory about the nature of law must rest on some normative assumptions, legal positivism included. I will examine this claim in some detail in Section D.

C. Substantive Normative Legal Positivism

In chapter four of *Law's Empire*, Dworkin purports to present an interpretation of legal positivism that he calls "conventionalism" on normative grounds. One immediate problem with it, however, is that very few legal positivists would recognize their work in this chapter. Since Dworkin does not attribute conventionalism to any particular theorist (none is mentioned in this chapter), perhaps he just invented this view as a friendly suggestion. If so, I believe that we need to say "thanks, but no thanks." Here is why.

"The heart of any positive conception of law," Dworkin claims, ". . . is its answer to the question why past politics is decisive of present rights."[29] Assuming that this is the main question, conventionalism is presented as a possible answer:

> Past political decisions justify coercion because, and therefore only when, they give fair warning by making the occasions of coercion depend on plain facts available to all rather than on fresh judgments of political morality, which different judges might make differently.[30]

---

28 Hart himself made it quite clear that such functional values are not necessarily moral or normative in the relevant sense, in his reply to Fuller's thesis about the rule of law virtues. See his *Essays in Jurisprudence and Philosophy*, 349–350. By this I do not mean to endorse Hart's view that the virtues of the rule of law are purely functional. In fact I have criticized this view in Ch. 1.

29 R. Dworkin, *Law's Empire*, 117.

30 *Ibid.*

This line of thought relies on Dworkin's thesis that the central question in jurisprudence is how to justify the use of collective force by the state, and how to justify the fact that certain forms of past political decisions warrant such use of coercive force, and to what extent.[31] Legal positivism is then presented as a possible answer to this question. So here is the argument, as I see it:

1. The law ought to be a legitimate institution.

2. In order to account for law's legitimacy, we must provide an answer to the question of why past political decisions justify the use (or monopolization) of coercive force.

3. Legal positivism claims that the answer to the question in 2 is given by the ideal of protected expectations.

4. The relevant kinds of expectations can be adequately protected only if law entirely depends on conventional sources.

5. Therefore, tying the identification of law to conventional sources is the best interpretation of legal practice.

There are two ways to read this argument. One is to see it as a form of what we've called Ethical Legal Positivism, namely, as a moral-political argument of the form: *it ought to be that P*. It would then be an argument that recommends something like legal positivism from the perspective of a political theory; namely, a prescriptive account about the role of law in society, and about how law should be practiced in order to be morally legitimate. As I have already argued, however, Ethical Positivism does not compete with descriptive jurisprudence, and therefore, cannot refute it either. And I don't think that this is what Dworkin has had in mind. Conventionalism is presented by Dworkin as a possible, albeit eventually wrong, *interpretation* of legal practice, not simply as a recommendation about the way law ought to be practiced.

But then there is a serious problem here: how can we get to a descriptive conclusion from answering a question about moral legitimacy? In other words, even if we follow Dworkin's argument until step 4, the move to step 5 remains a bit

31 *Ibid.*, 114.

of a mystery. If 5 purports to have a descriptive content, this could not follow from 4. "Ought" just does not imply "is," no matter how long or sophisticated the argument is. (Note that if 5 is understood in purely prescriptive terms, we are back to Ethical Positivism and its irrelevance to our concerns.) Of course it would have been a different argument if we replace premise 1 with

1A. The law is a legitimate institution.

Then perhaps something like 5 could somehow follow; not straightforwardly, but perhaps as a possible interpretation of law's legitimacy. But of course, this is a kind of assumption that legal positivism cannot endorse. No theory that begins with the assumption that law is a morally legitimate, or justified, institution can possibly be associated with legal positivism of any kind. As I have indicated earlier, one of the most important insights of legal positivism is that law is a social instrument, and that as such, it can be used for good or bad purposes; it can be used legitimately or illegitimately. Of course we can have a theory about what would render the law in this or that context legitimate, but this would not be a theory about the nature of law. It would be part of a moral-political theory about what constitutes good or justified law, not about what law is.

To sum up the problem here: If we begin with a question about what would make law legitimate, we cannot end up with conclusions about what the law is.[32] And if we begin with the assumption that the law is legitimate, we are no longer in the realm of legal positivism (or any other descriptive legal theory, for that matter).[33]

Undoubtedly, Dworkin would reply that I have ignored his account of what interpretation is, and how interpretation of such a practice as law necessarily combines elements of description and evaluation. I will get to this in a moment, when we consider Dworkin's version of the methodological argument, in the next section.

---

32 This should not be confused with a very different type of argument: Raz has argued that the law necessarily *claims* to be a legitimate authority, and therefore it must meet certain conditions to be the kind of thing that can make such a claim. *Ethics in the Public Domain*, Ch. 9. Raz's argument is not an attempt to derive an "is" from an "ought."

33 Since I find the argument structurally invalid, I did not go into the details of its concrete suggestion to view the ideal of protected expectations as central to the legitimacy of law, and its possible connection with an analysis of social conventions. In my *Positive Law and Objective Values*, 47–48, I have tried to explain why both of these aspects of Dworkin's suggestion are seriously misguided.

D. The Methodological Arguments

In his Postscript to *The Concept of Law*, Hart has reemphasized that his account of the nature of law is "descriptive in that it is morally neutral and has no justificatory aims; it does not seek to justify or commend on moral or other grounds the forms and structures which appear in my account of law."[34] The upshot of the methodological arguments I want to consider here is that this aspiration is conceptually misguided, and in any case, not attainable. Any jurisprudential account of the nature of law must be premised on moral and other evaluative views about the law. There are three main versions of this argument. The first, propounded by Stephen Perry, rests on the necessity to account for the functions of law. The second argument, espoused by Dworkin, Moore, and Waldron, focuses on the nature of the enterprise and its essentially evaluative presuppositions, and the last, suggested by all four scholars and others, focuses on Hart's own idea about the internal point of view and its importance for understanding law. I will consider these three arguments in this order and I will try to show that they all fail, and for similar reasons.

1. The Argument from Function

Perry's argument is best summarized by this quotation: "Jurisprudence requires a conceptual framework. The difficulty is that the data can plausibly be conceptualized in more than one way, and choosing among conceptualizations seems to require the attribution to law of a point or function. This in turn involves not just evaluative considerations, but moral argument."[35] I have already conceded the first main premise of this argument. It is, indeed, the case that we cannot possibly understand such a complex social practice as law without an elaborate understanding of its essential functions in society. The only question that remains is, why would it be necessary to engage in moral argument in order to understand the main functions of law, or its point, as Perry suggests?

Let us suppose that we want to understand a social practice largely, as Hart suggests, constituted by social rules or conventions. Perry is quite right to assume that knowing the rules would not suffice to explain the practice. At the very least, we must also understand their point. For example, we cannot hope to understand the game of chess, without understanding, more generally, what games are, and

34 Hart, *The Concept of Law* (2nd ed), 240.

35 S. Perry, "Interpretation and Methodology in Legal Theory" 123.

what is the point of playing them. We must understand, among other things, that the participants aim to win the game, which means that we must understand the complex idea of winning (or losing) a game, and such subtleties as winning it decisively, or gracefully, or barely. In other words, it is certainly true that an understanding of a normative social practice, like law, games, etc., must comprise an understanding of its functions, or points, and often of the values which would render intelligible the participants' relevant beliefs in their reasons for action. Needless to say, these purposes and beliefs can be put to critical scrutiny. One may wish to say that the putative values are not worth pursuing, that they are foolish or wrong, or that the practice may have had other, better values worth pursuing instead. But this kind of criticism is just an option that a critic may decide to pursue, or not. It is one thing to understand what the game of chess is, and quite another to decide whether it is a good idea to play it or not.

Consider, for example, a straightforward functional explanation of a social rule. Suppose we can show that the function, or rationale, of a social rule, say R, in a given society S, is to solve a recurrent coordination problem that members of S face under circumstances C. Solving the recurrent coordination problem is what explains the rationale of following rule R in society S under circumstances C. Such an explanation would typically rely on certain propositions about matters of fact, like the nature of the relevant circumstances, people's actual beliefs and preferences, and about the function, or the rationale, of the rule in their practical reason, given those factual assumptions. I find it very difficult to see, however, where the moral argument is hidden here. The explanation need not contend that the coordination problem that rule R is there to solve is one that *ought* to be solved, or that it *morally justifies* following R. It only explains the rationale of R, given certain observations about social facts. Morality is largely about the values that are worth pursuing. A descriptive account of a social practice, or any other type of theory about practical reasoning, need not rely on any particular views about the moral merit or worth of the functions or purposes that would make sense of the practice in question.

Perry's argument rests on the assumption that an account of the functions of a practice like law is either a "causal explanation of some kind" or "moral in character: it is grounded in a certain understanding of the moral point or value of the institution of law."[36] But this is clearly a false dichotomy. Take for example H.L.A. Hart's thesis, that one of law's most important functions is to guide human

36 *Ibid.*, 114.

conduct *ex ante*, "out of court," which forms the explicit target of Perry's argument. This is neither a causal explanation nor a moral evaluation. It is a complex thesis, based on certain assumptions about facts (e.g., that people typically know what the law relevant to their conduct, is; that they actually want to employ such knowledge in their deliberations about their conduct, that they often do so, etc.), and about some of the roles of legal authority in practical reasoning. When we talk about the practical function, or rationale, of a social institution, it need not be a causal explanation, or a moral evaluation. Once again, we can make sense of a social practice, render its rationale intelligible, without forming a moral or other evaluative judgment about the merit of the functions or purposes that render the practice rational for the participants.

Perry would be right to complain that rationality is not a value-free concept. But in this sense, theories are rarely, if ever, value-free, and Perry seems to be quite aware of this, since he is very careful to emphasize that it is *moral* evaluation that he ascribes to jurisprudence, not just theoretical evaluations in general. But this moral component is just not there. Essentially, what Hart was saying is that law is a tool, and tools can be used for good or bad purposes alike. Descriptive jurisprudence, of the kind Hart has had in mind, aims to explain what kind of tool the law is, and how its various features figure into its putative functions. We can say what purposes tools can be used for; this is what it normally means to explain what kind of tool a particular object is, yet at the same time we can remain entirely neutral about the moral merit of such uses. Generally speaking, the idea of usefulness is not necessarily a normative one. By suggesting, for example, that the sharpness of the knife makes it more useful, we are not committed to an evaluation of its uses. A sharp knife is more useful in cutting bread, and is also more useful in killing a person.[37] There is simply no argument to support Perry's assumption that an account of the functions of law, or anything else for that matter, is either a causal explanation, or else is necessarily premised on moral considerations.[38]

---

37 I do not mean to deny that in certain contexts an expression of the form "x is useful" is *meant* as a normative endorsement or positive appraisal. I only need to deny, as I do, that this is necessarily the case.

38 Although she does not focus on Perry's arguments, Julie Dickson has advanced a very similar line of reasoning against this methodological challenge in her *Evaluation and Legal Theory*.

2. The Argument from Interpretation

This false dichotomy between causal explanations and moral evaluation of a social practice sometimes informs Dworkin's methodological argument as well.[39] But I believe that we can present a clearer version of if without this fallacy. Jeremy Waldron suggests such a version, and it basically relies on three main premises. First, that it is a central issue in jurisprudence to determine whether certain types of normative claims are legal or not, whether they form part of the law or not. Second, that such disputes cannot be rendered sensible without "testing the respective theories against our sense of why it is important whether something counts as law or not."[40] Finally, Waldron maintains that an answer to this "why" question is bound to be normative; it is bound to rely on certain views about what makes law good and worthy of our appreciation. Therefore, Waldron concludes, jurisprudence necessarily relies on normative considerations.[41]

This is a very important argument, and it is almost persuasive. In fact, I think that the first two premises are quite right. Undeniably, it is a central question in jurisprudence what makes certain types of normative claims legal and others not. This is, basically, what the dispute over the conditions of legal validity boils down to. We want to understand what makes certain norms legally valid. And I think that Waldron is right to insist that such a theoretical dispute can make sense only on the background of some understanding about why it is important; why would it matter whether something is a legal norm, or not? So let me propose an answer: It matters to us, as theoretical observers, because we want to *understand what the law is*, as distinguished from other types of norms, and from what the law ought to be. (Note that for participants in the practice, for the subjects of a legal order, it may matter for other reasons; I will get to this shortly.)

---

39 Dworkin, *Law's Empire*, 64.

40 J. Waldron, "Normative (or Ethical) Positivism," 420.

41 *Ibid.* Michael Moore also makes a similar argument in "Hart's Concluding Unscientific Postscript." At one point Waldron is unnecessarily too hard on himself: He thinks that this argument commits him to the view that "in order to do positivist jurisprudence in the normative mode, one has to view law *as a good thing*" (428), and he rightly wonders whether this is not too strong. But I do not see how he is committed to this strong view at all. All that the argument commits him to (as opposed to Dworkin's argument, perhaps), is to say that normative positivism must have some views about what would make law good, or bad, views that would explain why it is important to distinguish legal from other normative claims. This is not tantamount to viewing law as a good thing. Suppose that somebody thinks that law is actually a bad thing. That would give him a very good reason to strive to distinguish what law is from what it is not.

Now you may think that I'm just pushing the question one step further. Why would we want to understand what the law is in this respect, as opposed to countless other questions we could have asked instead? Is this not a normative stance? Well, not more than any other quest for theoretical understanding. Theoretical questions always arise on the background of certain assumptions about what it is that needs explanation. Our sense of what needs explanation is typically path-dependent, emerging from the history of the discipline, and certain views that have been collectively shaped over time about what is theoretically or practically important.[42] Admittedly, any views about relative importance are partly normative, but if this is the only sense of normativity that Waldron has in mind, surely that would be too trivial. Any theory, in any given realm, is normative in *this* respect.

Dworkin has an interesting answer to this. It combines an emphasis on the interpretative nature of jurisprudence with the evaluative, normative nature of the practice it purports to interpret. Let me explain. The upshot of Dworkin's methodological argument is very simple: First, it assumes that jurisprudence is necessarily an interpretation of law (as a social practice). Second, it argues that all interpretations, as such, are essentially value laden. Interpretation, by its very nature, necessarily relies on evaluative judgments. Therefore, jurisprudence is necessarily evaluative.

One way to object to this reasoning is to reject its first premise, because it seems to trade on a crucial ambiguity. There is a broad sense of "interpretation" that would certainly make it plausible to claim that any philosophical account of the nature of law is necessarily interpretative. But in this broad, relaxed, sense of "interpretation," just about any theoretical explanation would be interpretative. Think of a zoologist who tries to figure out why apes spend so much time grooming each other. Surely, in a clear sense, the zoologist is trying to interpret the apes' behavior. Alternatively, "interpretation" can be understood much more narrowly, along the lines suggested by Dworkin's *constructive model.* Now the problem is that in the former case, the point has not been proved, since it is not clear that any interpretation in this broad sense is necessarily evaluative. (Think of our zoologist, again; she is not evaluating anything, she just tries to figure out the biological functions of the apes' behavior. She is certainly not trying to present their behavior in its best light.) On the other hand, if we assume a

[42] See, *e.g.*, J. Raz, *Engaging Reason*, 159.

narrow, evaluative, meaning of "interpretation," it is far from clear that we must concede that any philosophical account of the nature of law is necessarily "interpretative." I think that this is a serious worry, but I will not push it any further here. Dworkin's argument fails, even if we generously grant (most of) its main premises.

One of Dworkin's most important insights about interpretation consists in the way he regards evaluations essential to any interpretative project. One cannot even begin to interpret a text, he rightly claims, without first forming a view about the values that are inherent in the genre to which the relevant text belongs. After all, how can I begin to form an interpretation of, say, a novel, without having a pretty good idea about what makes novels good or bad, better than others, and the like? A certain vision of what the values inherent in the genre are is essential to any attempt to interpret texts which belong to that genre. The interpreter, Dworkin claims, must form an evaluative judgment of her own about those values which are inherent in the practice she purports to interpret. Such judgments, Dworkin claims, are not essentially different from the evaluative judgments of the practitioners themselves.[43]

This last move, however, is not so smooth, at least with respect to social practices like law. There is a crucial difference between forming a view about values that are inherent in a certain practice, and having an evaluative judgment about them. An anthropologist may form the theoretical view that a certain rite is valuable for the people who practice it because it enhances their social cohesion, without having any particular judgment about the value of social cohesion, certainly not one that is somehow competitive with her subjects' evaluative judgments. Similarly, a legal philosopher may suggest that the law is an essentially authoritative institution, without a commitment to any particular views about the legitimacy of legal authorities or their moral worth. Forming a theoretical view about a purpose or value that explains a given practice is not the same as forming an evaluative judgment about it, nor is the latter entailed by the former.

Arguably, different kinds of theoretical explanations of social practices face different methodological constraints. Presumably, it would not necessarily count against a scientific explanation of a social practice that the participants in the practice could not possibly come to recognize the explanation as something that

43 Dworkin, *Law's Empire*, 64. A very similar point is made by Waldron in "Normative (or Ethical) Positivism," 425–426.

rationalizes their practice. It is possible that a philosophical explanation is different in this respect. Perhaps a philosophical analysis must be such that it explains the practice in terms that the participants could, at least in principle, recognize as something that explains to them what the point of their practice is. Even so, the explanation need not be one that is based on moral or other normative judgments that compete with the judgments of the participants, to the extent that they have any.

In other words, there is a crucial difference between grasping a value and having an evaluative judgment about it. People can comprehend the values held by others, understand the point of those values, their relevance, etc., without actually forming any judgment of their own about those values. I can understand, for instance, that the glorification of Catholicism formed an essential purpose of the Counter-reformation Baroque architecture, without admiring Catholicism (or Baroque for that matter) myself, or actually having any particular evaluative judgment about these evaluative schemes.

Well, in one obvious sense this is not quite accurate. Our understanding of values is limited by our own past experience and conceptual-evaluative scheme. Sometimes people can come to understand new values by learning, but this is a relatively rare occurrence, it takes time and effort, and learning may not succeed. Does this mean that there are values of alien cultures which we could never come to understand? Not necessarily.[44] It does mean, however, that learning new values is relative to what we already know and to the values with which we are already familiar, and this certainly renders our ability to grasp values somewhat limited and dependent on our own experience and culture. Nevertheless, the distinction between grasping a value and having an evaluative judgment about it still holds. The fact that our ability to understand values or practices of other cultures is limited by our own cultural-evaluative background does not entail that understanding necessarily collapses into judgment (of the relevant kind). And if this distinction holds, it becomes very difficult to understand why jurisprudence, as an attempt to understand a social practice, must be engaged in moral evaluations of the kind Dworkin and Waldron envisage.

---

44 See, *e.g.*, Raz, *Engaging Reason*, 157.

3. The Argument from the Internal Point of View

It is possible to take the argument from interpretation one step further. Many legal philosophers maintain that it makes a crucial difference that the practice we aim to understand is itself a normative practice, one that purports to guide people's conduct and form reasons for their action. After all, it was Hart who introduced to legal philosophy the idea that an adequate explanation of law must take into account the "internal point of view," that is, the normative point of view of the participants in the practice. Committed participants, mostly judges and other officials, regard the rules of law as reasons for action. Therefore, they must regard the law as valuable or justified, at least in some respect.

This is undeniably true. It is true that we cannot attain an adequate understanding of the law without taking into account the perspectives of committed participants, and it is also true that the participants typically regard the law as something that gives them reasons for action. No doubt, the internal point of view is normative, at least partly in a moral-political sense.[45] But it still remains to be shown why a philosophical understanding of such a normative point of view would be committed to taking any stance on the values or normative assumptions it purports to explain. Why can it not remain essentially descriptive and morally neutral?

Consider the following analogy. Suppose I am told that Sarah had a choice, and was actually deliberating, whether to go to see movie A, say, a thriller, or movie B, a melodrama. I learn that she ended up going to movie A, and I also know that it reflects her choice. Can I conclude that Sarah has an evaluative preference of thrillers over melodramas? Or that she had such a preference on that occasion? Probably not. I still need to know more. I need to know why she had made the choice she did, what were her reasons, (e.g., perhaps the melodrama was shown in a theater too far away), and other similar aspects of her deliberation. An adequate understanding of her choice requires some knowledge of this, let us now say, "internal point of view." I need to know how she reasoned. But do I need

45 Hart, actually, resisted this last conclusion, at least as it is understood in moral terms. Hart insisted that even "when judges . . . make committed statements . . . it is not the case that they must necessarily believe that they are referring to a species of moral obligation." See his *Essays on Bentham*, 161. I have some doubts about the point of this debate. If we assume, as seems plausible, that a reason for Ø-ing entails that Ø is valuable, or that Ø-ing will bring about something valuable, then committed participants must be taken to presume that the reasons for following the law are reasons that derive from some values the law promotes. I tend to think that it matters very little whether we classify these values as necessarily "moral" or not. Morality has very fuzzy boundaries anyway.

to judge those reasons from my own evaluative perspective? Would my account of Sarah's reasoning necessarily rely on evaluative judgments at all, or some evaluative judgments competitive with hers? Nothing seems to compel such a conclusion. Once again, the opposite view seems to follow from a confusion between grasping a value or an evaluative reasoning, and forming an evaluative judgment about it. As I have already conceded, there are some inherent limits to values and evaluative reasoning we can grasp. To some extent, our ability to understand such things is shaped and limited by our own evaluative schemes and cultural habituation.[46] But this is not the same, not even close, to the conclusion that any understanding of evaluative reasoning collapses into judgment.

Dworkin's reply is not difficult to surmise. My attempt to explain Sarah's reasoning is an interpretation, he would say, and as such, it must purport to present its object in its *best possible light*, as the best possible example of the kind it belongs to. An attempt to present something in its best possible light, all things considered, necessarily relies on evaluative judgments of the kind that would be competitive with the judgments or reasoning one purports to interpret. But here we must part company. This is not the place to present an elaborate argument against Dworkin's theory of interpretation.[47] Suffice it to say that without this crucial assumption, that interpretation necessarily purports to present its object in *its best possible light*, the argument is not valid. And I think that very few of those who rely on the argument from the internal point of view share Dworkin's view about interpretation in this respect. But then they must come up with an alternative argument to fill in the gap.

Perhaps the following idea might help. Suppose it could be argued that "law" is an *essentially contested concept*. Participants rationalize their normative attitude to law, and their reasons for following legal rules, on the basis of different and competing conceptions of the concept "law." This would make sense if the concept of law was an essentially contested concept, more or less along the lines suggested by Gallie's analysis.[48] Would it not then follow that any account of the internal point of view is normative, just as any theory of justice, or theory of democracy,

---

46 Of course I could not understand Sarah's choice if I had no idea what thrillers and melodramas are, and what the differences between them are. But my understanding of Sarah's reasoning about such matters is simply not affected by my own views about the values of thrillers and melodramas, or such. My own evaluative preferences are simply not relevant here.

47 I have done that elsewhere; see my *Interpretation and Legal Theory*.

48 W. B. Gallie, "Essentially Contested Concepts."

must be normative? Such theories purport to defend a particular conception of a contested concept, and one that inevitably competes with other normative conceptions.

In order to assess such an argument, it is worth reminding ourselves what essentially contested concepts are. According to Gallie, there are five conditions: (1) The concept must be "appraisive," in that it stands for some kind of valued achievement. (2) This achievement must be internally complex and (3) any explanation of its worth must refer to the respective contributions of its various parts or features. (4) The accredited achievement must be of a kind that admits of modifications in light of changing circumstances. And, finally, (5) each party recognizes the fact that its own understanding of the concept is contested by other parties.[49] Gallie's own examples of essentially contested concepts include such things as democracy, art, social justice, and something like "the Christian way of life." Can we include the concept of law in this group?

I think not, because it is far from clear that law, in the relevant respect, is an "appraisive" concept in Gallie's sense. We must keep in mind that it is the concept of legal validity, and the conditions of legal validity, that form the focus of our interest here. Now, legality, or legal validity, is basically a phase-sortal concept: Norms are either legally valid, or not; they either belong to the law or they don't. Legal validity is not a kind of achievement that one can attain or fail to attain to a higher or lesser degree. Things can be more or less just, or more or less artistic, but this kind of appraisal is not something we can attribute to the validity of law. Of course, the enactment of *good* law is an achievement, and some laws are better than others, but surely not in terms of legal validity, per se; good law is good because it promotes some good, not because it is more legal, or more law, as it were, than some alternative.

To be sure, I do not wish to deny that one can fail to make law, or that there is some sense in which legality admits of degrees of success. Many legal philosophers who have written about the rule of law (including myself) share the view that there are ways in which one can fail to make law.[50] There are certain conditions that the law has to meet in order to be able to fulfill its pivotal function of guiding human conduct. Law's ability, as a social instrument, to guide human

---

49 *Ibid.*, 171–180.

50 See Ch. 1.

conduct necessitates certain features the law must possess in order to fulfill such a function, regardless of its specific contents. And then there is a sense in which success or failure in this respect is a matter of degree. But this is quite irrelevant to the argument from the internal point of view. First, even if there is a sense in which "legality" is a form of achievement, this does not, by itself, make it an essentially contested concept. Second, and more importantly, this is not the relevant sense of legality that concerns us here. As we have seen, the debate between legal positivism and its opponents is mainly about the conditions of legal validity; it is mainly about the question of what the law is, and what it is that renders certain norms legally valid and others not. In this respect, "law" is not an appraisive concept and therefore not an essentially contested one.[51]

So what is it about the concept of law of which participants and theorists can have competing and essentially contested conceptions? I suggest that it is not the concept of law, but the idea of good law, or legitimate law, that is, in a sense, an essentially contested concept. In other words, from the perspective of the participants, the law should be legitimate and justified. The legitimacy of the law in our society is something we have very good reasons to care about. And then we may have, as we do, very different conceptions about what the moral-political conditions of legitimacy are, and what would make various laws better or worse than others. But none of this shows that the concept of law is an essentially contested concept, even from the internal point of view.

To sum up: A theory about the nature of law must account for the internal point of view. It must explain the sense in which participants regard the law as reason for their actions and what are the kinds of purposes or values that would render such reasons intelligible. But this is still a form of understanding, not judgment. We can understand various forms of practical reasoning without forming any evaluative judgment about them. And if we do not need to form a judgment about such reasoning, then jurisprudence is still basically descriptive and morally neutral.[52]

---

51 For a similar argument, claiming that law is not an essentially contested concept, see Leslie Green, "The Political Content of Legal Theory," 16–20.

52 I am grateful to Scott Altman, Leslie Green, Martin Stone, and Joseph Raz for very helpful comments on earlier drafts of this paper.

CHAPTER 6

How Law Is Like Chess

There is a widespread view amongst legal philosophers, particularly in the legal positivist tradition, that there are certain norms that determine what counts as law in any given legal system. There is also a famous disagreement, though probably largely forgotten these days, about what kind of norms these are. Kelsen argued that a legal order can make sense only if one presupposes its *basic norm*, the norm that grants validity to the entire system.[1] H.L.A. Hart, on the other hand, famously maintained that there is a *rule of recognition* that determines what counts as law in a given society. The rule of recognition is not a presupposition, however, but a social rule or, as Hart later clarified, it is a social rule of a special kind, namely, a social convention.[2] Both of these views are very similar in that they both claim that there is some kind of a Master Norm that determines what counts as law in any given legal order. The disagreement is about the nature of this Master Norm: Is it, as Kelsen argued, a presupposition, or, as Hart would have it, a social convention? And if it is a social convention, what kind of convention is it?

I have three aims in this essay: First, to clarify this disagreement, arguing that Hart's view is, basically, the correct one. Second, to show that the rules of recognition are not coordination conventions, as some commentators claim, but conventions of a different kind. And, finally, to argue that there is a distinction between the *deep* conventions of law, largely determining what law is, and *surface* conventions of recognition determining what counts as law in a particular community. I will try to show that the distinction between deep and surface

---

1 See, *e.g.*, H. Kelsen, *Pure Theory of Law*; See also *General Theory of Law and State*. For a detailed bibliographical note on Kelsen's writings in legal philosophy, see my entry on Pure Theory of Law in the *Stanford Encyclopedia of Philosophy*.

2 H.L.A. Hart, *The Concept of Law*, Ch. 5. The explicit reference to the conventional nature of the rules of recognition is in Hart's Postscript, published posthumously in the 2nd edition of *The Concept of Law* at 256. For a very interesting account of the difference between the basic norm and the rule of recognition, see J. Raz, *The Authority of Law*, Ch. 7.

conventions can be employed to solve some of the puzzles about the nature of the rules of recognition.

A. The Hart–Kelsen Debate

Consider the following sequence of propositions:

1: According to the law in Si (at time t_1), it is the law that N_i.[3]

2: 1 is true because N_i had been enacted (prior to t_1) by P.[4]

Now 2 clearly presupposes something like 3—

3: If P enacts a norm of type N in Si, N is legally valid in Si.

4: 3 is true in Si because it is generally the case that X.

There is a logical sequence here: if there is a doubt about a statement of type 1, we would normally expect it to be resolved by an account of type 2.[5] And if there is a doubt about 2, we would expect it to be resolved by an account of type 3. And then we need an explanation of what makes 3 true, and so we get to 4. This much, I take it, is common ground. But now a question that needs to be answered is this: why is it the case that 4 has to be grounded in pointing to *norms*? Why could it not be something else?

Kelsen had a detailed answer to this question.[6] The law, according to Kelsen, is first and foremost a system of norms. Norms are "ought" statements, prescribing certain modes of conduct. Unlike moral norms, however, Kelsen maintained that legal norms are created by acts of will. They are products of deliberate human action. For instance, some people gather in a hall, speak, raise their hands,

---

3 N would typically stand for the following type of norm: "under circumstances Ci, A has a right/duty/power (etc.) to φ," where A is a defined class of legal entities, and φ is an action/omission type.

4 Assume that P stands here for an individual or an institution.

5 Dworkin famously denies that this is the only type of answer to the question of what makes statements of type 1 true. (see R. Dworkin, "The Model of Rules I.") But even Dworkin does not deny that a statement of type 2 can be, and often is, a perfectly adequate answer to the question of what makes 1 true.

6 See *supra* note 1.

count them, and promulgate a string of words. These are actions and events taking place at a specific time and space. To say that what we have described here is the *enactment of a law*, is to *interpret* these actions and events by ascribing a normative significance to them. Kelsen, however, firmly believed in Hume's distinction between "is" and "ought," and in the impossibility of deriving "ought" conclusions from factual premises alone. Thus Kelsen believed that the law, which is comprised of norms or "ought" statements, cannot be reduced to those natural actions and events that give rise to it. The gathering, speaking, and raising of hands, in itself, is not the law; legal norms are essentially "ought" statements, and as such, they cannot be deduced from factual premises alone.[7]

How is it possible, then, to ascribe an "ought" to those actions and events that purport to create legal norms? Kelsen's reply is enchantingly simple: We ascribe a legal ought to such norm-creating acts by, ultimately, *presupposing* it. Because "ought" cannot be derived from "is," and legal norms are essentially "ought" statements, there must be some kind of an "ought" presupposition in the background, rendering the normativity of law intelligible.

Thus, an act can create law, Kelsen argues, if it is in accord with another, "higher" legal norm that authorizes its creation in that way. And the "higher" legal norm, in turn, is legally valid only if it has been created in accordance with yet another, even "higher" legal norm that authorizes its enactment. Ultimately, Kelsen argued, one must reach a point where the authorizing norm is no longer the product of an act of will, but is simply presupposed, and this is what Kelsen called the basic norm.[8]

According to Kelsen, then, it is necessarily the case that an explanation of type 4 must point to a master *norm* that makes it the case that certain acts of will create law and others don't. Without assuming such a norm, the normativity of the entire legal order remains unexplained. H.L.A. Hart seems to have concurred,

---

7 Admittedly, there is something very simplistic in the way Kelsen understands Hume's is/ought distinction and I certainly do not want to endorse his position as is. It is possible, however, to articulate a more sophisticated conception that would retain the gist of Kelsen's argument. In particular, we need to keep in mind that Kelsen's main concern is the concept of normativity. Thus, roughly, when Kelsen speaks about "ought" what he has in mind is something like "reason giving": to say that one ought to φ entails that (or, according to some accounts, is entailed by) one has a reason to φ.

8 More concretely, Kelsen maintained that in tracing back such a chain of validity, one would reach a point where a first historical constitution is the basic authorizing norm of the rest of the legal system, and the basic norm is the presupposition of the validity of that first constitution.

with one crucial caveat: The master norm is not a presupposition, as Kelsen would have it, but a social norm, a social convention that people (mostly judges and other officials) actually follow. This is what the rule of recognition is: the social rule that a community follows, the rule that grounds the answer to the question of what makes statements of type 3 true or false in that particular society.[9]

But now, if you take Kelsen's question seriously, you should be puzzled by this. How can a social fact, that people actually follow a certain rule, be a relevant answer to Kelsen's question of what makes it the case that certain acts of will create the law and others don't? Crudely put, if you start with the question of how can an "is" generate an "ought," you cannot expect an answer to it by pointing to another "is." Has Hart failed to see this? Yes and no. Consider, for example, the game of chess. The rules of the game prescribe, for instance, that the bishop can be moved only diagonally. Thus, when players move the bishop, they follow a rule. The rule, undoubtedly, prescribes an "ought"; it prescribes permissible and impermissible moves in the game. What is it, then, that determines this "ought" about rules of chess? Is it not simply the fact that this is how the game is played? The game is constituted by rules or conventions. Those rules are, in a clear sense, social rules that people follow in playing this particular game. The rules of chess have a dual function: They constitute what the game is, and they prescribe norms that players ought to follow.[10] Similarly, Hart seems to have claimed, the rules of recognition define or constitute what law in a certain society is, and they prescribe (that is, authorize) modes of creating law in that society. Social rules can determine their "ought," as it were, by being followed by a certain community, just as the rules of chess determine their "ought" within the game that is actually followed by the relevant community.

This cannot be so simple, however. In fact, the complications go both ways. Something seems to be missing from Hart's account, but something is missing from Kelsen's account as well. Let me begin with Hart. The obvious difficulty with the chess analogy is that the rules of the game are "ought" statements, in the sense of giving reasons for action, only for those who actually decide to play this particular game. To the extent that there is any normative aspect to the rules of

---

9 There is a separate question here, that I will largely ignore, whether it makes sense to assume that in each and every legal order there is only *one* master norm of the kind Hart and Kelsen had in mind. It is probably more accurate to maintain that legal systems are constituted by a multiplicity of such norms that do not necessarily form a neat hierarchical structure that can be subsumed under one master norm.

10 This dual function of constitutive rules has been noted by J. Searle; see his *Speech Acts*, 33–34.

chess, it is a conditional one: *if* you want to play *chess*, these are the rules that you ought to follow. But of course, you don't have to play at all, nor do you have to play this particular game. Leslie Green was one of those who observed this difficulty in Hart's account of the rule of recognition. As he put it, "Hart's view that the fundamental rules [of recognition] are "mere conventions" continues to sit uneasily with any notion of obligation," and thus, with the intuition that the rules of recognition point to the sources of law that "judges are legally bound to apply."[11]

Green is wrong to focus the problem, however, on the notion of *legal* obligations. Hart's account of legal obligations is sound as is. The rules of recognition, just like the rules of chess, determine what the practice is. There is no particular difficulty in realizing that such rules have a dual function: They both determine what constitutes the practice, and prescribe modes of conduct within it. The legal obligation to follow the rules of recognition is just like the chess players' obligation to move the bishop diagonally. Both are prescribed by the rules of the game. What such rules cannot prescribe, however, is an "ought" about playing the game to begin with. But that is true of the law as well. If there is an" ought" to play the game, so to speak, then this "ought" cannot be expected to come from the rules of recognition. The obligation to play by the rules, that is, to follow the law, if there is one, must come from moral and political considerations. The reasons for obeying the law cannot be derived from the norms that determine what the law is.[12]

But now one could wonder whether we have contradicted Kelsen at all. Have we not just conceded that the normativity of law, like that of any other conventional practice, has to be presupposed? When a couple of people sit down to play chess, they just presuppose that the rules of chess are those they are obliged to follow. In playing chess, they presuppose its normativity. And in "playing by the law," lawyers, judges, and other participants presuppose the normativity of the legal order. This is basically what the concept of the basic norm is supposed to capture: The underlying presupposition of the normativity of the relevant practice. Is there anything more to it than a presupposition?

---

11 L. Green, "The Concept of Law Revisited."

12 One might think that at least judges and legislators must be presumed to regard the legal obligations as a species of moral obligation. But this is mistaken. Arguably, judges and other officials are under a moral obligation to follow the law that is stronger than the obligation of others. But this, again, is a moral obligation that must be grounded on moral reasons, not on the conventions that constitute what the law is. I have explained this in greater detail in my *Positive Law & Objective Values*, Ch. 2.

The problem is that even on Kelsen's own account, one can see that there must be more to it than a presupposition. Why is that? Because the specific content of any particular basic norm is crucially determined by actual practice. As Kelsen himself repeatedly argued, a successful revolution brings about a radical change in the content of the basic norm. Suppose, for example, that in a given legal system the basic norm is that the constitution enacted by Rex One is binding. At a certain point, a *coup d'état* takes place and a republican government is successfully installed. At this point, Kelsen admits, "one presupposes a new basic norm, no longer the basic norm delegating law-making authority to the monarch, but a basic norm delegating authority to the revolutionary government."[13]

Has Kelsen violated his own categorical injunction against deriving "ought" from "is" here?[14] Possibly, yes. The answer partly depends on the question of whether it is possible to distinguish between the role of the basic norm in answering the question of how we *identify* the law as such, and in answering the question of law's *normativity*. An answer to the question of what counts as law or as law-creating acts in a particular community cannot be detached from practice. As Kelsen himself basically realized, it is the actual practice of judges and other officials that ultimately determines *what* counts as law in their society. If the basic norm is a presupposition, it has to be an actual presupposition of particular people, and as such, a matter of fact. (Note that it does not matter for this argument how exactly we construe the idea of practice here, whether it consists of actions, propositional attitudes, or beliefs; all of these are within the "is" category.)

---

13 *Pure Theory of Law*, translated to English as *Introduction to the Problems of Legal Theory*, 59.

14 Kelsen was not unaware of the difficulty. In the first edition of the *Pure Theory of Law*, he suggests the solution to this problem by introducing international law as the source of validity for changes in the basic norms of municipal legal systems. It follows from the basic norm of international law, Kelsen maintains, that state sovereignty is determined by successful control over a given territory. Therefore, the changes in the basic norm which stem from successful revolutions can be accounted for in legalistic terms, relying on the dogmas of international law (*Pure Theory of Law*, 61–62). The price Kelsen had to pay for this solution, however, is rather high: He was compelled to claim that all municipal legal systems derive their validity from international law, and this entails that there is only one basic norm in the entire world, namely, the basic norm of public international law. Although this solution is repeated in the second edition of the *Pure Theory of Law*, 214–215, Kelsen presented it there with much more hesitation, perhaps just as an option which would make sense. It is not quite clear whether Kelsen really adhered to it. The hesitation is understandable; after all, the idea that municipal legal systems derive their legal validity from international law would strike most jurists and legal historians as rather fanciful and anachronistic. (We should recall that the development of international law is a relatively recent phenomenon in the history of law.)

Kelsen may still insist, however, that even if the identification of law is practice-dependent, the concept of (legal) normativity still requires something like the presupposition of the basic norm. Perhaps there is something to it, but there are some problems here. To begin with, Kelsen makes it very difficult to understand what he means by the idea of a presupposition: on the one hand, he emphasizes that for any normative system *to make sense* as such, namely, as a normative system, one must presuppose its basic norm. On the other hand, he also emphasizes that this presupposition is a matter of *choice*: One can either adopt the basic norm or not. But then how is this choice to be grounded? It cannot be grounded on the relevant normative system since it is the function of the basic norm to presuppose its normative validity. Thus the impression one gets is that there are countless potential normative systems, like law, religion, morality, etc., that one can either accept or not, just by presupposing their respective basic norms. But without any rational or objective grounding of such evaluative systems, the choice of any basic norm remains rather whimsical, devoid of any reason. It is difficult to understand how normativity can really be *explained* on the basis of such rationally groundless choices.[15] Second, it is also doubtful that a distinction can be drawn between the question of legal validity and an account of law's normativity, as Kelsen seems to maintain. If it is a social practice that determines what counts as law in a given community (as Kelsen admits), and laws are necessarily norms, then surely the practice determines how we identify laws *as norms*. There does not seem to be a separate question about how we identify or conceptualize the normativity of law. In short, even if we restrict the role of the basic norm to an explanation of the concept of systematic normativity, it is far from clear how helpful a tool it is. This is a complicated issue, however, and I will not try to substantiate this point here.

Whether there are rules of recognition is partly a matter of observation, not something that can be determined only by abstract argument. Nevertheless, there is an important lesson to be learned from the failure of Kelsen's antireductionism. The idea of the basic norm was intended by Kelsen to avoid a reduction of legal validity to social facts, precisely of the kind that Hart later suggested in the form of the rules of recognition. Kelsen thought that he could avoid such a reduction by insisting that the basic norm is a presupposition, not a social norm. But as we have seen, Kelsen's account of the basic norm actually violates his own

---

15 I have expressed this criticism in my entry on "Pure Theory of Law," in the *Stanford Encyclopedia of Philosophy*.

antireductionist aspirations. Even if, in certain respects, the basic norm is a presupposition, its content is always determined by practice. The basic norms of, say, the U.S. legal system, and that of the U.K., differ precisely because judges and other officials actually apply different criteria in determining what the laws in their respective legal systems are. The *content* of the basic norm is entirely practice-dependent. Once we see that this practice is rule-governed, namely, that in applying the criteria for determining what the law is in their legal systems, judges and other officials follow certain rules, it becomes very difficult to deny that there are rules of recognition, more or less along the lines suggested by Hart.[16]

B. Coordination Conventions and the Rules of Recognition

Two questions remain: What kind of social norms are the rules of recognition? And to what extent do those rules shape our understanding of what the law is? A widely held view, reinforced, perhaps, by some of Hart's comments in his Postscript to *The Concept of Law*, maintains that the rules of recognition are social conventions, more or less along the lines suggested by David Lewis.[17] Lewis claimed that conventions are social rules that emerge as practical solutions to wide-scale, recurrent coordination problems. A coordination problem arises

---

16 Dworkin denies that the criteria employed by judges and other officials in determining what counts as law are rule-governed, and thus he denies that there are any rules of recognition at all. But so far as I can see, Dworkin's argument is based on a single point, which is rather implausible. He argues that it cannot be the case that in identifying the law judges follow rules, since judges and other officials often disagree about the criteria of legality in their legal systems, so much so that it makes no sense to suggest that there are any rules of recognition. The problem is this: To show that there are no rules of recognition, Dworkin has to show that the disagreements judges have about the criteria of legality are not just in the margins; that they go all the way down to the core. But this is just not plausible. Is there any judge in the U.S. who seriously doubts that acts of Congress make law? Or that the U.S. Constitution determines how Congress is elected, and how it is supposed to enact the laws etc.? And what about their own role, as judges, and their authority to interpret the law—would they have deep disagreements about that too? Hart actually replied to this kind of objection in his critique of rule skepticism, see *The Concept of Law*, Ch. 7.

This should not be confused with a different and much more interesting claim that Dworkin also makes, namely, that even if there are rules of recognition, they do not settle the question of legal validity. Norms can be legally valid, Dworkin argues, even if they do not derive their validity from the rules of recognition. See Dworkin, "The Model of Rules I." This is a large topic that I will not address in this essay.

17 David Lewis, *Convention: A Philosophical Study*. Hart does not explicitly refer to Lewis but given the influence of Lewis in this area by that time, it is hard to imagine that Hart was not aware of it. For my critique of Lewis's account of social conventions, see my "On Convention." The thesis that the rules of recognition are coordination conventions was first suggested, so far as I know, by G. Postema in "Coordination and Convention at the Foundations of Law."

when several agents have a particular structure of preferences with respect to their mutual modes of conduct: Namely, that between several alternatives of conduct open to them in a given set of circumstances, each and every agent has a stronger preference to act in concert with the other agents, than his own preference for acting upon any one of the particular alternatives. Most coordination problems are easily solved by simple agreements between the agents to act upon one more or less arbitrarily chosen alternative, thus securing concerted action amongst them. However, when a particular coordination problem is recurrent, and agreement is difficult to obtain (mostly because of the large number of agents involved), a social rule is very likely to emerge, and this rule is a convention. Conventions, in other words, emerge as solutions to recurrent coordination problems, not as a result of an agreement, but as an alternative to such an agreement, precisely in those cases where agreements are difficult or impossible to obtain.

I have no doubt that many familiar types of social conventions are coordination conventions as Lewis explained. However, as I have argued elsewhere at some length, Lewis's analysis generalizes from some cases to all.[18] There are, as we shall see below, other types of social conventions. But before we get to this, we need a more precise definition of what social conventions are, and what makes them a unique type of social rules. There are two main features intuitively associated with conventional rules. First, conventional rules are, in a specific sense, arbitrary. If a rule is a convention we should be able to point to an alternative rule that we could have followed instead, achieving basically the same purpose, as it were. Second, conventional rules normally lose their point if they are not actually followed. The reasons for following a rule that is conventional are closely tied to the fact that others follow it too. In fact, both of these intuitive features of conventional rules derive from a single, though complex, feature that I will call "conventionality," defined as follows:

A rule, R, is conventional, if and only if all the following conditions obtain—

1. There is a group of people, a community, P, that normally follow R in circumstances C.[19]

---

18 "On Conventions," and in *Positive Law & Objective Values*, Ch. 1.

19 Note that *following* a rule (as opposed to just acting in accordance with a rule) is a complex condition. It probably entails that the agent regards the rule as a reason for action, and perhaps a reason to exert pressure on others to comply with the rule, etc.

2. There is a main, or primary, reason (or a combination of reasons), call it A, for members of P to follow R in circumstances C.

3. There is at least one other potential rule, S, that if members of P had actually followed in circumstances C, then A would have been a sufficient reason for members of P to follow S instead of R in circumstances C.[20]

A few brief clarifications are in place. The first condition indicates that conventions are social rules:[21] A convention is a rule that is followed by a population. It is crucial to realize that not all rules have to meet this condition. The content of basic moral rules, for example, is not affected by practice of compliance. In other words, if N is the content of a rule, in morality it makes sense to say that N is entailed by "it ought to be that N." However, "it ought to be that it is a convention that N" does not entail that "it is a convention that N." Conventions must be practiced by a population in order to exist.

Second, it is not part of this condition of conventionality that members of P must be aware of the reason, A, to follow R. People may follow conventional rules for various misconceived reasons or, in fact, for no reason that is apparent to them at all. The conventionality of a rule does not depend on the subjective conception of the reasons for following the rule by those who follow it, nor does it depend on people's recognition that the rule is conventional.[22]

---

20 Assume that we rule out the possibility of backtracking conditionals; and assume that the rules R and S are such that it is impossible or pointless to comply with both of them concomitantly in circumstances C.

21 A note on usage: I assume here that "rule" is the content of a linguistic form and thus rules can be valid or correct irrespective of practice. The word "norm" I will use to indicate a rule that is followed by a population or, at least, is regarded as binding by a population. Thus the terms "social rule" and "norm" will be used interchangeably.

22 See T. Burge, "On Knowledge and Convention." Note that there are three types of mistakes people can make about the conventionality of a rule: (1)people can be mistaken about the reasons for the rule, (2) people can mistakenly believe that the rule has no alternatives, and think that it is not a convention, whereas in truth it is (this is Burge's main point), or (3) vice versa, people can think that a rule is a convention because they believe that it has an alternative, though in truth, it does not. The third type of mistake is very uncommon. An example might be generative grammar: people may have thought that deep rules of grammar are conventional, but Chomsky and his followers argue that they are not, since those rules actually have no humanly possible alternatives.

The third condition explains the sense in which conventional rules are *arbitrary*. As Lewis himself emphasized, it is crucial to note that arbitrariness (thus defined) should not be confused with indifference.[23] This condition does not entail that people who follow the convention ought to be indifferent as to the choice between R and S. The rule is arbitrary, in the requisite sense, even if people do have a reason to prefer one over the other, but only as long as the reason to prefer one of the rules is not stronger than the reason to follow the rule that is actually followed by others.[24]

Arbitrariness is an essential, defining feature of conventional rules: A rule is arbitrary if it has a conceivable alternative. If a rule does not have an alternative that could have been followed instead without a significant loss in its function or purpose, then it is not a convention. Basic norms or principles of morality, for instance, are not conventions; properly defined and qualified, they do not admit of alternatives (in the sense defined above).[25] Admittedly, it is not easy to define what a *conceivable* alternative to a rule might be. Surely not every imaginable alternative to a rule would satisfy this condition. First, it has to be a rule that the same population could have followed in the same circumstances. Second, it has to be an alternative rule that is supported by the same reasons or functions that the original rule serves for the relevant population. Finally, in some loose sense that I cannot define here, the alternative rule has to be one that the relevant population can actually follow so that the cost of following it would not exceed the rule's benefits.

Lewis's account of social conventions easily meets these conditions. Rules that emerge as solutions to coordination problems are, indeed, arbitrary in this special sense, and it is pretty clear why the reasons people have for following coordination conventions are closely tied to the fact that others follow the same rule. But what about the rules of recognition: are they conventions of this kind?

---

23 See D. Lewis, *Conventions, A Philosophical Study*, 76–80.

24 In a sense, then, arbitrariness admits of degrees. We could say that a rule is completely arbitrary if the reason to follow it entails complete indifference between the rule, R, that people do follow, and its alternative(s), S, that they could have followed instead, achieving the same purpose. Then a rule becomes less and less arbitrary as we move away from complete indifference, up to the point at which the reason to follow the rule that is actually followed by others is just slightly stronger than the reason to prefer a different alternative.

25 This example might be controversial, of course, depending on one's preferred metaethical account of the nature of morality. Other examples, however, can be given. Some aspects of logic, and norms of rationality, are clearly not conventional.

There is some initial plausibility to an affirmative answer. After all, judges and other officials would need to follow those rules for identifying the sources of law that other judges and officials in their community also follow. Furthermore, as Coleman rightly noted, the coordinative rationale of the rules of recognition would also explain why judges and other officials have no particular incentive to defect; they would have no incentive to follow criteria of legality that differ from those followed by other officials.[26]

There are, however, three main problems with the view that the rules of recognition are coordination conventions. First, this view misses the constitutive function of the rules of recognition. It misses the point that these conventions constitute, to a considerable extent, what law is. Second, the idea that the rules of recognition are coordination conventions is not easy to reconcile with the apparent political importance of these rules. Finally, the coordination-conventions account blurs the distinction between the question of what law is, and what counts as law in a particular legal order. Let me explain these problems in some detail.

Consider, for example, the conventions that constitute the game of chess, or those that constitute artistic genres, like theater or opera. To say that these are coordination conventions, along the lines suggested by Lewis, entails the assumption that first there was some recurrent coordination problem, and then a convention has evolved as a solution to the problem. But this is implausible: Does it make sense to suggest that there had been a coordination problem between potential chess players before chess was invented, and now they play by the rules to solve the problem? Or that there was some coordination problem that the conventions of theater are there to solve, a problem that had existed before theater evolved, as it were? I do not want to deny that there are some coordination problems that are solved by such conventions. The point is that the social function of solving a recurrent coordination problem is simply not the main rationale of many types of social conventions. That is so, because prior to the emergence of those conventions, there simply was no coordination problem to be solved. Conventions evolve in response to a wide variety of social needs, and the need for coordination is just one of them. For example, conventions constitute various

---

26 See J. Coleman, *The Practice of Principle*, 93. Coleman himself, however, no longer holds the view that the rules of recognition are coordination conventions, though at some point he did. *Ibid.* at 94. See also G. Postema, "Coordination and Convention at the Foundations of Law."

ways in which we express respect for one another, both linguistically and otherwise;[27] conventions constitute artistic genres, games, and numerous social institutions; social conventions often regulate interpersonal relationships in such settings as a workplace, a party, an academic gathering, and such. In short, conventions serve numerous functions, by constituting ways in which people interact with each other and engage in socially valuable activities.

One might raise the following objection: Even if we grant that not all conventions are necessarily coordinative, it is plausible to maintain that all social practices are. We could not have a social practice without some cooperative intention or attitude shared by the relevant participants. Bearing in mind two caveats that I will mention shortly, I see no difficulty with this suggestion. It seems to me plausible to claim that social practices are sustainable only if the participants share some cooperative intentions or attitudes. The important point is, however, to keep these two issues separate: The main function of constitutive conventions is to constitute a social practice and regulate conduct within it. I have tried to argue that there is no need to assume that the main rationale of such conventions is to solve an antecedent recurrent coordination problem. This is quite compatible with the view, suggested here, that it is a condition of the existence of conventional (and other) practices that a certain cooperative aim is shared by its participants.

Now, one caveat that should be kept in mind is that social practices can exist and flourish even if their participants have different and incompatible conceptions of the point of the practice and its underlying rationale, at least to some extent.[28] Second, we should not assume that participation in a conventional practice is necessarily voluntary. Roughly, there are two kinds of conventional practices in this respect: those that potential participants need to opt in to (like chess, for example), and those in which we are participants by default, as it were, and the only relevant question is whether we can opt out of them (or how costly opting out is). Examples of the latter would be the conventional practices that form our everyday social interactions, like speaking a language or following basic rules of

---

27 Many natural languages, for example, have elaborate grammatical structures that constitute different ways in which a person should address another, according to various social requirements and expectations about the kind of respect that needs to be shown in various circumstances.

28 What I have in mind here is something like Gallie's idea about essentially contested concepts. People's conception of the practices they engage in, and their reasons for participation, might allow for different conceptions pretty much as Gallie describes (interestingly, Gallie's main example of how such conceptions work is an example of a game.) See his "Essentially Contested Concepts."

etiquette and civility. Consider, for example, the conventional aspect of language: some level of "opting out" is possible, in fact, quite familiar from poor, substandard, uses of language. But typically such substandard uses are subject to criticism and hostile reaction, and there is a limit to how much one can deviate from the conventions. At some point opting out would amount to one's inability to use language. To conclude this point, even if we admit that some cooperative intentions or attitudes must be largely present in any conventional social practice for it to exist, we should be careful not to exaggerate this point and, in particular, we should not be tempted to assume that it entails voluntary participation.

As Hart himself seems to have suggested, the rules of recognition are very much like the rules of chess: they constitute ways of creating law and recognizing it as such. Once again, it is not my purpose to deny that the rules of recognition solve various coordination problems. They do that as well. It would be a serious distortion, however, to miss their constitutive function. The rules that determine how law is created, modified, and recognized as law also partly constitute what the law in the relevant community is. They define the rules of the game, thus constituting what the game is.

There are two separate but closely related points here. First, we need to realize that social conventions tend to emerge as a response to many types of social needs, the need for coordination being only of them. Second, in many cases, the social conventions have a constitutive function in actually creating social practices that we are engaged in by following those conventions. Both of these observations apply to the rules of recognition. There is no reason to assume that the main function of such rules is to solve recurrent coordination problems, and it is important to bear in mind that the rules of recognition have a constitutive function in that they actually constitute the game, so to speak; they partly constitute what law is.

Why are these two points related? Basically, the reason is this: Coordination conventions do not tend to have a constitutive function. If there is a recurrent coordination problem, and a social rule evolves to solve the problem for the relevant agents, in this the rule has basically exhausted its function. The reason for having the rule in the first place, and the reason the agents have for following it in each and every instance, is basically the same: to solve the relevant coordination problem. There is a trivial sense in which we can say that here, too, the rule constitutes a practice, namely, the practice of following that rule. But in this sense, every social rule that is actually followed is constitutive of the practice of following it.[29] This, however, is not the sense in which the rules of chess constitute a social practice. The game of chess does not consist in the practice of following its rules, though it is certainly constituted by it. People can sit down in front of a chessboard and follow the rules of chess without actually playing the game.[30] Chess is a very complex social practice; it is an elaborate social interaction that embodies certain conceptions of winning and losing, values related to what counts as a good game and a bad one, or an elegant move and a sloppy one, and so forth. Following the rules is only part of this complex interaction. To be sure, I do not want to deny that the game is made possible by following its rules. On the contrary, as I have tried to suggest, the rules actually constitute the practice. But they do not exhaust it. The relation between the rules and their emergent social practice is not one of identity. There is no practice without the rules, and if the rules were different the practice would have been different as well, but there is more to the practice than just following its rules.[31]

At least one explanation for this non-identity relation consists in the complex social functions and needs to which conventions tend to respond. Chess has not evolved to solve a particular antecedent problem that we could identify irrespective of the game itself, and of the more general human activity of playing competitive games. Chess can be understood only on the background of understanding a whole range of social needs and various aspects of human nature, such as our need to play games, to win, to be intellectually challenged, to be able to understand a distinction between real-life concerns and "artificial" or "detached" structures of interaction, and so forth. In other words, there are always some reasons (or needs, functions etc.) in the background for having that kind of practice, and those reasons are closely entangled with the various values the practice instantiates. And then, once a conventional practice is in play, the practice may constitute further values that can only be instantiated by engaging in that practice. Once again, this complexity is typically not present in the case of coordination conventions. When the reason for having a social rule consists in solving an antecedent (recurrent) coordination problem, then following the rule to solve the problem is more or less all there is to it.

---

29 See J. Raz, *Practical Reasons and Norms.*

30 Notice that you can pretend to play chess; you cannot pretend to drive on the right side of the road, or to pronounce a word correctly.

31 See H. Schwyzer, "Rules and Practices."

If constitutive conventions tend to be responsive to a variety of human needs and values, as I claim that they do, you may wonder what makes such rules conventional at all. Basically, the answer consists in a combination of two facts: First, it is crucial to realize that the needs, functions, or values that such conventions respond to radically *underdetermine* the content of the rules that constitute the relevant social practice. Our need or desire to play some competitive intellectual board game does not determine the content of the rules of chess; the creative needs or desires to stage dramatic performances do not determine the particular theatrical genres that have emerged over time in various cultures; the reasons for showing respect to people under various circumstances do not determine the practices of etiquette that we have. Second, the reasons for following such constitutive rules are compliance-dependent reasons. The reasons for participating in a conventional practice crucially depend on the fact that the practice is there and its rules actually followed by the relevant population. Without some level of general compliance (in the relevant population), there is no social practice. To the extent that anyone has a reason to participate, the reason must partly depend on the fact that it is the practice that actually exists.

The combination of these two facts explains why constitutive rules of such practices are *arbitrary*, and thus conventional. In other words, the conditions of conventionality clearly apply here. Looking at the game of chess, for example, we can see that—

(1) there is a population that follows a set of rules, S_1, in circumstances C,

(2) there are some reasons, (real or perceived), call them A, for members of this population to follow S_1 in C, and

(3) there are some alternative rules, S_2, that if members of that population had actually followed in circumstances C, then A would have been a sufficient reason for them to follow S_2 instead of S_1 in circumstances C.

Basically, the idea is that chess could be played differently, and if chess were played somewhat differently from they way it is, that would be a sufficient reason for potential players to follow those rules that are actually being followed by others. This is why the constitutive rules of chess are conventional.

An obvious objection can be raised here: One can claim that if the rules of chess, for instance, were different from what they are, it would not be chess, but some other game. The identity of the game is substantially determined by the rules that constitute it; and if the rules are significantly different, the game is different as well.[32] I say "significantly" different because it is very doubtful that slight changes in the rules allow us to say that it would be a different game. Suppose, for example, that you have two communities of chess players. One plays the game with a rule that allows castling, while the other community plays it without this rule. Would we say that these two populations play a different game? I doubt it. We should say that they both play chess, albeit somewhat differently. However, if we imagine differences that are more and more substantial, at some point we would have to say that it is no longer the same game (though it may still be quite similar in its main functions and values), which is just another way of saying that such practices, like chess, are *constituted* by rules.

Now, it is true that the *identity* of a conventional practice crucially depends on its constitutive rules. But this does not mean that the rules cannot be conventional. As long as we can envisage alternatives to the rules that are actually being followed, that is, without any significant loss in the purpose or function of those rules, and the reasons for following the rules are compliance-dependent, the rules are arbitrary and thus conventional in the requisite sense. In other words, we have to admit that there might be some difficult questions about what counts as alternative ways of doing, roughly, the same thing. But rough identity is all we need here. As long as we can envisage alternative rules that would basically achieve the same purpose for the relevant population, or serve basically the same functions, etc., we should have no problem characterizing the rules as conventional.

Realizing that constitutive conventions tend to emerge as responses to complex social and human needs, and not just coordination problems, should make it much easier to understand why the specific conventions we happen to have may matter to us, sometimes a great deal. And the rules of recognition do matter, morally, politically, and otherwise. After all, it does matter to us who makes the law in our society, and how it is done. The rules of recognition of legal systems are often politically important. Consider, for example, one of the most fundamental rules of recognition in the U.S., namely, the rule that determines the supremacy of the

32 It is not entirely clear that only the rules determine the identity of the practice. It is arguable that the identity of such a practice, like chess, is partly path-dependent.

U.S. Constitution. It should be easy to recognize that this is no trivial matter; it is something that most Americans feel strongly about, to say the least.[33] There are political and moral values associated with rules of recognition, values that it would be much less rational to attribute to rules that are simply there to solve a coordination problem. There are, of course, many coordination problems that it is very important to solve; but it is usually not very important how exactly we solve them, as long as the solution is reasonably efficient.[34]

Finally, the coordination account of the rules of recognition makes it very unclear how these conventions of recognition relate to the concept of law. Consider chess, again: Without the conventions that constitute this game, there is neither a game of chess nor, consequently, a concept of chess. The rules of chess have a crucial constitutive role to play in constituting our concept of chess. On the other hand, if we think about a standard coordination convention, the picture is quite different. Consider, for example, a convention that determines on which side of the road to drive, or in which hand to hold the fork and the knife, or how to greet an acquaintance, or such. In these cases we normally have the concept of the relevant activity irrespective of the conventions. In fact, this is typically so, since the whole point of coordination conventions is to solve a problem that had been there before the convention emerged, so it must be the case that we have a concept of the relevant activity irrespective of the conventions that have evolved to regulate it. Once again, it seems that law is more like chess than the coordination cases; without the social conventions that constitute ways of making law and recognizing it as such, it is difficult to imagine what kind of concept of law we could possibly have.

Or maybe not? Hart comes close to making the suggestion that the concept of law is not really dependent on the rules of recognition. That he does when he considers (in a different context) the hypothetical of a "primitive" legal system that has no secondary rules, and thus no rules of recognition.[35] Hart seems to suggest that

---

33 It is possible, of course, that people tend to project greater importance on the rules of recognition than would be morally or politically warranted. However, even if the precise content of these rules is less important than people tend to presume, I think it is safe to maintain that they are not entirely mistaken.

34 As we have noted earlier, there is no reason to assume that coordination conventions emerge only when the agents are indifferent among the various options of conduct open to them in the relevant circumstances. The only assumption is that their preference for concerted action is stronger than their preference to act on any particular alternative. But this would still not explain why we attach moral or political significance to the solution that has emerged. And, if our main concern is the one of coordination, we are normally satisfied with whatever solution emerges, as long as it is reasonably efficient in solving the relevant coordination problem.

35 *The Concept of Law*, Ch. 5.

such a legal order is possible, even though, as he argues, it would be very defective and quite remote from law as we now understand it. So it seems that if we can imagine a legal system without rules of recognition, then the concept of law is not constituted in any significant way by such rules. Perhaps law is not like chess, after all?

Let us reconstruct the exercise. Imagine "law" in a certain community that consists solely of primary rules, namely, a set of rules of conduct, and no secondary rules whatsoever. Roughly, there are certain rules of conduct most people follow; they expect others to follow those rules, and react in some hostile manner if they do not. So far, this set of social norms does not even come close to an example of a legal system. Almost any set of some rudimentary social norms fits the bill.[36] What makes it law? Nothing, as far as I can see. If there are no rules of recognition, how can these people tell the difference between following the law, and any other set of norms they follow, or think that they ought to follow? Suppose, to illustrate, that these people think that they ought not to steal another's possessions. And then they also think that people should greet a friend by a kiss on the cheek, never hold a knife in the left hand, pray to God twice a day, and show respect to their elderly. All this is their law? If this is a possible concept of law, it hardly resembles anything we would call "law" in our world. In other words, Hart's example of a "primitive" legal system is not *legal* in any meaningful sense; it is just a set of social norms. As Hart himself was at pains to argue, law is much more than *this*; and without the rules of recognition we couldn't possibly tell the difference.

Does it mean that the rules of recognition constitute the concept of law? In order to answer this question, we must distinguish between deep and surface conventions. Once we clarify the distinction, and the idea of deep conventions, I hope that the answer to this question will be easy to provide. This is the topic of the next section.

---

36 To be more accurate, Hart indicated some restrictions on the primary rules of such a "primitive" society, restrictions that have to do with the content of the norms. (See *The Concept of Law*, 89.) But those restrictions are somewhat *ad hoc*, and in any case, would not really answer the concerns I point out here.

C. The Deep Conventions of Law

There are some reasons for having law, reasons that explain the main functions of law in our society: for example, the reasons to have some authoritative rules of conduct, the need to resolve conflicts in society, to create public goods, to solve collective-action problems, etc. And then there are, as we have seen, social conventions that determine what counts as law in a given community, namely, the rules of recognition. I want to argue that between the general reasons to have law, and the local conventions that determine what counts as law in particular legal system, there is an intermediary layer of *deep conventions*, conventions that partly constitute the concept of law. The deep conventions of law are typically manifest in the surface conventions of recognition that are specific to any given society, or legal system.[37]

Deep conventions differ from surface conventions in the following ways:

1. Deep conventions emerge as normative responses to basic social and psychological needs. They serve relatively basic functions in our social world.

2. Deep conventions typically enable a set of surface conventions to emerge, and many types of surface conventions are only made possible as instantiations of deep conventions.

3. Under normal circumstances, deep conventions are actually practiced by following their corresponding surface conventions.

4. Compared with surface conventions, deep conventions are typically much more durable and less amenable to change.

Needless to say, all this is very schematic and needs to be shown. Let me follow the example of chess, and explain what I mean here. The rules constituting chess are constitutive conventions. They constitute what chess is and how to play the game.

---

37 I have presented the general idea that there are deep conventions and the distinction between deep and surface conventions, in my "Deep Conventions" (forthcoming in *Philosophy* & *Phenomenological Research*). This section draws on that much more detailed account.

In part, they constitute the point of playing the game and some of the specific values associated with it. But all this is possible only against the background of a deeper layer of shared understanding about what competitive games are. In order to play chess as a competitive game of a certain kind, players must follow a fairly elaborate set of norms, or deep conventions, determining the concept of games and the essential point(s) of engaging in such a practice. Chess, as a game of a particular kind, is only an instantiation of a more general human activity that we call "playing a (competitive) game."

Admittedly, it is not easy to define a particular set of norms that constitute the activity we would call "playing a competitive game." Nevertheless, some basic conventions are clear enough:

1. Playing a competitive game is basically a rule-governed activity. This means at least two main things. First, that in playing a game, the participants follow some rules. Second, that the rules of the game define, among other things, what the game is, and what counts as success or failure in the game, what counts as winning or losing, etc. And, of course, these norms can be violated, so that putative players might break the rules or deviate from them in various ways.

2. Games involve a certain element of detachment from real-life concerns. The level of detachment varies considerably between different types of games, and in different contexts and cultures. But even when the detachment from real-life concerns is minimal, games have a certain artificiality that is quite essential to our understanding of what games are. A violation of such norms typically involves a confusion; it typically manifests a misunderstanding of the situation.[38]

3. Games have a fairly sharp demarcation of participants. Players are typically recognized as such and can be distinguished quite clearly from spectators, fans, and other nonparticipants. Again, these are norms that can be violated on particular occasions, as when, for example, fans or spectators attempt to participate as players and thus disrupt the game.

---

38 Consider the instances in which we say to someone "this is *just a game*"; it happens when people take the game too seriously, as it were, and get confused about this detachment norm.

Let me clarify two points here. First, these three features are meant to be examples of deep conventions determining what games in our culture are. This list is not meant to be exhaustive, of course, and it is certainly not meant to be a definition of what (competitive) games are.[39] Second, I do not wish to claim that first we must have an abstract concept of games, and then we can invent concrete instances of the abstract concept. This is not how our social and conceptual world develops. Abstract concepts emerge gradually, I presume, concomitantly with the particular cases that they instantiate. In any case, I do not purport to speculate about how people started to play games. In order to play a game like chess, I argue, participants (players and spectators) must also follow a set of background norms that determine what playing a game is.[40] Without such background norms of what, say, a competitive game is, the specific conventions constituting particular games, like chess, would not make sense; they would not be possible at all.

Now, the feature that makes it the case that these background rules are conventional is the fact that they are basically arbitrary norms; the particular shape they take is underdetermined by the reasons that explain their emergence. And what makes them *deep* conventions is the fact that such norms are responsive to relatively deep aspects of human society and human nature, and that they are normally practiced by following the corresponding surface conventions of the particular games we play.

Let me try to explain, beginning with the idea of depth. It is very easy to imagine a world in which people don't play chess, or soccer, or any particular game that is familiar to us. However, it is much more difficult to imagine a world in which people do not play any competitive games whatsoever. Or, if we can imagine such a world, we would realize that it has to be very different from our own. Playing games is not something that we just happen to do, it is something that reflects some deep aspects of human culture and human nature.[41] But now you may wonder: If deep conventions are responses to such deep aspects of our nature,

---

39 I believe that I do not need to take a stance on the question of whether "game" is a family resemblance concept, as Wittgenstein has famously maintained. I have confined my interest here to one central case of the concept of games, namely, those that are fairly structured and competitive. The question of how other uses of the word "game" are related to this central case, whether by some defining features or only by some loose family resemblance, is a very difficult one, that I need not try to answer here.

40 It may be argued that the deep norms or conventions I have in mind are shared *beliefs*, not norms, and thus not conventions either. I have responded to this in detail in my "Deep Conventions."

41 To believe what we see on *National Geographic* channels, many animals seem to play games as well. I don't doubt that animals play, but I doubt that we can say, strictly speaking, that they play *games*.

what makes these norms conventional at all? The answer consists in the fact that the norms are underdetermined by the reasons, functions, needs, etc., that give rise to them. The same needs could be satisfied, as it were, by an alternative set of norms that would serve us just as well. Perhaps we could have had some rituals that were not games but would have served similar functions; or we could have had "games" that were not winnable; or we could have had "games" that were not detached from real-life concerns, such as the Roman gladiators' "game" for their lives.

Deep conventions tend to be rather elusive because they are typically practiced by following their corresponding surface conventions. We do not play competitive games in the abstract, but particular games like chess, or soccer, that are constituted by surface conventions. (Although it is worth noting that small children sometimes come close to playing an abstract game, as it were; they just play something and invent the rules as they go along. It is almost as if they practice what it is to play a game.)

Let me give another example, from a different domain. In our culture there is an underlying convention that requires dress codes under certain circumstances, and then there are conventions about what counts as an appropriate outfit on particular types of occasions. The social practice appears to us in the practice of following the latter norms: what you see when you observe social behavior is the practice of following the surface conventions. But it is still the case that the deep convention is the underlying norm that people follow, albeit indirectly, that is, by following the corresponding surface conventions on the appropriate occasions. Suppose that the reasons, or needs, functions, etc., for having dress code norms in our society are *P*. Let us assume that *P* consists in the reasons to show respect for people by some outward appearance. Now, it shouldn't be difficult to imagine a different society where *P* is instantiated by a different kind of social practice, for instance, that people paint their faces in various colors in comparable circumstances. (Perhaps they wear feathers, or different sizes of earrings; the possibilities are numerous.) And then, of course, if you live in this different society, it would be pointless for you to associate the social functions of *P* with any particular dress code. This is what makes the underlying norms of dress codes conventional.

In other words, here is how the conventional setting works: In our culture, one way in which we manifest respect for people is by dressing in certain ways on certain occasions. In other societies, the same social function of showing respect on comparable occasions can be practiced by other means, such as painting one's face or wearing feathers, etc. This is the relevant deep convention. But such deep conventions can be practiced only by following their corresponding surface conventions. So there might be a convention that if men attend a wedding they should wear a suit and a tie. This is how they are expected to manifest the relevant kind of respect for such an occasion. And then this suit and tie norm is the surface convention men would follow on such occasions. And of course there are many other surface conventions that instantiate the same underlying deep convention (of showing respect by dressing in certain ways).

Deep conventions typically come to our attention when we face some deviant behavior or some doubts about the practice we are engaged in. My history professor at college used to say that when his king is threatened by checkmate, he would simply declare a republic. Taken seriously (which I am almost sure he did not), this is not just a violation of the rules of chess; it is a violation of the deep conventions constituting what counts as playing a competitive game.

Finally, note that surface conventions often come in layers with different degrees of shallowness, so to speak. Consider, for example, the deep conventions of representational art, say, in medieval Europe. As we know, they were instantiated by an elaborate set of surface conventions. But some of those surface conventions were probably deeper than others. I would guess that conventions of religious symbolism, composition, and perspective were deeper than specific conventions of, say, color-symbolism (e.g., that blue represents virginity); and conventions of color-symbolism may have been deeper than conventions about paint material or the size of the works, etc. Similar degrees of depth and shallowness are present in other cases. The deep conventions of theater, to take another example, are instantiated by surface conventions of particular genres of theater, and those, in turn, may be practiced by following even shallower conventions, say, about the number of acts, stage setting, etc.

If this is the case, you may wonder whether there is a categorical distinction between deep and surface conventions at all; perhaps we are entitled to say only that there is a *deeper than* relation of conventions. In response, two points: First, it should be noted that deep conventions can rarely be followed on their own, as it were; deep conventions are actually practiced by following their corresponding surface conventions. When we play competitive games we follow the deep conventions that constitute what competitive games are by following the surface conventions of particular games. Surface conventions, on the other hand, can be followed on their own even if there are further, even shallower conventions, that people follow in those circumstances as well.

Another main difference between the deep and the surface conventions is that the deep are constitutive of the practice in ways that the "deeper than" is not necessarily. Without the deep conventions of theater (such as, for example, the convention about suspension of disbelief), there is no theater, at least not in any form that we are familiar with. Without the deep conventions of competitive games that we mentioned above, there would not be a practice that we can call "competitive games." The deep conventions constitute what the practice is. In contrast, the surface conventions that are deeper than others do not necessarily serve this constitutive function (though sometimes they may). For example, the conventions about color symbolism could easily be replaced with different ones (say, a different color or none at all), without any necessary relation to the deeper conventions about the religious significance of the work, composition, perspective, etc. Surface conventions generally *instantiate* the deeper ones; they are different ways of *doing that*. Shallower conventions within the setting of other surface conventions do not necessarily instantiate the deeper ones. Their relation to the deeper conventions is typically more incidental.[42]

Let us now return to law. The rules of recognition, of the kind Hart had in mind, are surface conventions. They determine what counts as law in a particular legal system, in a particular community. These surface conventions of recognition are instantiations of deep conventions about what law in our culture is. Roughly, the idea is that the rules of recognition relate to the deep conventions of law as particular games relate to deep conventions about what it is to play a competitive game. What would be the deep conventions of law?

Consider these three (hugely simplified) possible models of what the law is. According to one familiar conception, law is a product of the act of will of particular individuals or institutions. Let me call this the institutional model of law. At least two other models, however, are familiar from history: The customary

42 Note, however, that even if I am wrong about this, and the most we can say is that conventions come in layers, some deeper than others, my basic contention that there are deep conventions remains basically intact. Even if there are just layers of depths and shallowness, it can still be the case, as I argue here, that many shallow conventions instantiate deeper ones; and that without the relevant deeper layer, certain shallow conventions would not make sense.

model, and the religious one. According to the customary model, law is not created by acts of will, but by long-standing social customs; roughly, law is just those norms of conduct (or, more likely, some subset of them) that have been followed in the community for a long period of time. And then there is a third familiar model that is essentially religious: Law is the expressed wish of God, grounded on the interpretation of some holy scripture, like the Bible or the Quran. To be sure, I am not claiming that these are the only models we are familiar with, and I am certainly not committed to historical accuracy here. I present these models here just to exemplify the fact that our deep conventions of law are indeed conventional, that they could be quite different from what they are.

Now, these three models exemplify very different conceptions of legal authority. They instantiate different conceptions of what the law is. As one should expect, they have a great deal in common. That is why they are different models *of law*; they form conventional solutions to similar problems and social needs: for example, the social needs to have mechanisms for resolution of conflicts in society, to solve collective-action problems, to produce public goods, and so forth. These and similar concerns constitute the basic reasons for having law and legal institutions in our societies. But these reasons, universal as they may be, can be instantiated by different sets of deep conventions. According to the institutional model, the one that more or less prevailed in the modern world, law is, by and large, the deliberate product of recognized and institutionalized authorities. According to religious models, law is the expressed will of God, not of human institutions. And then there were times and places where law was just a little bit of both of these, but mostly consisted of the customs and traditions that have been followed for generations. The normative manifestations of these different models of law are examples of the deep conventions I have in mind. As with any other type of deep conventions, they are actually practiced by their corresponding surface conventions of recognition that are particular to the specific society in question. For example, a religious practice of law must have certain surface conventions that determine what counts as the relevant holy scripture, the "expressed" will of God, who gets to determine its interpretation, and so forth. Similarly, a customary model must have some surface conventions of recognition about what counts as a legal custom as opposed to norms about, e.g., etiquette, or desirable, but not obligatory, behavior, and about who gets to resolve interpretative questions about such matters, who gets to apply them to particular conflicts, etc.

Let me sum up: The conventional foundation of law consists of two layers. There are deep conventions that determine what law is, and those deep conventions are instantiated by the surface conventions of recognition that are specific to particular legal systems. The concept of law is constituted by both layers of conventions. Our concept of law partly depends on the deep conventions that determine what we take law and legal institutions to consist in, and partly on the specific institutions we have, those that are determined by the rules of recognition. Basically, this is just like chess. Without the rules of chess, we would not have a concept of chess. But we can only have such a concept because we already possess the deeper concept of playing competitive games, of which chess is just one instance. Both are profoundly conventional, and in this general insight, I think that Hart was quite right.

Needless to say, all this was a very sketchy account. I am sure that more needs to be said about the precise nature of the deep conventions of law, and about the ways in which the deep conventions are manifest in specific rules of recognition. However, there is one point I would like to develop a bit further here. There is, I think, an interesting difference between the ways in which deep and surface conventions are amenable to change. All social conventions change over time. Some of them dwindle and cease to exist, others get modified in substantial ways. But there is this important difference: Surface conventions can be modified or abolished at will, and they often are, whereas deep conventions are much more durable and typically resist deliberate, institutional modification.

Surface conventions are often codified and thus replaced by institutional rules.[43] The rules of chess, for example, have been largely replaced by codified rules during the twentieth century.[44] Similar codification has occurred with many competitive sports. In other domains, like the arts, or the conventions of a natural language, codification is very rare, and surface conventions change much less institutionally. They typically change either by losing their point, so to speak, and then gradually fading away, or sometimes by a revolutionary change, one that brings

---

43 As I have argued in "Deep Conventions," there are two ways in which conventions can be codified: I called them *legislative codification* and *encyclopedic codification*. Legislative codification of rules purports to determine, authoritatively, what the rules are. In contrast, encyclopedic codification only purports to report what the rules are, without actually determining their content for the future (such as codification of grammar rules in textbooks, or dictionaries, etc.). It is the legislative form of codification that I am concerned with here in the text.

44 So far as I could ascertain, the first official international codification of chess rules occurred in 1929, by FIDE, the World Chess Federation, in Venice.

about a new convention replacing the old one. All these modes of change are also present in the law. Rules of recognition sometimes fade away and cease to be followed; other times they may be changed institutionally. The formation and development of the European Union, to mention a clear example, has brought about a considerable change in the rules of recognition of its member states. And then, of course, there are revolutionary changes as well.

Legal theorists often thought that it is a particular strength of Kelsen's account of the basic norm, compared with Hart's conventional rule of recognition, that it is capable of explaining the idea of a legal-political revolution. When a revolutionary change takes place in a certain regime, like a *coup d'état*, Kelsen argued, the success of the revolution determines its legality.[45] A revolution is successful when judges and other officials actually presuppose a new basic norm, and apply it instead of the basic norm of the old regime. If that change occurs, Kelsen argued, a new legal system is in place. As we have already noted, this observation is actually not a strength of Kelsen's account but reveals one its main weaknesses. Realizing that it is the practice of judges and other officials that actually determines the content of the basic norm violates the antireductionist aspirations of Kelsen's theory. In addition, however, we can now see that there is nothing particularly mysterious or problematic in the idea of a revolution for a conventional account of law's foundations. Once we realize that the rules of recognition are surface conventions, it should be much easier to understand how they can change by a political revolution. Surface conventions, as we noted, often change by deliberate, institutional intervention. Changes that occur in the deep conventions, on the other hand, are much less obvious and typically much more profound.

Deep conventions typically change very gradually, over a long period of time. The deep conventions we mentioned above, like those that constitute our practices of playing competitive games, or those that constitute forms of art, such as theater, etc., have changed over time, perhaps even quite substantially, but those changes were very slow, spanning centuries. Sometimes, however, a radical change does occur even at the level of deep conventions. For example, the emergence of abstract art at the beginning of the twentieth century may have been such a radical change in the deep conventions of painting and sculpture. And it was a fairly rapid and quite a radical change. It is a difficult question, that I cannot really answer, how such radical changes occur in deep conventions. My only purpose

45 Not, to be sure, its moral legitimacy. That is a separate issue.

here is to point out that such changes are, basically, what we would normally call a social revolution. A political revolution, if successful, brings about a change in the surface conventions; in law, it is the rules of recognition. Whether the revolution also amounts to a radical *social* change, depends, I suggest, on the question of whether the deep conventions have changed as well.[46]

---

46 I am indebted to Scott Altman, David Enoch, Leslie Green, and Gideon Yaffe, for helpful comments on earlier drafts.

CHAPTER 7

Should Like Cases Be Treated Alike?

It is a familiar slogan in legal circles that "like cases should be treated alike." This idea is often confused with two others: the rationale of analogical reasoning in adjudication, and the value of coherence. I would like to keep these three issues separate, at least for a while. What is unique about the idea of treating like cases alike? I would suggest that the interesting cases (and by "cases" I do mean judicial decisions, to which this essay is confined) are those in which legal decisions are not entirely *determined* by reasons. If two similar cases are actually determined by the reasons that apply to them, then there is no need for the principle of treating like cases alike: the determining reasons would do all the work of justifying similar rulings. This is what makes the principle of treating like cases alike uniquely problematic, and separate from the questions of analogical reasoning and coherence. In analogical reasoning, for example, the assumption is that if there is a good reason that determines a decision X under circumstances C1, and we now face a similar case C2, then the reason that determines X in C1 may also determine (or support) the decision X under C2. In other words, analogical reasoning typically appeals to the reasons that underlie the previous decision(s) and extends the application of *those reasons* to the new case.[1] (I will qualify this account of analogy in the last section.)

But now think about those cases in which decisions are *underdetermined* by reasons, because the decision involves, to some extent, an arbitrary choice, or because the decision involves a choice between incommensurable values, or because the relevant reasons are indeterminate (due to moral vagueness, for example). Outside courtrooms, in the ordinary course of our lives, we might try to avoid such decisions or, more commonly, we just make a decision and move on. But the courts

---

1 See J. Raz, *The Authority of Law*, 201–206.

must decide, and often judicial decisions, especially of higher courts, actually make the law. So here is the question of treating like cases alike: are there any good reasons to treat previous judicial decisions as legally binding in similar cases, just because they are similar, that is, even if the underlying reasons of the previous decisions underdetermine the result?

One might be tempted to think that coherence has something to do with this. But this is far from clear. Coherence would seem to call for a consistent application of reasons.[2] You do not exhibit incoherence by making different decisions under similar circumstances, if the decisions were not quite determined by the reasons that apply to those circumstances. If we assume that the principle of treating like cases alike pertains to decisions which are underdetermined by reasons, coherence, by itself, would not answer our question; at least not generally. (An exception will be discussed in the last section.) Furthermore, this should also alleviate an immediate worry: One could have thought that if similar cases are treated differently, it must follow that (at least) one of them was wrongly decided. If we confine our attention, however, to those cases in which legal decisions are not entirely determined by reasons, this conclusion does not follow.[3]

A. Examples

Let me outline three types of cases where the principle of treating like cases alike is relevant. Consider, first, the case of a judicial decision that is partly based on an arbitrary choice. Determining the exact levels of punishment is a good case in point. Suppose, for example, that a previous legal decision, call it D1, determined that the punishment for an armed robber is ten years of imprisonment. Let us assume that there are no particular reasons that would support imprisonment for

---

2 I am not suggesting that coherence is synonymous with consistency. That is certainly not the case. I do assume, however, that coherence applied to practical reason would call for a consistent application of reasons. This assumption does not seem to beg any questions here.

3 There is a vast amount of literature, both in philosophy and in law reviews, on treating like cases alike in the context of equality. In fact, one gets the impression that when people think about this topic, they think about equality. I cannot possibly do justice to this literature in this short essay. What I propose here is an alternative argument, and I can only hope that the reader will come to realize that equality is not the issue, at least not in the context in which the principle of treating like cases alike is discussed here. But this is not something that I can take up here directly. For some of the recent literature that focuses on equality, see, *e.g.*, P. Westen, "The Empty Idea of Equality," K. Greenawalt, "How Empty Is The Idea of Equality?," and C. Peters, "Equality Revisited."

ten years, as compared with, for example, nine or eleven.[4] Now assume that a very similar armed robbery comes before a new court (that is, assume that the cases are identical in all relevant respects, whatever you take the relevant respects to be), say D2. To suggest that there is *a principle* of treating like cases alike, amounts to the suggestion that even if there are no particular reasons to prefer ten years over eleven (or nine), the court in D2 ought to follow the decision in D1 and impose the ten years. And this would suggest that it would be wrong for the court in D2 to opt for a different level of punishment of, say, eleven years.

It is tempting to say that none of this should matter. After all, the assumption was that within the range of nine to eleven years, any decision would be just as good as any other. So why should we care? Well, for one, the convict would care, and quite a bit. Could he not reasonably complain that if the convict in D1 was punished with ten years of imprisonment, it would be wrong to put him away for eleven years? (Recall that we have assumed that the cases are identical in all relevant respects.) True, the convict in D2 cannot claim that the eleven years would be, in itself, somehow disproportionate or inappropriate. We have assumed the contrary. But can he claim that *given* the previous decision in D1, it would be wrong or unfair? And if the convict is right about this, shouldn't we care about it too?

Now consider the case of a judicial decision that is based on a choice between incommensurable values. Suppose that the court in case D1 had faced a choice between two decisions, A and B, and that the difference between these options is as follows: Option A would score higher on promoting value P (say, economic efficiency) and somewhat lower on promoting a competing value Q (say, environmental protection), whereas option B would amount to the opposite; B would score higher on promoting value Q and somewhat lower on promoting value P. Let us assume, further, that the comparison between A (P>Q) and B (Q>P) is basically incommensurable or, in any case, not determinable by reasons.[5] Now suppose that the court in D1 opted for A. Should this choice amount to a binding

4 In other words, you have to assume here that whatever it is that you take to constitute the proportionality and adequacy of punishments allows for a certain range of actual punishments that would be appropriate to the case at hand, and assume that in our case, the range is between nine and eleven years of imprisonment.

5 A choice between A and B is incommensurable if it is the case that none of these relations between A and B obtain: "A is better than B," "B is better than A," and "B is equal to, or on par with A." For an interesting distinction between standard accounts of incommensurability and indeterminacy of evaluative comparisons, see J. Broome, "Is Incommensurability Vagueness?" For my purposes here, however, it does not matter which type of indeterminacy applies.

decision so that in a future case, D2, which is similar in all relevant respects, the court ought to follow D1 only because like cases should be treated alike? Or would it be warranted on part of the court in D2 to recognize that the choice in D1 was not supported by reasons which can determine a preference of A over B, and therefore the court in D2 should be free to opt for decision B?

Finally, consider the case of moral vagueness. Judicial decisions often have to determine whether to apply a certain moral (or other evaluative) concept to the case at hand.[6] The case may turn on the question of whether, say, action P is really "dishonest," or not. Honesty, let us assume, is a moral concept, and like any other concept, it would have some borderline cases due to its inevitable vagueness. A deliberate lie, for instance, is typically dishonest, but not always. Some "white lies" are not dishonest at all, and some would be borderline cases. (Consider this example: Teachers and educators may encourage a troubled student by slightly exaggerating his or her achievements or talents, etc. Surely, at some point, the exaggeration would become dishonest, but it is unidentifiable at what point such "white lies" become dishonest.) In other words, there is no reason to assume that moral concepts are free from vagueness.[7] And there is no reason to deny that some of the decisions courts have to make are about the application of such concepts to borderline cases. But then, if it is a morally borderline case, the decision of the court cannot be described as one which is determined by the relevant moral reasons. (Perhaps the decision is warranted by other relevant moral reasons, but that is beside the point now.) If the court has to decide whether action P is "dishonest," and P falls within the borderline of "honesty," then the decision is, ex hypothesis, underdetermined by what "honesty" really requires.

You might think that such legal decisions on morally borderline cases should be avoided. Perhaps so, but they cannot be avoided, not entirely anyway. It is true that in some cases the law purports to have a margin of safety, phasing out borderline cases as if they are "no" cases. A good example is the *rule of leniency* in

6 Needless to say, courts have to make decisions on borderline cases (due to vagueness) in countless non-moral cases as well. I have chosen the example of moral vagueness for two reasons: First, in order to make my own case stronger, purporting to show that even in morally significant decisions, like cases need not be treated alike. Secondly, in many of the non-moral cases, a decision on borderline cases would be one of the examples mentioned in the first category, namely, decisions which are based on basically arbitrary choices. On the relation between arbitrariness and decisions on borderline cases, see T. Endicott, *Vagueness in Law*, 186–190.

7 I share the view of Russ Shafer-Landau that moral vagueness does not necessarily entail antirealism about morality, even though, as he rightly claims, vagueness in morality stems from a real fuzziness of moral predicates. See his "Vagueness, Borderline Cases and Moral Realism."

criminal law, prescribing that unless an action falls well within the meaning of the offense, it should be regarded as if it doesn't. This is a noble attempt to phase out borderline cases, but it doesn't always work. First, these kinds of precautions are rare outside the sphere of the criminal law, and even there, they are not (and perhaps cannot be) consistently applied. Secondly, and more importantly, as we know very well, vagueness cannot be eliminated, and even if you employ a generous margin of safety, you are still left with second-order vagueness (viz., vagueness about where the borderline cases begin).[8]

So now suppose that the court in D1 decides that action P, which, we assumed, is a borderline case of "honesty," is dishonest. Should this decision be legally binding on future courts? (I am not asking whether it *is* a legal duty, but whether it *ought* to be one.) If the court in D2 faces a very similar case (that is, again, assume that D2 is identical in all relevant respects), should it be bound to decide D2 according to D1, just because the cases are similar, or should it be allowed to reach the opposite conclusion?

These three types of cases are not meant to be exhaustive. Other cases would have a similar structure. What they all have in common, however, is the fact that the *reasons* that would justify the previous ruling of the court do not determine the decision in the new case, even when the new case is basically identical in all the relevant respects.[9] Thus the question is whether the mere similarity of the new case to the previous ones is sufficient to consider the previous rulings legally binding; should the new case be decided alike, just because it is alike, even if it is underdetermined by the reasons justifying the previous rulings?

B. Justice Should Be Seen

There are two main principles that could justify an affirmative answer to this question. Let us consider, first, the idea that is (loosely) expressed by the saying that "Justice should not only be done, but should manifestly and undoubtedly *be seen*

8 On the idea that vagueness in law cannot be eliminated, see T. Endicott, *Vagueness in Law*, 188–192.

9 You may complain that no two cases can be really identical in all the relevant respects, and that is probably right. I need not insist on such identity claims here. I am happy to admit that similarity between legal cases is itself vague, and that we would inevitably face borderline cases here. None of this affects my arguments about the principle of treating like cases alike. Surely two legal cases can be very similar, or roughly identical, in all relevant respects, and that is all we need here.

to be done."[10] Admittedly, this is a rather crude formulation, since we have seen in detail that there is no real issue of justice involved here. But there may be a value to uniformity of legal decisions in being seen as uniform by the parties concerned, even if there is nothing else to commend the decision but its similarity to previous decisions. This value, call it the need for justice to be seen if you like, consists in the assurance that litigants may gain by coming to realize that they are treated equally with others in similar situations. The more you can come to recognize that you are being treated exactly like others, the less you have reasons to suspect bias, prejudice, and other distortions that may have affected judicial decisions.

This is a complex value that has both an epistemic and a symbolic aspect. The epistemic aspect relates to the value of uniformity as a safeguard against potential bias. Consider, for example, the case of our armed robber who faces punishment. If he knows that the judge has the discretion to disregard the previous ruling that set the punishment at ten years, he would not be unreasonable to suspect that if he receives eleven years of imprisonment, it may have been a result of a particular prejudice against him. After all, as we have assumed, there is no particular reason that compels this decision, and therefore the suspicion of bias or prejudice might loom large. Dispelling such suspicions, even when they are actually unfounded, may be valuable in itself. Furthermore, there is a symbolic value to uniformity of decisions that is not insignificant. By requiring the courts to treat like cases alike, the law purports to assure the litigants that they are treated equally by the law. Even if this is actually an equality that is not called for by the relevant reasons that should determine the case, a public affirmation of such equality may have a symbolic value that is desirable in itself.[11]

The main problem with this reasoning is that it provides some support for the principle of treating like cases alike, but not a very strong one. Generally speaking, concerns about appearances are typically weak and easily defeasible. Consider, for example, the concerns about the possibility of judicial bias or prejudice. One way to alleviate the worry that we may have about the possibility of bias on part of judges is to try to reduce their discretion as much as possible. But this can be a very costly way of achieving what we want. After all, we need judges partly because

---

10 Attributed to Baron Of Bury Hewart (1870–1943), Remark, Nov. 9, 1923. "Rex v. Surrey Justices," vol. 1, King's Bench Reports (1924).

11 For an interesting account of why appearances matter morally, see J. Driver, "Caesar's Wife: On The Moral Significance of Appearing Good."

we expect them to exercise discretion. There may be other ways of reducing the suspicion of bias and prejudice that are just as good, or perhaps even better. The requirement for judges to provide detailed justifications of their rulings that are rendered public, the possibility of appeals, and other forms of institutional checks and balances may constitute more effective ways of convincing potential litigants that they have not been discriminated against.

You may think that this is just a rough generalization, and of course, it is. Furthermore, there may be certain situations in which the danger of a particular bias or prejudice looms large, and then perhaps in those cases, no precaution would be too much precaution. (Unfortunately, certain situations in which racial prejudices are all too present is a notable example that comes to mind.) In other words, it would be fair to say that in some cases the value of justice being seen and not just done is more important than in other cases.[12] Nevertheless, and as a rough generalization indeed, I would venture to suggest that public scrutiny and institutional constraints would work better than a practice that would require judges to "treat like cases alike." After all, if the judge is indeed biased or prejudiced, it would not take a great deal of ingenuity on her part to show that the case in front of her is not really like the other cases. Judicial resourcefulness in distinguishing cases is almost unlimited.[13]

C. Protected Expectations and the Value of Predictability

Perhaps a much stronger case for the principle of treating like cases alike can be made by reference to the value of protected expectations. Potential litigants may have relied on previous judicial rulings and formed expectations about the law that would be wrong to frustrate. But we must proceed with caution here: Not every expectation potential litigants may have about the law is one that would be wrong to frustrate. The expectation must be reasonable and legitimate. Part of what makes expectations about the law reasonable and legitimate is that the relevant type of expectations is supported by legal practice. To take an extreme example, in a legal

12 Scott Altman suggested to me that the stakes may also matter here. The higher the stakes, the more important it might be that justice be seen, since the suspicion of bias or prejudice might be greater. I am not sure what to think about this. I suspect that as an empirical generalization this is too rough.

13 I take this also to prove that there is not much to support the idea that a principle of treating like cases alike can serve as a serious deterrent against the potential prejudice of judges.

system that does not recognize a doctrine of precedent, potential litigants cannot rely on judicial decisions to make legitimate predictions about the law. If the law tells you that the decisions of higher courts are not binding, you cannot have a legitimate expectation that they would be. So the question of what expectations about the law are legitimate is partly, but crucially, a matter of legal practice. This, in itself, makes the argument about treating like cases alike somewhat circular: Unless there is a judicial practice of treating like cases alike, how can you claim that you have had a legitimate expectation that such cases would be treated alike?

This is not so simple, however. Sometimes we want to make an argument about the importance of protecting expectations even if the kind of expectations in question is not yet supported by legal practice. In such cases we argue that legal practice *ought to* protect the relevant expectations because that would be a good thing to do. Certain social goals are better achieved if the judiciary follows bright-line rules that parties can rely on and thus predict, with greater accuracy, the content of the law that the courts will enforce. This is the kind of argument that is often made on behalf of clear canons of statutory interpretation: The more such canons of interpretation are clearly laid out and consistently followed by the courts, the greater stability and predictability the law would have, and this, it is argued, is generally a good thing.[14] So can we make a parallel argument about the principle of treating like cases alike? Can we say that even if it is not a practice-based expectation that needs to be protected here, it is the kind of expectation that should be positively encouraged by the courts?

It seems to me that such an argument would be more cogent in some cases than others. For instance, it is rather doubtful that accurate predictability is valuable in the case of punishments. There is no reason to assume that potential criminals should be able to predict, as accurately as possible, what their punishment might be. It would probably not enhance the deterrent effect of the penal system,[15] and, as long as punishment is kept well within permissible boundaries, fairness should not be a concern either. Criminal punishment is not like a tax that criminals have to pay on their antisocial behavior. Taxes should be predictable indeed, because people should be allowed to calculate the costs of their economic activities *ex ante*, and make their relevant choices. In contrast to tax law, criminal law is

14 I am not suggesting here that this is a good argument on behalf of clear canons of statutory interpretation. This is just an example of the form such an argument would have to take.

15 This, of course, is an empirical question. See, for example, Baker, Harel, & Kugler, "The Virtues of Uncertainty in Law: An Experimental Approach."

there to prescribe modes of conduct that are not permissible. It is not the general purpose of the penal system to enable potential criminals to calculate in advance whether they would rather follow the law and not be punished, or violate it and pay a fixed penalty for it. To be sure, I am not suggesting that we have no reason to maintain a principle of proportionality in punishment. Far from it. My only suggestion is that *within* the range of punishments that are fair and proportional to the crime, accurate predictability serves no desirable social goals.

It may be tempting to think that the case of punishment is unique. In most other areas of the law, it may be argued, the greater the uniformity and predictability of judicial decisions, the better. On closer scrutiny, however, it should become clear that even as a rough generalization, this is not true. Increasing the predictability of judicial decisions is never costless, and often the costs will outweigh the benefits. The more judicial decisions are predictable, the more rigid they are. Generally speaking, rigidity is undesirable because it tends to impede judicial experimentation, innovation, and other potentially desirable social changes. It is a truism, but nonetheless an important one, that there is always a delicate balance that needs to be maintained between the values of predictability of judicial decisions and the values which call for their flexibility.

Consider, for example, the case of judicial decisions that reflect a choice between incommensurable values. To remind ourselves of the example: We have assumed that the court in D1 had faced a choice between option A, that scores higher on value P and lower on a competing value Q, and option B, which is the opposite, scoring higher on Q and lower on P. We have also assumed that the choice between A and B is basically incommensurable. Now the question is whether faced with a similar case, the court in D2 should follow the decision in D1, only because the cases are similar and a decision in D1 had already been rendered, say, to prefer A over B. Admittedly, an affirmative answer could be justified by an appeal to the ideal of predictability of judicial decisions. But this can hardly settle the issue. There is something to be said in favor of the opposite answer, allowing the court in D2 to experiment with a different choice of values, which is, ex hypothesi, not necessarily inferior to the choice of the court in D1.

But why should we allow the courts, you may ask, to engage in social experimentation? For two main reasons. First, there is an epistemic issue here. The actual effects and ramifications of some judicial decisions are often very difficult to assess in advance. It may take years, if not decades, to realize and adequately appraise the social consequences of some judicial decisions. Experimenting with different decisions under similar circumstances might facilitate a better assessment of the effects of various evaluative and other social choices that the courts make.[16] Second, and perhaps more importantly, there is an issue of pluralism and diversity that might be involved here. Even if certain choices between values or mixed goods are, objectively speaking, incommensurable (or otherwise underdetermined by reasons), different people might nevertheless have a preference for one over the other option that is not irrational. In other words, incommensurability does not entail indifference. (Even if we assume, for example, that the choice between the life of an academic and that of a merchant banker is basically incommensurable, it doesn't mean that my choice of the former is arbitrary or something that I should not deeply care about.[17]) Thus, allowing the courts to make different choices under similar circumstances may be justified by the need to cater to different populations with divergent needs and preferences. As long as the relevant judicial decisions are morally and otherwise within the bounds of permissibility (as we have assumed all along), courts should be allowed, at least in certain cases, to reach different decisions that reflect different preferences amongst otherwise incommensurable values. The uniformity of decisions that is dictated by the principle of treating like cases alike seriously undermines the courts' ability to respond to the needs of diversity and pluralism.

To be sure, I am not suggesting that these reasons for forgoing uniformity are necessarily present in each and every case. Far from it. But often one, or both of them, are, and this should count against the assumption that the value of predictability of judicial decisions ought to prevail. Thus, treating like cases alike is not necessarily desirable or even warranted.

D. The Role of Analogy and Coherence Reconsidered

So far I have considered only the principle of treating like cases alike in those cases in which the rulings of previous courts are underdetermined by reasons. It may

---

16 Needless to add, there are certain conditions that would have to obtain to make such judicial experiments desirable. For instance, experimentation would be pointless if there was no feedback mechanism that would allow us to monitor different effects of judicial decisions. It may also be noted that in federal systems, courts can experiment with different decisions on a regional basis. The desirability of this is manifest in the fact that in most federal systems, the doctrine of precedent is not applied horizontally. This practice is very much in line with my argument in the text. But it should be noted that the possibility of such regional diversity does not exhaust the need to experiment with different decisions under similar circumstances; after all, the issues are not always tied to regional differences.

17 For a detailed discussion of incommensurability in this and similar contexts, see J. Raz, "Incommensurability and Agency."

be worth exploring another possibility: The principle of treating like cases alike may be thought to apply to cases that are determined by *similar reasons*. In order to explain what I have in mind here, let me draw a distinction between two forms of analogical reasoning in adjudication. Let us call it strong and weak analogy.

In the case of *strong analogy*, the court draws on previous rulings in order to extract the underlying justification for those rulings and seeks to apply that justification to the novel case. Suppose, for example, that a court decided in D1 that automobile manufacturers must fully disclose the exact technical specifications of the safety features of the cars they manufacture. Now suppose that the new case, D2, concerns a requirement to disclose safety features of mechanical toys. A reasoning by analogy would run as follows: The court in D2 must first try to surmise *what is the underlying reason, or principle*, that actually justifies the court's ruling in D1 to require full disclosure in case of automobile manufacturers; suppose it is principle P. Now, having realized that P justifies the ruling in D1, the court should decide whether P also justifies a similar ruling in D2, with respect to mechanical toys. If it does, the same principle is applied by analogy to the new case. Thus the effect of reasoning by strong analogy is that a certain principle or reason, previously relied on by the courts, is extended to novel cases, but this is only an extension of application, not of the underlying principle itself.[18]

By contrast, reasoning by *weak analogy* does not apply the very same reason or principle that justifies the previous rulings. Instead, roughly, we would want to say that the court relies on *a similar principle*, one which would be in accord with it, even though it is not the same. Thus consider the following cases: In D1, the court decided that liability exemption clauses in standard-form contracts should be subject to a requirement of "reasonableness." Suppose that the underlying reason for this ruling, call it P1, consists in concern about the disparity of information and bargaining power in standard-form contracts between the two types of parties to such contracts. Now suppose that the new case, D2, concerns a question

---

18 This is also why it is correct to say that analogical reasoning typically *extends* previously recognized reasons to determine novel cases. (See J. Raz, *The Authority of Law*, 201–206.) Suppose that a judicial decision runs as follows: D1: A, B, C, and D → X, where A, B, etc, stand for the legally relevant circumstances of the case, and X for the court's decision. Now assume that in a new case, D2, we only have circumstances A, B, C, but not D (*e.g.* it is not an automobile manufacturer, etc.) The question of analogical reasoning is whether we should extend the ruling of D1 to D2 as well; and this, of course, cannot be a mechanical decision. It must be based on the answer to the question of whether the underlying reason(s) which support X in D1 would also support X in D2. If the answer is yes, then the court in D2 basically decides that the principle underlying D1 is actually broader in scope than we had previously thought, or that it ought to be such.

about the validity of liquidated damages of standard-form contracts and the question is whether any upper limit should be imposed on such liquidated damages. Presumably, the underlying justification for the ruling in D1 is that P1, does not, by itself, apply to the new question of limits on liquidated damages. After all, different considerations may apply to questions about exemption clauses and remedies. But there is a clear sense in which a similar principle might be at work in D2, one which would be in accord with the justification of D1, namely, a concern about disparity of power between contractual parties to standard-form contracts and the need to protect the relatively weak and vulnerable side. So there is a sense in which a decision by the court in D2 to impose some limits on liquidated damages of standard-form contracts would be justified by a principle, say P2, that is *similar* to P1, which justifies the ruling in D1. Similarity is a very vague concept, of course. But we can make it more precise: We could claim that given P1, P2 is required, or at least justified, by considerations of coherence. The assumption would have to be that P2 coheres better with P1 than its alternative. Therefore, it would also make sense to say that *given* P1, P2 would be legally justified.

You may think that there is a different type of reasoning that is going on here: Perhaps the court in D2 simply takes the principle underlying the previous ruling, P1, to a higher level of abstraction, and then it applies the more abstract principle to the case at hand. Perhaps this is so, but then you have to keep in mind that the higher we ascend in levels of abstraction, the less determinate the principles become. In any case, I suspect that this description does not undermine my point. Once you try to justify the application of the more abstract principle to the new case, the same types of concerns will be present: The court in D2 would have to justify its assumption that the more abstract principle has sufficient legal support, as it were, and ex hypothesi, support for the abstract principle and its legal relevance can only come from its similarity to, or coherence with P1 (and other similar previous decisions).

To sum up: the use of strong analogy in adjudication is not an instance of treating like cases alike because it actually amounts to the application of basically the same reasons to novel cases. In contrast, it is arguable that the use of weak analogy can be rationalized as an instance of treating like cases alike, and one which is justified by a direct appeal to the value of coherence in adjudication.[19]

---

19 The distinction between strong and weak analogy is probably continuous, rather than dichotomous, and it is probably vague, and that means that there are bound to be borderline cases between these two modes of reasoning.

Notably, however, once we invoke the concept of coherence here, it should become clear that it takes more than one or two previous rulings to justify reasoning by weak analogy. There must be a larger set of previous decisions pulling in a certain direction, as it were, to make sense of a coherence justification of new decisions. That is so because any pair of noncontradictory propositions can be made to form part of a coherent set, under some set of other propositions. Unless there is a relatively large set of previous rulings that instantiate a significant number of related reasons or principles, a coherence justification can hardly yield any specific results.

Be this as it may, the value of coherence, I suggest, constitutes both the rationale and the limits of applying the principle of treating like cases alike in the context of weak analogy. The rationale must be derived from the value of coherence in adjudication, and the limits of this value would also point to the limits of weak analogy. A detailed account of the value of coherence in adjudication would exceed the scope of this essay.[20] I will confine myself to two concluding remarks. First, I wanted to show that, generally speaking, coherence is not the underlying justification for the principle of treating like cases alike, with the notable exception of weak analogy. Second, as I hope it is clear by now, it should not be assumed that weak analogy is necessarily justified whenever an occasion for its use presents itself. As in other cases of treating like cases alike, there may be very good reasons to treat like cases differently. All this, I admit, is very inconclusive. But sometimes the conclusion of a normative analysis is that there should not be any conclusive answer to the question dealt with. The principle of treating like cases alike is one of those issues.[21]

---

20 For an extensive critique of the value of coherence in adjudication, see J. Raz, "The Relevance of Coherence." My own stab at this complex issue is in my *Interpretation and Legal Theory*, Revised Second edition, Ch. 4 and, in the context of legislation, Ch. 2 in this volume.

21 I am indebted to Scott Altman, David Enoch, Elizabeth Garrett, and Leslie Green for invaluable comments on earlier drafts.

CHAPTER 8

The Immorality of Textualism

Textualism is a doctrine about statutory interpretation. In fact, there are two versions of textualism. One branch of textualism is basically a negative view. It maintains that in statutory interpretation judges should not strive to consult legislative intent and legislative history. Let me call this view *negative textualism*, since it allows courts to interpret legislation in countless other ways, as long as the interpretation does not purport to retrieve the actual intentions or purposes of the legislature.[1] *Negative textualism* is not the kind of textualism I will discuss in this essay. My concern here is with *positive textualism* (often referred to as "new textualism"). The latter endorses the negative view, but also maintains that statutes and statutory regulations should be interpreted, first and foremost, according to the *ordinary meaning* of the language of the relevant statutory provision. Since the plain meaning of statutory provisions is not always clear enough, textualism would have judges rely on canons of statutory interpretation, as long as those canons are clear, bright-line rules, and they are consistently applied.[2] Hereafter in this essay, "textualism" will refer to this positive version of it.

Textualism in this positive sense is increasingly popular in federal courts and perhaps even more so in certain neoconservative political-ideological circles

1 Jeremy Waldron, in his *Law and Disagreement*, for example, defends such a view on the basis of an account of the values associated with legislative procedures in democratic assemblies. Deference to legislative intent, Waldron argues, undermines the values and political ideals that confer dignity and moral respectability on the process of lawmaking in democratic assemblies. I have argued against Waldron's version of textualism in my *Positive Law & Objective Values*, Ch. 5.

2 Here is one of Justice Scalia's formulations the official doctrine: "I thought we had adopted a regular method for interpreting the meaning of language in a statute: first, find the ordinary meaning of the language in its textual context; and, second, using established canons of construction, ask whether there is any clear indication that some permissible meaning other than the ordinary one applies. If not and especially if a good reason for the ordinary meaning appears plain we apply that ordinary meaning." See Chisom v. Roemer, 501 U.S. 380, (Scalia, J., dissenting).

in the U.S.[3] The connection between statutory interpretation and politics should not be surprising. Views about statutory interpretation are partly views about the role of judges in making law and their authority in determining what the law is. To the extent that law matters to us, politically, morally, and otherwise, it matters a great deal who gets to determine what the law actually is. Textualists, like others, are rightly concerned about the close connection between the *how* and the *who* questions—how judges determine what statutes mean significantly determines who gets to make the law. Roughly, the intuitive idea is this: The more discretion or interpretative freedom judges have in statutory interpretation, the greater their role, personally and institutionally, in determining what the law is. And this is the upshot of textualism: textualists do not want judges to make the law.

This, at least, is the official doctrine, and it sounds very democratic. Lawmaking should be left to the legislature, textualists maintain, since it is a political business, and as such, it should be left to the elected representatives of the people. The judiciary is not a democratic institution, and thus it should not be allowed to usurp the power of making law by using various "liberal" or "creative" means of statutory interpretation.[4] But there is also an unofficial view, one that is more complex. In fact, one should suspect that there is some hidden story here, since it is not evident why distrust of common law and the judiciary should be part of a neoconservative political agenda. On the contrary; at least from an historical perspective, one could have expected that a distrust of judicial power should come from liberals and progressive political movements, not from conservatives. After all, the judiciary is typically a rather conservative institution, hardly ever at the forefront of social radicalism. Why would conservatives like Justice Scalia, President Bush, and countless other neoconservatives, find themselves aligned with a rigid doctrine about separation of powers that originates in the social radicalism of the French Revolution? What is the source of this neoconservative deep distrust of the judiciary in the U.S.?[5]

---

3 I use the term "neoconservatives" in a rather loose fashion here, only to indicate the contemporary dominant strand in American conservative ideology. It is a difficult question that I cannot answer here how these new conservatives, mostly in control of the government these days, differ from their traditional ancestors.

4 See J. Manning, "Textualism As A Nondelegation Doctrine" (advocating this version of textualism on the basis of the constitutional doctrine of nondelegation).

5 Is textualism just a reaction, albeit somewhat delayed, to the progressive liberalism of the Warren Court? Perhaps it is, but I doubt that this goes deep enough. This shallow political explanation does not really explain the particular focus on statutory interpretation. The legacy of the liberal Warren Court, to the extent that it still exists, is mostly in the constitutional domain, not in the field of statutory interpretation. Some commentators have argued that textualism is a reaction to the Hart & Sacks Legal Process theory,

I believe that the underlying motivation of textualism derives from a neoconservative conception of the regulatory state, much more so, anyway, than from a concern with principles of democracy and separation of powers. The upshot of this concern is the familiar libertarian ideal of "the minimal" state and its deep distrust of the "big government."[6] Essentially, the connection is this: textualism urges judges to interpret statues and statutory regulations as literally as possible. The plain literal meaning of the statute is what judges should apply to the case at hand. But of course this is deceptive: Judicial interpretation of statutes is typically needed (and cases get to higher courts) precisely because the meaning of the relevant statutory provision is not clear enough to yield a particular outcome (or, sometimes, because the literal meaning entails results that are plainly unjust or otherwise unacceptable). In other words, from the perspective of a theory of interpretation, just telling judges that a statutory provision means what it literally states is mostly quite unhelpful. Unless, that is, one also assumes a default rule, whereby unresolved interpretative issues ought to remain unresolved by judges. And this, I submit, is precisely the unofficial story of textualism: The unregulated disputes ought to remain unregulated, because regulation by the state, in any legal form, is very suspect to begin with. In other words, I will argue that textualists cannot be blind to the logical absurdity of their interpretative position. They must know perfectly well that difficult cases get to be litigated at higher courts primarily because the language of the relevant statute is not clear enough to resolve the issues at hand. Their underlying political agenda, however, is to leave those unregulated issues as they find them. By advocating a theory of statutory interpretation that is preoccupied with literal meaning, and purportedly relies on bright-line rules or canons of statutory interpretation, textualism strives to effectuate a broader ideological agenda that seeks to reduce the state and its regulatory functions to the necessary minimum. The deep distrust of neoconservatives is not really a distrust of judges, it is a distrust of regulation and state intervention.

---

rather than a reaction to the Warren Court liberalism. See, for instance, Nicholas S. Zeppos, "Justice Scalia's Textualism: The "New" New Legal Process."

At an academic level, I think that this is right. But it still doesn't quite capture the politics of textualism and its conservative motivation.

6 This account of the motivation behind textualism is not entirely unofficial: Frank Easterbrook has made it quite explicit in "Statutes' Domain."

A. Ordinary Meaning and Unintended Consequence

The effect of textualism is most clearly present in the familiar types of cases where the literal meaning of a statutory regulation would lead to unacceptable results. These cases typically raise the problem of unintended consequences: The legislature enacts a statute without realizing that under a certain set of circumstances, a literal or straightforward application of the statute would lead to consequences that were neither intended nor, typically, would make much sense. A wonderful case in point is *U.S. v. Marshall*[7]. According to a law that sets mandatory punishment for various drug offenses, the mandatory minimum is triggered by the weight of the drugs sold, defined by the statute in terms of "a mixture or substance containing a detectable amount" of the relevant drug. As it turns out however, LSD is distributed on a particularly heavy carrier viz., typically sprayed over paper or gelatin. The defendants in this case sold relatively small amounts of LSD, but the weight of the mixture of LSD with its carrier substance triggered the mandatory minimum sentence.[8] Marshall, one of the defendants, sold fewer than 12,000 doses of LSD and was sentenced to 20 years in prison. Judge Posner clarified, however, that to receive a comparable sentence for selling heroin, Marshall would have had to sell ten kilograms, which would yield more than a million doses (!); and in case of cocaine, he would have had to sell fifty kilograms, or something like 325,000 doses. Judge Posner rightly noted that this must have been an unintended consequence: "Congress simply did not realize how LSD is sold." And then he poses the relevant question here: "Well, what if anything can we judges do about this mess?" The majority, headed by Judge Easterbrook, provided the standard textualist answer: nothing at all. The meaning of "mixture of or substance containing a detectable amount" clearly applies, Judge Easterbrook held, to the drug with the weight of its carrier, and not only to the pure drug. To be sure, Judge Easterbrook did not deny that the legal consequence here would be somewhat absurd; he just thought that it was not his judicial responsibility to rectify it.[9] And indeed, this is what the debate is about: Should judges clear up the mess created by poor legislative drafting, or not? And textualists reply that they should not.[10]

---

7 908 F.2d 1312 (7th Cir. 1990).

8 In fact, the weight issue is even more absurd: The weight of the pure LSD is so light compared to the carrier that it is mostly the weight of the carrier that is measured, and the choice of the carrier is pretty much arbitrary. So the whole weight issue is completely arbitrary, as it depends on whether the LSD was distributed on sugar cane, or gelatin, or blotter paper.

9 The Supreme Court agreed. See Chapman v. U.S., 500 U.S. 453 (1991).

10 There is a widespread debate about textualism's willingness, or unwillingness, to correct scrivener's error. (See, for example, J. Manning, "The Absurdity Doctrine.") I will not deal with this particular debate here.

The argument supporting this stance has both a backward-looking and a forward-looking aspect. Textualism seems to maintain that if the legislature is unhappy with the particular judicial result, it can always rectify it by legislative amendments that may, if the legislature deems necessary, apply retroactively. As to the forward-looking argument, textualism advocates a kind of educational policy: the more textualism is consistently applied by the courts, the more legislators will realize that drafting errors will not be corrected by the courts, and thus lawmakers will become more vigilant and meticulous in their drafting of legislation.

Both of these arguments raise many difficulties. The backward-looking argument is particularly weak. First, it assumes that the legislature can be expected to find the time, resources, and political will to monitor and, if necessary, rectify judicial decisions whenever such unintended consequences are applied by the courts. This is both unrealistic and morally questionable. It is unrealistic because legislative resources are very limited. Given the number of courts and the vast number of judicial decisions, it is naïve, at best, if not deliberately deceptive, to assume that every unintended consequence of a legislative act can be corrected by the legislature. Even when the information becomes available and the problem salient (which is not often the case), the legislature may lack the political will to interfere in judicial decisions and make the necessary amendments, especially if to do so would require retroactive application.[11]

More importantly, however, the textualist position is morally problematic. Litigation is not a theoretical exercise; there are particular parties to the dispute whose fates are at stake. Consider the case of Mr. Marshall, who ended up at least a decade longer in prison than he should have, being told, effectively, that if the legislature so wishes, it can amend the law retroactively and set it right for him. It is difficult to see how this can be morally justified. Nobody claimed here that Marshall actually deserved this harsh sentence. Does it make moral sense to put the responsibility on the U.S. Congress to solve this by an act of retroactive legislation? That hardly seems fair. But the main moral concern here is not fairness, it is

---

To the extent that textualism is committed to ignoring even such technical errors, my arguments in the text would be more forceful, and to the extent that textualism allows for an exception with respect to scrivener's error, its consistency may be in some doubt.

11 In fact, the problem is even more troubling, since there are some *legal* constraints on the ability of congress to rectify such problems retroactively, some of them imposed by the court itself! See, for example, Dellmuth v. Muth, 491 U.S. 223 (1989).

the concern of using people only as means to an end. A textualist strategy that puts the responsibility on the legislature to eliminate inequities resulting from poor legislative drafting actually amounts to using the particular litigants only as means to an end, without due respect for their personhood and moral agency. It is a blunt violation of the famous Kantian principle that one should never treat another person as means only, but also as an end in itself.[12]

I am not trying to suggest here that the Kantian principle is unproblematic or that its application is always as clear as we could have wished. But at least at its core, it is one of the basic principles of humanist morality, and there are many clear cases of immorality in its violation. Consider, for example, the case of a nanny who deliberately neglects to feed the child in her care, in order to make a point to her employers that next time they should leave her with clearer instructions about the food that the child likes. Surely, we would say, there must be other means for the nanny to make her point without using the suffering of the child as means to an end. And, crucially, this remains the case even if it is true that the parents have neglected their own responsibility in leaving clear instructions for the nanny. Similarly, in the case of Marshall and his codefendants, they were used as means to a political end, without respecting their personhood, that is, without respecting the principle that they ought to be punished according to the severity of their deeds.

And this brings us to the second issue, the forward-looking argument. Some commentators have focused on the empirical aspects of this argument, claiming that textualism's working assumption that Congress can be induced to be more meticulous in its legislative drafting is problematic, at best, and most likely, unrealistic.[13] But even if we assume that these commentators are wrong, and that textualism's educational project is empirically feasible, difficult moral-political questions remain.

First, there is a moral question about the role of the courts here: Why should it be the business of the courts to educate the legislature on how to draft statutes and enact laws? Is it because nobody else is there to do it? Surely that is false. Legislation is scrutinized by countless interest groups, watchdogs, lobbyists, the general press, and eventually, by the public at large during campaigns and elections.

---

12 See I. Kant, *Groundwork of The Metaphysics of Morals*.

13 See, *e.g.*, J. Schacter, "Metademocracy: The Changing Structure of Legitimacy In Statutory Interpretation," and E. Garrett, "Legal Scholarship in the Age of Legislation."

Ample institutions are out there to tell the legislature how to do its job and how to improve it. I am not suggesting that all these institutions have an interest in particularly clear and unambiguous legislative drafting. But surely, clarity is only one of the virtues of good legislation. Legislation often has to reach a compromise between conflicting considerations, and then other institutions, like agencies and the courts, should fill in the gaps. In any case, it is surely false to assume that the courts are the only institution that scrutinizes legislative drafting. Many other institutions fulfill a similar function, and they all have an important advantage over the courts: They do not need to sacrifice the interest of individuals in order to make their point.

Note that this question about the courts' role in educating the legislature is even more pressing when considered on textualism's manifested political grounds. If textualists are so concerned about respect for democratic procedures, it must be because they attach a high value to the respect we owe to the authority of legislative institutions. But one does not normally express respect for the authority of another by trying to educate the latter. In this respect, textualism displays a certain arrogance towards the legislature that is not easy to reconcile with its alleged respect for the authority of democratic institutions.[14]

Secondly, and more importantly, this educational project is at odds with the fiduciary duty that courts owe to the legislature and thus, indirectly, to all of us. The courts are entrusted with a precious task of applying the law and determining authoritatively what the law is in particular cases. In fulfilling this role, courts must assume a fiduciary duty to carry it out in good faith and to the best of their judgment. Consider this analogy with employment relations: The employer entrusts the employee with certain tasks. Sure, a good employer will give instructions and try to make it as clear as desirable under the circumstances what the employee is expected to do. But both parties know, as they should, that there is a limit to the detail and accuracy of such instructions, and then the expectation is that when the employee lacks explicit directions, he should use his own judgment and act in good faith to fulfill his tasks.[15] In short, we do not expect the employee to act like a textualist. Imagine yourself having to work with a textualist employee,

---

14 And this is particularly the case if it is true that the legislature's institutional ability to live up to the textualist ideal is very limited. See Eskridge, Frickey & Garrett, *Cases and Materials on Legislation*, Ch. 4.

15 Note that the level of detail for such instructions typically depends on the relative expertise and seniority of the employee; high level employees are typically expected to act on their own without detailed instructions. After all, that is what they are paid to do.

who is constantly pressuring you to give him the clearest instructions, and when the instructions are not clear enough, he does nothing at all in order to induce you to be more precise in the future. My guess is that you would fire him. Textualist employees tend to lose their jobs very quickly, and rightly so, we should think; basically, they breach the fiduciary duties that form an essential part of any employment relationship.

Textualists are bound to object that the courts do not work for the legislature. That is partly true, but not entirely. In a moral-political sense, to some extent courts do work for the legislature, and thus indirectly, for all of us. In the context of statutory interpretation, the courts are entrusted with an important task: to carry out the "instructions" of the legislature in applying the law to particular cases. Though not, of course, a straightforward employment relationship, such a task does carry with it a similar fiduciary duty to act in good faith and fulfill responsibilities according to the agent's best judgment. In any case, I believe that the analogy holds in this crucial respect: Just as employees are expected to know that there is a limit to the instructions they can receive and, once on their own, they must act according to their best judgment in fulfilling their employment tasks, so the courts should be expected to know that there is a limit to the legislative instructions they can get. At some point they must act like a good employee when the instructions have run out: use your own judgment and solve the problem as best as you can.

To sum up: Textualism's educational project, even if it is deemed feasible, is morally unjustified. It should not be the business of the courts to enlighten the legislature on how to make laws or how to make them more precise. The moral obligation of the court is first and foremost to do justice to the litigants in front of them and, to the extent that their rulings have the force of binding precedent, their duty is to make the law the best it can be (given the conventional constraints of the legal practice). Trying to teach the legislature how to make legislation better should not be the business of the courts, especially when it involves injustice to the litigating parties or when it entails bad law.

B. Ordinary Meaning and the Limits of Language

First-year law students are taught that legal results often depend on what words and sentences in a statute mean. If a statute prescribes, to use a worn-out example, that "No vehicles are allowed in the public parks," then, students are told, the law depends on what the word "vehicles" means: Does it include, for instance, electric wheelchairs? Roller skates? Bicycles? But how can we determine whether the word "vehicle" means, among other things, bicycles or electric wheelchairs? Is it really a question about *the meaning of a word in English*? Textualists would have us believe that the answer is basically yes, and then judges have only to verify what words or linguistic expressions mean in the ordinary use of language. The result of this attitude (strangely shared by non-textualist judges as well) is that judges find themselves quarreling over dictionary definitions of words, running word checks in literature or, sometimes, using sheer wit to convince us that their grasp of the English language is correct and thus mandates the legal result they seek. Allow me to demonstrate this with a quotation from Justice Scalia's dissent in *Smith v. U.S.*:[16]

> Section 924(c)(1) mandates a sentence enhancement for any defendant who "during and in relation to any crime of . . . . uses . . . a firearm." [In this case, the defendant exchanged a firearm for drugs in a barter deal. The majority held that § 924 applies, even if the firearm was not used as a weapon.]
>
> In the search for statutory meaning, we give nontechnical words and phrases their ordinary meaning . . . To use an instrumentality ordinarily means to use it for its intended purpose. When someone asks "Do you use a cane?" he is not inquiring whether you have your grandfather's silver-handled walking-stick on display in the hall; he wants to know whether you walk with a cane. Similarly, to speak of "using a firearm" is to speak of using it for its distinctive purpose, i.e. as a weapon.

A noble result, perhaps, but the argument is a non sequitur. The phrase "use an x" can mean quite a number of different things, depending on the context of the utterance. To use an object can either mean, for example, "use" in relatively a narrow sense, namely, for the object's intended purpose, or it can mean "use" in a number of broader senses, for whatever purpose context may allow. Generally, the literal meaning of words used in language often does not, by itself, determine what *is said (or asserted) by a speaker* in a context of speech. Contextual background may be

16 508 U.S. 223 (1993).

necessary to determine what the semantic/assertive content of an utterance is.[17] Just to mention a few familiar examples, consider these speech situations:

1. Speaker: "He is standing in the corner"; assuming that both speaker and hearer know who is referred to, say, Jim, then this sentence *asserts* that Jim is standing in the corner.[18]

2. Speaker A: "Do you have two children?"; speaker B: "Yes." In this case, we normally assume that speaker B has said that he has *two and only two* children. Now compare with –

2a. Speaker A: "Do you have a two dollars?"; speaker B: "Yes." In this case, contrary to 2, we normally assume that speaker B said that he has *at least two* dollars, but maybe more.[19]

3. Speaker: "I have just finished reading Joseph's book." What does "Joseph's book" mean here? Only contextual background, normally shared by speaker and hearer, can clarify whether "Joseph's book" means a book that Joseph owns, or a book that he wrote, etc.

Now, consider Justice Scalia's example: Suppose B tells A that he "used a cane." Is it obvious that "use" was meant here in the narrow sense, such as using a cane for walking? That just cannot be determined without the contextual background. Consider the following conversation between A and B:

A: How did you break the window?
B: I used a cane.

---

17 There is a great deal of controversy in philosophy of language about the distinction between what has been *said* by a speaker (normally called "semantic content") and what has been *asserted* by a speaker, or assertive content. How to draw the line between these two is far from evident and for some philosophical purposes, it makes a difference. For us, however, these subtleties make no difference and I have not made an effort here to reflect the distinction. For different views about this, see the references in notes 18 and 19, infra.

18 D. Kaplan, "Demonstratives" in Almog et al, eds., *Themes from Kaplan*; S. Soames, "Direct Reference, Propositional Attitudes, and Semantic Content."

19 This pragmatic aspect of numerical ascriptions has been elaborated by Soames, in "Drawing the Line between Meaning and Implicature – and Relating both to Assertion," forthcoming in *Nous*.

Now we know that **B** did not walk with a cane; he used it to break the window. A perfectly sensible use of "use" (though perhaps not a very sensible deed).

Similarly, the question of whether "using a firearm" is to be understood in a narrow sense (using it as a weapon), or in a broader sense (using it for whatever crime-related purpose), cannot be determined by a better grasp of what the word "use" means in English. In English it can mean both, depending on the context of its expression.[20]

Similar considerations apply to the problem of vagueness. Most concept-words we use in a natural language are vague: In the application of the word to concrete instances, there are bound to be borderline cases. Can we tell whether John, weighing 240 pounds, is "obese" or not? And is John "tall" if he is 6 feet? And is he "bald" if he has 200 strands of hair on his head? The problem of borderline cases due to vagueness is that they are inquiry-resistant. No amount of further information can determine whether John is really bald, or tall, or obese, etc.[21] But what if a legal decision depends on it? Then judges should try to determine why it should depend on the relevant factor, and strive to reach an adequate result on the merits of the case. An attempt to figure out what "tall" or "bald" really means in ordinary English can only reveal that these terms are vague and thus would necessarily have borderline cases. If you happen to face a borderline case, no further amount of knowledge of English can tell you how to classify such a case.

One might be tempted to reply that in such cases judges should rely on canons of statutory interpretation like, for example, *expressio unius* (expression of one thing suggests the exclusion of others), *noscitur a sociis* (interpret a general term to be similar to more specific terms in a series) and such. But the assumption that application of canons of interpretation would solve the problems left open by linguistic indeterminacies, is too naïve to be taken seriously. Let me state the obvious: First,

20 In fairness to Justice Scalia, I should mention that he proposed another argument in his dissent that is much more sensible: He argued that if "using a firearm" is ambiguous in this case, *the rule of leniency* in criminal law requires interpretation of the ambiguity in favor of the defendant. I am not suggesting that this is an appropriate application of the rule of leniency, only that the argument is much better. Notably, however, it undermines the first argument.

21 I should qualify this somewhat: According to one philosophical theory about vagueness, borderline cases are inquiry-resistant only in an epistemic sense. Such philosophers claim that there is a truth of the matter about borderline cases, even if those truths are not knowable (see T. Williamson, *Vagueness*, London). This so-called epistemic theory of vagueness, however, is very controversial, and in any case, hardly affects my argument in the text: For all practical purposes, it remains true that borderline cases are inquiry-resistant, even if it is true that in some deep metaphysical sense there is a truth of the matter about borderline cases.

canons of statutory interpretation are formulated in a natural language (impressive Latin phraseology notwithstanding), and thus all the indeterminacies of natural language would plague them as well. Second, canons of statutory interpretation often conflict. (And the more such canons you employ, the more likely it is that they will conflict.[22]) One rule may stipulate, for example, that later statutory provisions ought to prevail over earlier ones; and another rule may dictate that specific provisions should prevail over general ones. What are we to do if the later provision is more general?[23]

But of course the problem goes deeper than this. Vagueness, ambiguity, and other linguistic indeterminacies just cannot be eliminated. Consider vagueness, for example. In some cases, particular borderline cases can be legally resolved, as it were. The law can stipulate that, say, concept X under circumstances C, would include (or exclude) borderline cases **a**, **b**, and **c**. But then **a**, **b**, and **c** would have their own borderline cases, so the vagueness of X would not be eliminated, or even reduced; it would only be shifted to other potential cases.[24] It is true that in some limited areas, the law purports to have a margin of safety, phasing out borderline cases as if they are "no" cases. A good example is the *rule of leniency* in criminal law that basically prescribes that unless an action falls well within the meaning of the offense, it should be regarded as if it doesn't. This is a noble attempt to phase out borderline cases, but as a general strategy, it cannot work: even if the law employs a generous margin of safety, we are still left with second-order vagueness viz., vagueness about where the borderline cases begin.[25]

To be sure, I do not intend to claim that the meaning of legal rules does not profoundly depend on the semantics of the relevant natural language. Of course it does. We can understand the law only because we understand the language. Furthermore,

---

22 In one recent casebook I have counted over 120 canons allegedly used by the Supreme Court during the period of 1986–1993. See Eskridge, Frickey & Garrett, *Cases and Materials on Legislation*, Appendix B.

23 To be sure, I am not claiming that canons of statutory interpretation are completely useless. They may be very useful in numerous contexts for various specific purposes of statutory interpretation. My only claim in the text is that it is mistaken to believe that such canons can generally solve the deep problems that stem from the indeterminacy of language. There is nothing new about this observation; it has been made dozens of times before.

24 Here is an example: Consider the case of the "no vehicles in the park" rule. Suppose the legislature stipulates that for the purposes of this rule, "vehicle" will not include (*inter alia*) "bicycles." So now the question might arise whether "bicycles" includes, for example, tricycles, or bicycles with small electric engines, etc.

25 On the idea that vagueness in law cannot be eliminated, see Endicott, *Vagueness in Law*, 186–190. See also my "Should Like Cases be Treated Alike?," Ch. 7 in this volume.

I have long argued that there are necessarily "easy cases" in law, cases in which there is no doubt that the law applies, or not, to the particular case at hand simply because it is what the relevant linguistic expression means.[26] Had Mr. Smith pointed the loaded gun to the face of the drug dealer and demanded the drugs by threatening to shoot him, there would have been no doubt that he "used a firearm" according to § 924(c)(1). This would have been an "easy" case, precisely because such a use of a gun is a clear case of what "using a firearm" means. The point is, however, that such easy cases rarely get to be litigated, especially in higher courts. Litigation is typically pursued and allowed to reach appellate courts in "hard cases," where statutory language is indeterminate due to ambiguity, vagueness, or other semantic or syntactic indeterminacies.[27] And then it would be absurd to say that in such cases the law should depend on what words and sentences *literally mean*; there is nothing one can further inquire about the meaning of such expressions in English. Ambiguities, or borderline cases due to vagueness, cannot be resolved by a better grasp of natural language. There is nothing more about language one can possibly know that would resolve such cases on the basis of "ordinary meaning," to use Justice Scalia's expression.

One might suspect that this is too obvious to have been overlooked by textualists. This I am happy to concede. Textualism is not a theory about the semantics of statutory language; as such it would have been too obviously mistaken. I believe that the preoccupation with "ordinary meaning" reflects a political stance, and one which is mostly concerned with the desirable limits of statutory regulation. The more judicial interpretation of statutes is confined to their "ordinary meanings," real or imagined, the more the ability of the legislature to achieve broad regulatory policies is constrained. In any complex organization, broad policy changes can be accomplished only if those who determine the policy and those who are supposed to carry it out act in concert and share the spirit of the general goals to be advanced. Imagine, for example, a large corporation that strives to implement a new policy. If the mid- and low-level executives required very detailed instructions on every move they made, and then tried to follow the instructions to the letter in a textualist fashion, it is difficult to imagine how the new policy could ever be implemented. Textualism is motivated precisely by

---

26 See my *Interpretation and Legal Theory*, Chs. 2 & 7.

27 To be sure, I do not intend to claim here that all "hard cases" in statutory interpretation necessarily derive from linguistic indeterminacies. There are many possible reasons for the need to interpret statutory law, besides those that derive from language. Conflicts between different statutory provisions, or between them and other parts of the law, would be another example.

denying the legislature this spirit of cooperation that is needed to implement broad regulatory policies.[28] Vulgar semantics is just one more casualty in this war against a "big government."

C. Conclusion

You may think that I have been unfair to textualism. After all, there is nothing new about the phenomenon; courts have always acted in an ideological fashion, often driven by ideological and political commitments of the prevailing judiciary. Liberal courts strove to advance a liberal political agenda, and now conservative courts work to advance their own agenda in a different direction. The fact that every judicial political agenda requires adjustments of theories of statutory interpretation is hardly news.

I certainly agree with both of these observations. The problem is that textualism is actually different, and in two respects. First, as I have tried to argue here, textualism involves an impoverished theory of interpretation, one which simply ignores the obvious complexities of language. Second, and more troubling from a moral point of view, textualism differs from previous politically driven theories in its ideological opacity.

Admittedly, courts are often in a very delicate political situation. Higher courts have typically more political power than people tend to assume. Courts get to determine what the law is, often prevailing over the democratically elected legislature. This disparity between actual power and public perception has always put considerable pressure on the courts to conceal some of the power they actually have, typically by presenting judge-made law (that is often inevitable) as an act of law application. This is understandable and not necessarily a bad thing. The problem I see with textualism is that its theory of statutory interpretation is ideologically opaque, not to say straightforwardly deceptive. With very few exceptions, textualism is presented by its adherents as an interpretative practice that respects the authority of legislatures, and that respects democracy and democratic division of labor between the courts and the legislature. But in fact, as I have tried to show here, textualism actually does the exact opposite: The whole point of textualism is

---

28 I realize that there may be exceptions to this. Sometimes the cooperation that the legislature needs is actually a literalist attitude. For instance, if the legislature is forced to enact a very uncomfortable compromise, it may actually rely on the courts to interpret the compromise as literally as possible. (See Easterbrook, *supra*, note 7) But these are exceptional cases, and they do not undermine the general point.

to undermine the ability of the legislature to pursue broad regulatory goals. When you make a point of following authoritative directives literally, strictly abiding by the letter of the directives, you actually behave in an uncooperative fashion. Authorities do not want to be understood literally. Authorities purport to govern, and complex, large-scale governance requires cooperation in the spirit of its goals, not a strict adherence to the letter of its directives.

But now, you may wonder, why is this ideological opacity needed at all? Why not make the ideological goal explicit, especially now, when the executive branch and the majority of Congress largely share this textualist ideology anyway? I venture to guess that the answer resides in the following. One of the ironies of neoconservatism is that in the complex world we live in, it takes a substantial amount of legal regulation to implement its antiregulatory ideology. Why? Mostly because governance is no longer the exclusive domain of a central administration sitting in Washington and dictating to citizens across the country how to live. Governance has long spread to low-level political institutions, local authorities and bureaucracies, and grassroots organizations, which often utilize the courts, and these entities generate a huge amount of legal regulation. It is just no longer the case (if it ever has been) that a libertarian government can avoid excessive regulation by abstention, as it were. Libertarians find themselves in the uncomfortable position whereby they need to use regulation by a central government in order to curb the regulatory regime of local authorities and numerous agencies.[29]

If I am right about this, it would seem that textualism is bound to fail on its own terms. But this is not necessarily the case. Nothing prevents the courts from acting in a way which is theoretically incoherent. Textualism is a tool, and it can be used selectively, only when it serves the ideological purpose. But then, when you want to rely on an incoherent theory, opacity is the price you have to pay for it; an incoherent theory is difficult to make transparent. In other words, neoconservatives cannot easily proclaim that their theory of statutory interpretation is designed to curb the regulatory means of government, because they know that often they need that regulatory mechanism to curb regulation that originates elsewhere. So I do not think that textualism is bound to fail. But on its own ideological grounds, textualism is bound to be a flip-flop theory, one that cannot be applied consistently across the board. Textualism is thus inherently deceptive and consequently immoral.[30]

---

29 Not to speak of the conservative agenda to dismantle the welfare state, which takes a lot of legislating.

30 I am indebted to Elizabeth Garrett and Scott Soames for comments on this essay.

PART III

Rights and Equality

CHAPTER 9

On the Limits of Rights

According to conventional philosophical wisdom, there are two main questions pertaining to rights discourse. There is the analytical, interpretative, question of what it means to have a right, and there is the moral-political issue concerning the question of what rights people ought to have. Few philosophers doubt, however, that these two issues, the analytical and the political, are closely related and the answers to them interdependent. In this essay I wish to make a modest contribution to the discussion of the relations between the analysis and the political morality of rights discourse.

My aims, however, are very limited. I will concentrate on only one analytical conception of rights, called "The Interest Theory of Rights," which I find most plausible. I will try to show that there are two interesting conclusions that follow from it concerning the appropriate *limits* of rights: namely, that rights, properly conceived, are both inherently limited and inherently, or unavoidably, controversial. Though these two conclusions seem to pull in different directions, I will try to show that they teach us the same political lesson, namely, that there is something both misleading and unattainable in the aspiration to political neutrality.

The discussion will follow traditional paths. In the first section I will provide a very brief outline of the interest theory of rights, emphasizing those of its features which make it, to my mind, the most plausible and attractive analysis of the nature of rights. In the second section I will outline one conception of the limits of rights, that I call the Newtonian conception, arguing that it cannot be maintained. This conception basically holds that rights can only be limited in order to secure some other right (or the same right for somebody else). I call this conception Newtonian because it depicts the force of rights in a way similar to the Newtonian law of inertia: a right will continue to be in force as long as it does not collide with another right that conflicts with it. As opposed to this, I will try to show that rights have inherent limits as well; each right partially imposes its own limit even before any "collisions" occur.

Finally, in the last section, I will try to show that something unique about rights discourse renders decisions about the limits of rights unavoidably controversial. More precisely, I want to show why rights discourse is particularly suitable for pluralistic societies, and that the reason for this is also the reason for the unavoidable controversies concerning the limits of rights.

A. The Interest Theory of Rights

It is tempting to think that an analysis of a concept like "right" is either an explication of its common social or linguistic usage, or a novel definition that claims to serve some philosophical or political purpose. A reasonable account of the nature of rights, however, must encompass both, and more. Such an account must not only expose common usage, but should also *explain* it; it should answer not only the question of how "right" is used in a certain context, but also, insofar as is possible, why it is used in that way, and what purpose it serves. On the other hand, the dependence of definitions on political theory, though perhaps unavoidable, should not ignore prevailing discourse. An analysis of rights, in other words, is partly a matter of interpretation; it is an interpretation of certain aspects of our existing legal and political culture and, as such, it must fit the practice. Finally, as rights are extensively used both in legal and nonlegal contexts, I will assume that it is a virtue of any such theory on the nature of rights that it gives us a unified account of "rights" in both the legal and nonlegal contexts.

Notably, not all the familiar theories of the nature of rights were so ambitious. For example, Hohfeld's celebrated analysis of legal rights was initially confined to the legal context, and was meant to be primarily expositive of common legal usage.[1] Or, to take another example, Dworkin's theory of "rights as trumps"[2] presented rights discourse exclusively against a politically utilitarian background. Thus, Dworkin's account, whatever one thinks of its merit, could not explain rights discourse in many other nonpolitical contexts, such as one's right to have a promise kept, for example. The interest theory of rights, on the other hand, is an account of *the nature* of rights as such.[3] Basically, the theory maintains that A's having a right to something means that there is an aspect of A's well-being (i.e. an interest of A)

---

1 W. N. Hohfeld, *Fundamental Legal Conceptions*.

2 R. Dworkin, "Rights as Trumps."

3 This theory of the nature of rights was developed by Neil MacCormick and Joseph Raz. See MacCormick, "Rights in Legislation." For Raz's work, on which I mainly rely here, see his *Morality of Freedom*, Ch.7. See also Jeremy Waldron, *The Right to Private Property*, 79–94.

important enough to justify imposing a duty on some other person(s) in order to protect that interest.

The most important element in this conception of rights is the justificatory relation it maintains between rights (or the grounds for rights) and duties. As opposed to the traditional Hohfeldian analysis, which conceived of a right to be *correlative* to a duty, the interest theory holds the right to be the *normative ground* for the imposition of duties. In other words, the relation between a right and its corresponding duty (or duties, as we shall see below) is not symmetrical; the relation is a justificatory one. Rights justify the imposition of duties but not vice versa.

Consequently, two further aspects of the Hohfeldian thesis of correlation between a right and a duty should be modified. First, it should be noted that a right may often provide the grounds for the imposition of numerous duties on others, and not only one. If A has a right to x, then A's interest in x is taken to be a good reason for imposing various duties on others; namely, all those duties which are reasonably required to secure A's interest in x. Secondly, the duties imposed on the basis of one and the same right may vary from case to case, depending on the particular context and circumstances.[4] Thus, for example, the nature and the extent of the duties imposed on the state in order to secure its citizens' right to free speech may vary according to the specific conditions which happen to prevail in the society, such as who controls the media (state or private ownership), how affluent the society is, how tolerant, and the like. As these conditions tend to change over time, so should the corresponding duties change, even if they are required by the very same right, namely, the right to freedom of speech. Take, for example, the dispute over the question as to whether the state should take active measures to secure equal access to the mass media for all its citizens. Clearly, the answer to this question would depend in part on the particular circumstances of the society concerned, and primarily on who controls the media and how monopolistic it is. These are matters that would certainly affect our judgment about the kind of duties that should be imposed on the state with respect to the right of freedom of speech. But it is not the nature of the right that varies here, only the nature of the duties which are required to secure the interests protected by the right.

4 Raz called this the "dynamic aspect of rights." See Raz, *ibid.*, 171.

The essential point is, however, that rights are grounded in the interests of the potential right holder, and that duties are grounded in rights.[5] Before I venture to draw my conclusions from this analysis of rights, I would like to say a few more words about its intuitive appeal, though this will take us on a small detour.

One of the most interesting features of rights discourse, meticulously analyzed by Jeremy Waldron,[6] is the possibility of A's having a right to do something which A ought not to do. The right to do wrong, as Waldron called it, is a very prevalent element in rights discourse, and examples are well known. For instance, one has a right to vote for a political party even if one should not vote for it. People have a right to say things which are wrong for them to say (if the expression is stupid, insulting, humiliating, etc.). Finally, suppose John and Susan want to get married. We would think that they have the right to get married even if we are convinced that it would be a terrible mistake (as they actually hate each other and the marriage is bound to ruin their lives).

The right to do wrong, as these and many other examples show, is a very common feature of rights discourse. But it is puzzling and markedly opposed to the way we think about duties. A duty to do wrong is surely an oxymoron. Why, then, is the right to do wrong a plausible concept? As a first approximation, we should note that an important asymmetry exists between rights and duties: Duties are taken to constitute *reasons for actions*. The proposition that "A has a duty to do x" entails that A has a reason to do x. No such relation of entailment exists in the case of rights; rights do not constitute reasons for action. Having a right to do something does not entail that one has a reason to do it.

This asymmetry is clearly manifested in the difference between invoking duties and rights in the context of explaining one's action. When a question arises about explaining a particular action one performed, invoking a duty to explain the action is normally a sensible thing to say. "I did it because it was my duty . . . " is, normally, a good explanation for what you did. However, it is rarely a sensible

---

5 The interest theory, as Raz expounded it, focuses exclusively on the relationship between rights and *duties*. However, it is possible, and probably desirable, to extend its scope to encompass a larger variety of normative structures. It may well be the case that rights grounded in interests justify not only the imposition of duties but perhaps immunities, liberties, and powers as well. I cannot explore these possibilities here. In any case, I believe that such an extension of the interest theory would not affect my arguments in this paper.

6 See Waldron, "A Right to do Wrong."

explanation of an action that one had a right to do whatever one did. "I did it *because* I have a right to . . . " is, under normal circumstances, a bad reply to the question of why you did it; it is normally beside the point.

Now, the fact that rights do not constitute reasons for action merely explains why "the right to do wrong" is not an oxymoron. However, we still need an explanation of its prevalence. Why is it so often the case that people should be accorded a right to do something which they ought not to do? The answer, I suggest, is rather simple: The right to do wrong pertains to cases in which one of the main interests grounding the right in question is that of personal *choice*. By this I refer to those cases where we think that it is more important for the agent to choose for herself than to choose correctly (within a certain range of reasonable options, of course).

It is not difficult to see that the interest of personal choice is one of the main interests grounding numerous familiar rights. It is certainly important in the case of the three rights I mentioned earlier, namely, the right to vote, to freedom of speech, and to marry, and it is equally important in the case of such rights as the right to bodily integrity, the right to practice religion, the right to private property, and many others. In all these cases, and many others, *one* of the main interests grounding the right in question is the interest of personal choice. Thus, for example, one of the reasons for having a right to get married consists in the importance we attach to personal choice in these matters; we think that it is more important for a person to choose her spouse for herself than to choose correctly. Hence the right ought to protect wrong choices too.

Personal choice, however, is not essential to all rights. Certain familiar rights are grounded in interests which have very little to do with personal choice. Thus, for example, one's right not to be exposed to oppressive means of interrogation, or simply not to be tortured, is a right grounded in interests concerning people's personal safety and dignity; the element of personal choice is marginal. And so is the "right to do wrong" in these cases. One would be very hard-pressed to find an example of the right to do wrong in the case of the right not to be tortured. And this is as it should be; the right to do wrong pertains only to those rights where one of the main interests grounding the right is the interest of personal choice.

There is no reason to think that this is so in the case of all the rights we should acknowledge.[7]

Many other aspects of the interest theory of rights are certainly worth exploring, but I cannot do this here.[8] Instead, let me return to my own concerns about the limits of rights, beginning with the Newtonian conception.

B. The Newtonian Conception of Rights

There are two main versions of what I call here the Newtonian conception of the limits of rights. Although the differences between the two are substantial, both share the Newtonian conception; a right is conceived to have inherent inertia which can only be limited externally, namely, when it collides with a conflicting right. Now, according to one view, rights are basically unlimited. Let us call this

---

7 The interest of personal choice I invoke here should not be confused with the so-called Choice Theory of Rights. The latter dwells on a very different aspect of the relations between rights and personal choices, namely, on the control a right gives to the right holder over another's actions. The choice theory of rights is a position H.L.A. Hart at some point maintained and later discarded. For references and discussion see Waldron, *supra* note 3, 95–99.

8 Here are three more examples:

a. *Duties without correlative rights.* One important implication of this theory, pointed out by J. Raz, has to do with the capacity to have rights. One of the embarrassing dilemmas that we inherited from the Hohfeldian correlativity thesis between rights and duties pertains to the duties we think we owe to animals, endangered species, perhaps to embryos, and the like. According to the Hohfeldian tradition, acknowledging A's duty towards B entails the correlative right of B. Hence the embarrassing question arises whether animals or endangered species have rights. No such question necessarily arises, however, under the interest theory. The latter is compatible with the view which accords us duties towards creatures or entities that are incapable of having rights.

b. *Rights and desires.* Yet another puzzle about the capacity to have rights stems from the uneasiness people feel about according rights to somebody who either does not wish to have them, or more problematically, is incapable of desiring them. According to the interest theory, however, one's capacity to have a certain right depends on the potential right holder's interests. Hence, it follows that one may well have a right to something one does not wish to have, or one is incapable of desiring. Thus, for example, my newborn baby can be said to have a right to a decent education because it is in her interest to have it. The fact that she is incapable of desiring the object of the right is rendered irrelevant.

c. *Core and derivative rights.* People often have rights to things of trivial importance; my right to scratch my head at the moment, for example, can hardly be thought to protect an important interest; surely, I can do without scratching my head at the moment. Why is it protected by a right, then? A simple answer is given by Raz's important distinction between core and derivative rights. The interest theory concentrates, as it should, on the core rights, namely, those rights which derive from interests worthy of protection by the imposition of duties on others. Derivative rights, like my right to scratch my head, are those which follow from core rights (the right to bodily integrity, in this case) by a process of justification. See Raz, *supra* note 3, 168–170.

view the Absolutist conception of rights. This conception, associated with the philosopher Robert Nozick,[9] maintains that rights have an absolute force, and that an infringement of a right is never justified. In other words, according to the Absolutist conception of rights, rights never really conflict; hence, there is no need to determine their limits. According to Nozick, rights are thought of as *side constraints*: Limits on the kinds of action individuals are entitled to perform. Thus, rights are negative in character; they require individuals and state organs to refrain from certain forms of conduct. Rights can never require an agent to perform a certain act. Now, if the only type of behavior imposed by rights is omission, it is not difficult to see why rights have no limits. As Jeremy Waldron rightly pointed out, rights are in conflict when the duties they imply are not compossible.[10] According to the Absolutist conception, however, rights are basically incapable of being in conflict, simply because there is an unlimited and indefinite number of things one can refrain from doing.

I do not think that we need to dwell too much on this Absolutist conception of rights, since it is clearly inadequate, even with respect to those few rights where it seems most at home, like the classical liberal rights of free speech, or the freedom of assembly, the right not to be tortured, and the like. Even in these cases, we believe that there is much more to having a right than the requirement to refrain from interference.[11] More importantly, however, the theory of rights as side constraints severely limits the types of moral concerns that can be cast in a rights framework. The right to have a decent standard of living, or reasonable access to education, and the like, are rights that require the imposition of considerable duties on the state and on others—duties to perform certain actions, not only to refrain from interference.

The second Newtonian conception of the limits of rights, far more plausible and pervasive than the Absolutist conception, maintains that rights can only be limited to secure some other right, or the same right to someone else. John Rawls's *first principle of justice*, though not explicitly formulated in terms of rights, is undoubtedly the most influential version of this Newtonian conception. In all its various formulations the first principle of justice clearly suggests that people's rights, at least those rights that are meant to be covered by the first principle, are

---

9 R. Nozick, *Anarchy, State and Utopia*, Ch. 3.

10 See J. Waldron, *Liberal Rights* 206.

11 See Waldron, *ibid.*, particularly Ch. 1.

to be limited only when this is essential for securing the more pressing rights of others.[12] This Newtonian conception fits nicely with Rawls's anti-perfectionism: It would seem to suggest a politically neutral formula for the resolution of rightscon-flicts. According to Rawls, and to many others who share his conception of liberalism, it is the role of the state to secure the most extensive set of human and civil rights compatible with the same rights for others; hence the state (or the courts, for that matter) need not act on reasons which are based on any preferred conception of the good. If rights are to be limited, or set aside, it must be because this is required by the more pressing rights of others.[13]

This Rawlsian view is often contrasted with the utilitarian conception, which maintains that rights can sometimes be set aside, or limited, for the sake of the collective good. In this contrast with the utilitarian framework, the Newtonian conception gains a considerable advantage. We must recall that much of the impetus towards contemporary rights discourse stemmed from objections to the way in which moral and political conflicts are resolved in the utilitarian framework. Many people felt that the utilitarian calculus allows for the unwarranted sacrifice of important human interests when these are traded off against considerations intrinsically much less important, but which gain their weight in the utilitarian calculus only because of the numbers involved.[14]

Be this as it may, it is not the anti-utilitarian element of the Rawlsian picture of rights I wish to emphasize here, but its anti-perfectionism. As long as rights are viewed as inherently unlimited, the resolution of rights conflicts would seem to require only a kind of quantitative "balancing." Namely, the role of the state and

---

12 J. Rawls, *A Theory of Justice*, 60–65. It may be thought that it is not the first principle of justice which entails this Newtonian conception of rights, but Rawls's insistence on the priority of the first over the second principle of justice. I do not think that this would be a correct interpretation, however. There is no reason to think that only the first principle is concerned with rights; the second principle is also concerned with rights, only of a different (i.e. socioeconomic) kind. Hence, the priority principle should be seen as a further constraint on the Newtonian conception I have outlined, a constraint maintaining that rights of one kind, namely, those covered by the first principle, may not be limited or put aside, for the purposes of enhancing the rights covered by the second principle.

13 Notably, liberal-minded courts were only too happy to endorse this Rawlsian conception of rights discourse. Such a Newtonian conception of the limits of rights enables the courts to present the resolution of numerous moral and political conflicts in politically neutral rhetoric: As long as the limits imposed on someone's rights can be justified by reasons derived from someone else's rights, the "balancing" required by this conflict can easily be presented in quantitative, and hence politically neutral, terms.

14 This anti-utilitarian element of rights constitutes, for some philosophers, the main reason for having rights in the first place. See, for example, R. Dworkin, *supra* note 2. See also Waldron, *supra* note 10, 210.

the courts would only be to try to secure the set of rights that would *maximally* satisfy the most extensive set of rights for each person which is compatible with the similar rights of others. In other words, only the "collision" of rights calls for balancing, and then the balancing can be done by calculating relative weights and forces.[15]

But is this Newtonian picture reasonable? Can it be supported by an adequate theory of rights? Not if we think that rights are grounded in interests, as the theory I have outlined above maintains. It is not difficult to see that rights, according to the interest theory, should be seen as inherently limited. The reason is basically this: Acknowledging the right of A to x necessarily involves the imposition of duties on others. Being under a duty is a burden, and it is a burden that must *initially* be taken into account when the interests of the potential right holder and others are compared. This initial balancing of interests and burdens is unavoidable. Sometimes, even the most pressing interests of people do not receive the recognition of a right, as this would involve too costly a burden imposed on others.[16] Even when the right is recognized, however, the burdens it imposes on others must be justified as such. This process of cost-benefit justification lies at the foundation of the recognition of each and every right.

According to the interest theory, then, the Newtonian conception of rights is misconceived; it ignores the fact that conferring a right is always a costly matter. A's right to x can only be justified, initially, if we think that A's interest in x is important enough to warrant imposing a duty on others, and *only to that extent.* Namely, to the extent that the burden involved in the imposition of the duties does not outweigh the importance of the interest protected by the right in question. This is why the limits of rights are not only external, but inherent as well. Each and every right holds, to some extent, its own limit.

In other words, once we are willing to recognize that the basis of a right is the interest of the right holder, an interest important enough to justify imposing a duty on others, we must also acknowledge that the duties are limited; no interest is so important as to justify the imposition of unlimited duties on others. Even one's interest in the preservation of life, for example, does not justify the imposition of unlimited duties on others. For example, your right to life may impose a duty on me to drive my car with caution, but it does not justify imposing a duty

15 Cf. H.L.A. Hart, "Rawls on Liberty and its Priority."

16 An example of this is discussed in Ch.10 of this volume.

on me to refrain from using my car altogether. We do not need to invoke the possibility of a conflict of rights here (which may well exist, of course); suffice it to recognize that there is a cost involved in the imposition of duties, as such.

Perhaps a kind of diagnostic explanation is called for at this stage: why has this simple point about the inherent limits of rights been generally overlooked? There are two main reasons, I believe. First, as we noted earlier, much of the impetus towards rights discourse in the first place stemmed from its anti-utilitarian motivation, acknowledging, as I claim that we should, that the cost-benefit calculus necessarily involved in the determination of the existence of a given right tends to contaminate rights discourse with precisely the kind of evaluations it was meant to avoid, namely, the trade-offs between the interests of some people and the burdens imposed on others. Furthermore, it is naturally feared that once trade-offs are allowed into the calculus, numbers may matter. After all, we may be driven to ask, how many people should share the burden of securing the interests of others? Can we set aside the vital interest of some, only because large numbers are involved on the other side? Understandably, then, the Newtonian conception of rights seemed to have avoided these embarrassing questions. If the only reason for limits imposed on a given right must be drawn from the more pressing rights of others, the resolution of rights conflicts would seem to be free of the much feared utilitarian-like calculus. But this neat solution, as I have tried to argue, is not viable. The considerations of trade-offs and the weighing of opposing interests come into the picture even before rights turn out to be in conflict; they are essential in determining whether one has a right at all.

There is another explanation for the prevalence of the Newtonian conception of rights. As Raz pointed out, there is an interesting puzzle about the limits of rights: Quite often, he says, "the value of a right, the weight it is to be given, or the stringency with which it is to be observed do not correspond to its value to the right holder."[17] Rights, in other words, normally receive, as they should, much more weight and protection than the extent that such protection would seem to require by the interests of the right holders. Most people's interests in free speech, for example, are hardly so valuable to them as to warrant the current protection of the right to freedom of expression in Western democracies.

---

17 J. Raz, *Ethics in the Public Domain*, 30.

Undoubtedly, this apparent discrepancy between individual interests forming the foundation of rights, and the extent of the protection of these rights, calls for a serious discussion, one which I cannot hope to provide here. However, I believe that the problem itself explains the currency of the Newtonian conception. If we agree that a right deserves wider protection than that which is required by its value to the right holder, it would seem natural to maintain that a right can only be limited for the sake of securing somebody else's more pressing right.

But, in fact, it is the other way around. Whatever the precise solution of this puzzle should be, it would point to the fact that rights benefit not only the right holder, as such, but the community as well. Rights receive extensive protection, because they serve the common or collective good. In other words, it is often the combination of private and public interests that lies behind the extent of a given right's legal protection. Living in a community where a certain right is protected is in itself a general good over and beyond the good it serves for those individuals whose right is potentially protected. Needless to say, the nature of this general good is prone to be controversial. Is it, for example, a "common good," as Raz maintains, in that it is supposedly conflict-free, non-exclusive and non-excludable, or is it a "collective good," which is not free of conflict and exclusion? These are difficult questions which I cannot hope to resolve here.[18] Nevertheless, perhaps I should say that I do not share Raz's optimistic view of rights serving the common good in the conflict-free way he describes. On the contrary, my own view is that rights serve collective goods, which are prone to conflicts and trade-offs. For example, think of one of the standard feminist reactions to pornography in the context of the right to freedom of expression. Undoubtedly, the latter is a collective good, as it serves the interest of the community as a whole, but in the context of the protection of pornographic publications, it may well serve the good of some (men, I presume), at the expense of the same kind of good, namely, freedom of expression, for women. Pornography, it may well be argued, serves the value of free speech for men, occasionally at least, at the expense of free speech for women. To take another example, which is, I hope, less controversial, think of the effects of economic deregulation of the media in the context of the freedom of expression. In one sense, deregulation certainly contributes to more extensive speech opportunities and, in that respect, it is good for the public at large. On the other hand, deregulation tends to increase the private ownership of the media and its resources, and this is not so good for the speech opportunities of the poor and

---

18 See Raz, *ibid.*, 37ff. For a more detailed account of the distinction between collective, common, and public goods, see Ch.10 in this collection.

unprivileged segments of society. In whichever way we go, we will create some collective good at the expense of the collective good of others.

Be that as it may, the public aspect of the protection of rights, far from supporting the Newtonian conception of rights, rather explains its inadequacy. Once again, it points to the fact that determining the extension of a right initially involves the kind of calculus that the Newtonian conception is so anxious to avoid. It involves a cost-benefit calculus where, *inter alia*, the communal good, and hence, inevitably, opposing conceptions of the good, play a part too.

The skeptical reader may conclude at this stage that I have in fact been arguing for the endorsement of a utilitarian conception of rights. But such a conclusion would be unwarranted. There is nothing in the interest theory of rights I espouse here that should lead one, inevitably, to a utilitarian framework. The balancing of interests and costs which I claim to be essential for the determination of the existence of each and every right is not necessarily a utilitarian one. The way we think about these matters depends on numerous evaluative considerations, pertaining, eventually, to the fundamental values we hold and their relative importance as compared with each other. When we ask ourselves, "What are those interests which are worthy of protection by imposing duties on people, and to what extent?" we certainly engage, *inter alia*, in cost-benefit calculations, but these need not be based on utilitarian or any other consequentialist grounds. Cost-benefit calculations of this kind are not necessarily a quantitative matter; the *intrinsic* values and relative importance of the interests in question matter too. As Jeremy Waldron rightly emphasized, "what is wrong with utilitarianism is not that it contemplates trade-offs but that it combines the idea of trade-offs with a doctrine of the quantitative commensurability of all values."[19]

On the other hand, it is impossible to try to answer such questions without considering the most fundamental values we hold and our conceptions of the good. How else could we determine, for example, whether the interests of women in their personal autonomy justifies the imposition of duties on the state to enable them a reasonable access to abortions? Or, whether the interests of some people in a higher standard of education for their children warrants the imposition of a higher income tax on others, or not? And how can such questions be avoided in a modern democratic state? The interest theory of rights points to the fact that

19 Waldron, *supra* note 10, 211.

rights discourse renders such questions inevitable at the stage of determining the existence of rights; how these questions should be answered, however, is a matter left open by the interest theory of rights.

C. Rights and Pluralism

The thesis that rights are inherently limited should not be taken to entail that determining the limits of rights is not a controversial matter. In fact, I would like to show that the contrary is true. Determining the limits of rights, I will claim, is unavoidably a controversial matter, and for reasons which are worth exploring. We can begin by looking at the political structure of our societies. We shall see very clearly, I think, that it is generally much easier to settle on the rights people have than on their limits. It is, in fact, a prominent feature of rights discourse that people with very different and opposing moral views, people with conflicting conceptions of the good and the right, can nevertheless agree on a list of universal human and civil rights. How can we explain all this?

It is all too tempting to think that there is really nothing that needs explaining here. After all, cynics could remind us, it is very easy for the politicians and the courts to declare that they cherish an impressive list of human rights, without actually intending to bear all the consequences. But this cynical attitude only begs the question. If we do actually know what the ramifications of having a certain right are, it is very difficult to understand why people with conflicting views on the matter should subscribe to one and the same right. If, on the other hand, the cynics maintain that rights discourse is basically lip service, we would still want to know what it is lip service to; and why do we need such a discourse cast in the framework of rights?

Let me propose a less cynical answer. According to the interest theory of rights, rights are actually *intermediary conclusions* in arguments that begin with the evaluation of interests and end with conclusions about duties which should be imposed on other people. When we say that A has a right to x, we say that A's interest in x justifies the imposition of duties on others in respect to that interest. From a strictly analytical point of view, however, the concept of a right is, in a sense, redundant; it is just an intermediary step in a moral argument leading from the values of certain human interests to conclusions about the need to impose certain duties. Therefore, the question arises: Why do we need this intermediary step cast in the form "a right"?

Joseph Raz gave two answers:[20] One partial answer might be that it simply saves time and energy; it is often the case that practical arguments proceed through the mediation of intermediary steps simply because there is no need to begin each and every practical argument from first premises—that would be too tedious. There is, however, a much more important reason: Intermediary steps, such as rights, enable us to settle on a set of shared intermediary conclusions, *in spite of considerable disagreement about the grounds* of those intermediary conclusions. In other words, people can settle on the recognition of rights, despite the fact that they would deeply disagree about the reasons for having those rights. Rights discourse enables a common culture to be formed around some intermediary conclusions, precisely because of their intermediary nature.

Furthermore, it is crucial to recall that there is an important asymmetry between rights and duties. Rights, unlike duties, do not entail that the right holder has any particular reasons for action. The proposition: "A has duty to x," *entails* that A has a reason to x. But having a right to do something does not entail that one has a reason to do it. (Your right to freedom of speech, for instance, does not give you any reasons to say something.) This analytical point is very important: It explains why people with different and competing sets of fundamental values are bound to disagree about the duties they have.[21] But this need not be the case with rights, since there is no immediate relation of entailment between rights and reasons for action. True, there is an indirect relation of entailment: Rights justify the imposition of duties on others. But since this entailment is indirect and not immediately transparent (certainly not in its details), people can agree on the existence of a given right even if they actually disagree on the nature and scope of the duties that the right justifies. Thus, it is normally easier for people with different conceptions of the good to agree on a shared set of rights than duties, as rights do not entail immediate reasons for action.

It is, however, the intermediary nature of rights discourse which is quintessential. It explains why rights discourse is particularly fit for pluralistic societies. Societies where different groups of people are deeply divided about their conceptions of the

---

20 See Raz, *supra* note 3, 181. I do not intend to suggest that Raz would agree (or not) with the main thesis that I advocate here in the next few paragraphs.

21 Unless, of course, the duties in question are very abstract, like the duty not to cause unnecessary suffering, or the duty to respect others. I am not suggesting that people with conflicting conceptions of the good and of ultimate values cannot agree on some duties we should all have. My point is relative: that it is easier to agree on a list of relatively specific rights than on duties.

good need to settle on a set of rights they can all acknowledge, in spite of deep controversies regarding the grounds of those rights (and their ramifications). Hence it is not surprising or accidental that in homogeneous societies there is very little rights discourse; such societies normally share a common understanding of ultimate values, and consequently of the various duties people have, and they do not need this intermediary step from ultimate values to duties. It is only in those societies where people do not share a common understanding of ultimate values, namely, in pluralistic societies, that rights discourse is prevalent.[22]

But this social function of rights discourse also points to its own limits. The intermediary nature of rights discourse explains why determining the limits of rights, and their relative weight in competition with other rights or values, is bound to be a controversial matter. In order to determine in a reasoned manner the limits of a given right, or its relative weight in a situation of conflict, one would naturally need to go back to the reasons for having the right in the first place, and it is precisely at this point that agreement breaks down. As a matter of fact, more often than not we will discover that there was never an agreement there to begin with. In other words, precisely because of those reasons which explain the widespread consensus on the rights we have, there is bound to be disagreement over the boundaries of those rights and their desirable ramifications. Widespread consensus on how to resolve various conflicts between rights, or between rights and other values, is only possible in the framework of a shared culture of moral and political views, but it is typically in such cases that rights have relatively little cultural and political significance. If rights discourse is prevalent in a given society, it is mostly because there is little agreement on anything else, in particular, on the ultimate values people cherish.[23]

In his book *Liberal Rights*, Jeremy Waldron tries to offer a partial solution to this problem of unavoidable conflicts of rights. Waldron claims that it is possible to recognize the lexical ordering of certain moral considerations involved in the

22 Admittedly, this last point is actually a piece of armchair sociology. But not a particularly fancy one. I think that we are quite familiar with this phenomenon, namely, that rights discourse is much more prevalent in pluralistic societies than in homogeneous ones. It is quite likely that there are other explanations for this difference, besides the one I offer here. I do not intend the explanation to be exhaustive.

23 It is probably true, though not universally so, that the prevalence of rights discourse in a given society does reflect a deeper level of consensus about the acceptance of pluralism and perhaps even individualism. But this deeper level of tacit consensus, to the extent that it exists, is very abstract and quite unlikely to have significant bearing on how to determine the limits of rights.

conflicts of rights, if we notice that certain pairs of such considerations are *internally* related to one another. As an example of such an internally related argument of lexical ordering, he gives the famous account of John Stuart Mill of the grounds for the right to free speech. "Since the whole point of free expression is to challenge received opinion and shake up complacency, the discomfiture attendant on that challenge is to be given no weight at all against free speech," says Waldron.[24]

I find it difficult to share Waldron's optimism, however. I think that it should be clear by now that, in most cases, there is no such thing as "the whole point of free expression is" such and such. In pluralistic societies, and it is in those societies that rights are most needed, people are bound to disagree about the point of having a right to free expression, even if they agree that they should have the right. Thus for example, "the whole point of free expression" that Waldron adopts from Mill may well be the point of this right for the educated majority of a democratic society; the ground for this right for an oppressed ethnic minority, or for, say, an ultraorthodox religious minority, may well be quite different! In other words, the lexical ordering of the conflict of rights is possible only in the framework of a shared culture of moral and political views, but it is precisely in such cases that rights have relatively little cultural and political significance.

By way of conclusion, let me pull some of the strands together. In the previous section, I argued that the Newtonian picture of rights is misconceived, and that rights should be seen as inherently and not only externally limited. In this section I have tried to show that there is something unique to rights discourse in pluralistic societies which renders the questions concerning the limits of rights unavoidably controversial. It would be a mistake, however, to think that these two points pull in opposite directions. The idea that rights are both inherently limited and inherently controversial, in the ways I have described, leads to one and the same conclusion, namely, against the aspiration to political neutrality. I have tried to show that a certain conception of rights, namely, the interest theory, which is distinctly *liberal* and basically *individualistic*, cannot offer, and to my mind, should not be required to offer, a politically neutral formula for the resolution of rights conflicts.

---

24 See Waldron, *supra* note 10, 221.

It is the common ground of those liberals who have misconceived both points to believe that the liberal conception of rights can offer such a politically neutral formula for the solution of rights conflicts. Those who hold that rights can only be limited for the sake of securing other rights conceive of liberal rights discourse in terms of political neutrality. But this Newtonian conception of rights, I have tried to show, is simply wrong. Rights also have their inherent limits, and the determination of those limits is bound to depend on conceptions of the good and the right, conceptions without which we could never determine the initial necessary balance between the fundamental values of certain kinds of human interest, and the costs that it is reasonable to impose on others for the benefit of securing those interests. This controversial nature of rights, exemplified by both points I have tried to make, should cause despair only to those who cherish political neutrality. I have tried to show that the interest theory of rights, liberal and individualistic as it is, does not support their view.[25]

25 I am indebted to Meir Dan-Cohen, John Gardner, Ruth Gavison, Joseph Raz, Noya Rimalt, and Ariel Porat for their helpful comments on a draft of this essay.

CHAPTER 10

Do We Have a Right to Common Goods?

Individuals have rights. I will assume that this means that individuals have interests which are important enough to justify the imposition of duties on others in order to secure those interests. Groups of individuals, such as nations or ethnic minorities, plausibly have rights as well. Groups of individuals may have groupinterests appropriately protected by the imposition of duties on others, typically, on governments, or on other larger political entities. My concern in this essay is with the question of what individuals or groups may have *a right to*. In particular I want to explore the question of whether people can have a right to common goods, such as the flourishing of their culture or national heritage. First, I will explain the concept of a common good and its distinction from other, similar, concepts such as collective and public goods. Second, I will argue that individuals should not have a right to common goods, unless a particular distributive principles applies to the good in question, and then the individual's right is the right to a certain share in that common good. Finally, I will explore the question of how this analysis applies to group rights.

A. Conceptual Framework

According to Raz's influential "interest theory of rights," which I will basically endorse here, rights protect interests of potential right holders.[1] An interest of an individual is an aspect of his well-being. Needless to say, not every aspect of a person's well-being should be protected by rights, that is, by the imposition of duties on others. Some aspects of a person's well-being are too trivial to deserve such protection; they simply do not justify the imposition of any burden on others. Other aspects of a person's well-being, in spite of being important and worthy of

1 See Raz, *The Morality of Freedom*, Ch. 7 and *Ethics in the Public Domain*, Ch. 1.

protection, such as, for example, a person's interest in being loved and cherished by others, cannot be plausibly protected by the imposition of duties on others, because the duty would either be disproportionately burdensome or practically impossible to impose.[2] Whenever a right exists, however, it is a right to a certain good that is in the interest of the right holder.

Many goods that potentially ground rights are essentially individualistic. For instance, the right not to be subject to torture is based on aspects of people's well-being which are individual in character. Neither their production, nor their enjoyment, requires a community. Other goods, however, are communal; in one form or another, such goods take a community to produce, sustain, or enjoy. However, there are important differences between the various ways in which goods have a communal aspect, and it is crucial to be clear about this. In particular, we should distinguish between collective goods, public goods, and common goods.

The concept of the collective good is the easiest to define: Collective goods are those which require some form of collective action to produce.[3] What marks this concept of a good only concerns its typical production process. There is a considerable variety of goods in our societies which can only be produced collectively, that is, by the concerted action of numerous individuals, institutions, and agencies. Consider, for example, the goods of national security, the protection of the environment, democratic decision procedures, adequate health care, and perhaps also science and education; all these goods require collective action to produce. Note, however, that there is an element of contingency in this characterization. The production of goods may vary with circumstances. In some societies, or under certain circumstances, the production of a given good may require collective action, whereas in others, it may not. Consider the good of clean air, for example. The production of clean air becomes a collective-action problem only in societies which actually face a problem of pollution. If there is no pollution, such

---

2 Not always: We do tend to assume that parents, for example, have a duty to love their children.

3 There are two main types of collective action, and I intend to include here both of them: First, there are those cases in which the production of the good simply requires *coordination* amongst numerous participants. Second, there are those cases in which the creation of the good by a number of individuals requires more than simple coordination because participants would have a strong incentive to defect, free-ride, etc. Prisoner's Dilemma situations form the paradigmatic example of this latter category. The main difference between these two types of collective action problems consists in the fact that in the second category some form of sanction is needed to solve the collective-action problem, whereas in simple cases of coordination, it is typically enough to secure common knowledge of one course of action everybody can pursue. On the difference between these two types of collective-action problems I have elaborated in my *Positive Law and Objective Values*, Ch. 2.

as in distant rural communities, perhaps, there is no need to produce clean air, and clean air becomes a good people can enjoy without any communal aspect whatsoever. On the other hand, certain goods are essentially of such a nature that their production involves a collectivity. Democratic political procedures, for example, are of such an essentially collective nature. People cannot produce or have a democracy by themselves.

Be this as it may, the essential point is that the communal aspect of collective goods consists in their means of production. Public goods, however, are communal regardless of the prerequisites of their production. By the term "public good" I mean to refer to those goods which can be enjoyed by a multiplicity of persons in such a way that the use or enjoyment of some does not substantially subtract from the use of others. In other words, public goods are goods which, once produced, benefit a whole community. Street lighting is a classical example often given for such goods. Regardless of why or by whom a street light has been installed, it benefits a whole community of potential pedestrians, and their benefit is not mutually exclusive. Similar considerations apply to public parks, or the beauty of a building, or some of the examples we have mentioned above, such as clean air or national security. As these examples show, some public goods are also collective goods, and others need not be. What marks a good as public is the possibility of a nonexclusive enjoyment, not its means of production.[4]

Nonexcludability, so to speak, is a matter of degree. Whether the use or enjoyment of one person subtracts from the use or enjoyment of others greatly depends on circumstances. There is rarely a case of perfect nonexcludability. City parks can be used and enjoyed by many, and under normal circumstances, if people behave in a civilized manner, the park can be enjoyed by all without substantially subtracting from the enjoyment of others. But only up to a point, of course. The more people use the park, at some point the less enjoyable it becomes. Few goods, however, are entirely nonexcludable.[5] Consider, for example, the beauty of a public building. It seems to be true that once a beautiful building has been constructed, all those who enjoy it can do so without the exclusion of others and without subtracting from anybody else's enjoyment. But even this relatively easy case is not as

4 Nonexcludability is Raz's main characterization of public goods. See his "Right-based Moralities": However, the distinctions I mention here between collective, public, and common goods, more or less follows the insights of Denise Rèaume, "Individuals, Groups, and Rights to Public Goods" and Jeremy Waldron, *Liberal Rights*, Ch. 14.

5 The political importance of this has been discussed in Ch. 3.

easy as it seems. Arguably, at least according to a certain "aristocratic" conception of aesthetics, the more people come to appreciate the beauty of an object, the less appreciable it may become. So even the passive enjoyment of the beauty of an object may not be a perfect case of nonexcludability.[6] But perhaps it is; I do not want to insist on this point.

Finally, common goods are quite different. As Jeremy Waldron rightly observed,[7] the essential character of a common good is that it cannot be *enjoyed* without its communal aspect. The communal aspect of the good is an essential ingredient of what makes it a good. Consider, for example, such goods as culture, national heritage, democracy, solidarity, fraternity, or, to mention one of Waldron's nicest examples, the conviviality of a party. All these, and countless other examples, refer to goods which gain their quality as goods only in connection to a community. The good is something that occurs at a collective, communal, level, and its communal aspect is an essential ingredient of what makes it a good that individuals can enjoy. The communal aspect of common goods is typically twofold. First, such goods typically take a community to create and to sustain. Culture, democracy, a natural language, and such, cannot exist without a community which sustains them. The good can only be maintained by the existence of a community that actually practices those elements that constitute the good in question. Second, but not as a necessary consequence, such goods can only be enjoyed as goods in their communal manifestations.

Consider the goods of a culture, for example. Such goods cannot be sustained by an individual acting on her own. It takes a community to create and sustain a culture. Note, however, that the creation of such goods doesn't necessarily require a collective, concerted, effort. Most common goods are actually created by something like an invisible-hand mechanism. Individuals behave *as if* they are driven by a certain communal purpose, whereas in fact, it is typically the case that no such communal purpose had ever been anybody's actual intention. The creation of some common goods, however, such as democracy or solidarity, does require certain forms of collective action. Be this as it may, the essential point is that common goods typically require a community to create and sustain. This aspect of common goods, however, does not necessarily entail the further element, which is crucial, namely, that the enjoyment of the good is essentially communal.

---

6 Rèaume, *ibid.*, 12.

7 See Waldron, *supra* note 4, 355 and Rèaume, *ibid.*, 10–11.

In other words, the characterization of common goods should take into account their consumption, and not only their production end. What makes a good common, in a morally interesting way, is the fact that its consumption is essentially communal. This is so, despite the fact that it would be very difficult to think of a common good which is not also produced communally.[8]

Consider, for example, the importance people attach to their national identity and national-historical heritage. For many people identification with their nation and its historical and cultural heritage is an important good. The flourishing of one's nation or ethnic group is something which contributes to people's well-being. This is undoubtedly a common good. Quite apart from the fact that national heritage and the flourishing of a national culture can only be produced by a community, it is also true, and crucially so, that people cannot enjoy such a good without its communal aspect. The flourishing of one's national culture is a good people can enjoy only in concert with others who share their appreciation of it and take pride in its achievements. In this respect, the values of nationality and national culture are very much like the conviviality of a party; they can only be enjoyed in concert with others who willfully participate in the same enterprise. Note, however, that in the case of common goods, there is typically an intimate, almost inextricable, connection between the production of the good and its enjoyment or consumption. Common goods involve communal enterprises in which the distinction between the production and the consumption of the good is often very difficult to draw. Often participation in the communal enterprise is both the production and the enjoyment of the good.[9]

Now, before we discuss the question of a right to common goods, it is worth noting that neither collective goods nor public goods create a special problem for the rights theorist. Consider collective goods first. The fact that the production of the good involves certain forms of collective action may have a bearing on the cost of the relevant right, and on the question of who it is a right against, but these

---

8 As a possible example of a common good which is not produced commonly, I hesitate to mention the example of the arts, such as painting or literature. In some respects it is true that art is typically created by individual achievements, and the communal aspect of its production is at least not always on the surface. But we should not ignore the fact that the creation of art is very genre-dependent, and genres are common goods.

9 See Rèaume, *supra* note 4, 11. Unlike Rèaume, however, I am somewhat less certain that this is an essential element of common goods. Some common goods do allow for a division of labor between producers and consumers. To a considerable extent, we can distinguish, for example, between producers and consumers of literature.

are practical problems, endemic to the production of most goods in our societies. There seems to be no theoretical difficulty with the idea that people have a right to collective goods. Consider, for example, people's right to clean air. People's crucial interest in clean air grounds a right because it justifies the imposition of duties on others, and this is so, even if it is the case that discharging those duties requires collective action.[10]

Similarly, there is no particular difficulty with the idea that people have a right to some public goods. Consider, again, the right to clean air. Once the object of this right is produced, it happens to be a public good. Clean air can be enjoyed by everybody without thus subtracting in any significant way from the enjoyment of others. Furthermore, it is arguable that the protection of a great many traditional rights in itself creates certain public goods by creating a social-political environment which is good in itself, and can by enjoyed nonexclusively by the community at large.[11] A society which does not tolerate torture, for instance, is a society in which a certain public atmosphere exists, and this public atmosphere is a public good, enjoyable by the community at large. The protection of rights often creates positive externalities which amount to public goods. Positive or negative externalities, however, bear on the cost and the desirable extent of the protection of the right in question; externalities do not create any special problem of principle for the determination of whether a right can be acknowledged or not.

B. A Right to Common Goods?

Jeremy Waldron claims that there cannot be a right to *common* goods because the benefit such a right would secure to individuals cannot be adequately captured by particular benefits to individuals considered on their own. "An individual has a right to G when the importance of his interest in G, considered on its own, is sufficient to justify holding others to be under a duty to promote G." But the whole point of a common good, Waldron claims, is that such goods have worth only to members of the group considered *together*, and not as individual recipients

---

10 The fact that the production of a good requires concerted action on a large scale is typically a good reason to impose the duty of the production of the good on institutions, such as the state, or some other public agency.

11 See Raz, *Ethics in the Public Domain*, Ch. 1. Raz also claims, however, that such public good externalities tend to be noncompetitive in their nature. I have expressed my doubts about this optimism in the previous chapter.

of benefit.[12] Therefore, Waldron concludes, individuals cannot have a right to common goods. This is not quite accurate, however. The fact that a good is common, namely, that it can be consumed only at a communal level, does not entail that the consumption of the good is not of paramount importance to individuals considered on their own. Culture, for example is a common good; it can only be consumed communally. From this communal aspect of culture, however, it does not necessarily follow that individuals considered on their own, namely, as the recipients of the benefit of culture, do not have an interest in culture sufficient to justify holding others to be under a duty. Even if culture can only be enjoyed communally, its benefit to individuals can be considered on its own, as an individual benefit worthy of protection. The fact that I cannot enjoy something on my own does not entail that the good in question is not a good *for me*, considered on my own.[13]

Waldron's mistake is not so obvious, however. Some of his formulations suggest that his understanding of the idea of a common good is somewhat different from mine in a way which might explain his conclusion. At certain points he seems to suggest that the idea of a common good is not exhausted by the fact that the good in question can only be consumed at a communal level. The good in question, he claims, is *"primarily a property of the group."*[14] A common good is good *for the community*, considered as a certain community, and not for the individual participants. If this characterization of common goods is correct, it would seem to justify Waldron's conclusion. But I don't think that it is, nor is it supported by any of Waldron's examples. It is true that many properties which constitute common goods are properties of groups and not of individuals: It is the party that is convivial, the society that is democratic or cultured, and so on. But we should be careful not to confuse the semantic-conceptual nature of the properties of aspects of the world which give rise to common goods, with the goods, understood normatively, that they give rise to. The fact that the party is convivial is *good for its participants*, not for the party. And the fact that a society is democratic, or cultured, is *good for its members*, and not for "the society," considered in some abstraction.

---

12 Waldron, 359 (emphasis added).

13 I think that Rèaume (in "Individuals, Groups, and Rights to Public Goods" *supra* note 4, 9 and 11) makes a very similar point to Waldron's, which I find flawed for the same reason. Cf. Alon Harel, "Review Essay: Free Speech Revisionism: Doctrinal and Philosophical Challenges" and Michael Hartney, "Some Confusions Concerning Collective Rights," 298–300.

14 Waldron, *supra* note 4, 355.

The problem with common goods, then, does not consist in the fact that they cannot ground individual interests. In fact, contrary to Waldron's thesis, I do not think that there is any *conceptual* problem with a right to common goods. The problem is a *moral* one, and it concerns the nature of the duties which would be required to secure an individual's interest in a common good. Goods are common, as we have seen, if individuals can enjoy the good only at the communal level, in concert with others who participate in the same communal enterprise. Such a communal enterprise, however, is typically a normative, evaluative matter. People can enjoy common goods because there is a whole community which enjoys them with them, that is, a community of people who *share those values which make it a good of a certain kind.*[15] A duty to provide a common good, therefore, would typically mean, *inter alia*, a duty to share certain values with others, and this is a type of duty which is morally very disturbing. In a liberal society, committed to the profound importance of freedom and personal autonomy, we would rarely wish to impose a duty on people to share certain values with others. People ought to have certain duties to promote valuable things, but this is very different from saying that they should have a duty to value those things. Perhaps people, and more plausibly institutions, should have a duty to do certain things which, for example, promote culture or solidarity. But this is, again, very different from suggesting that people should have *a duty to value* such things as culture or solidarity. However, having *a right* to such common goods as culture, or solidarity, would necessarily mean that others are under a duty to value certain things, since without such a communal sharing of values, culture or solidarity cannot become common goods. In other words, the duties which would be required to secure people's initial interest in a common good are too burdensome, morally speaking, since such duties are essentially duties to value as others do; the value cannot be realized unless it is shared by the relevant community.

In a similar line of reasoning, Denise Rèaume suggested that it may be impossible, not just morally wrong, to impose duties on others to share values which constitute common goods. She believes that "willing participation" cannot be imposed

---

15 I say that common goods *typically* involve such a normative aspect just in order to be on the safe side. I find it very difficult to think of common goods which can be sustained and enjoyed as goods without there being certain values which are shared by most members of the relevant community. As Wittgenstein famously showed, even the use of a natural language necessarily involves "agreement in judgment" shared by the community of speakers. But again, I might be wrong about the generalization, in which case, I readily admit that my argument is restricted to those goods which require the members of the community to share the values which make it a common good.

as a matter of duty. For example, if we think about an alleged right to culture, we would have to assume that it is possible to impose a duty on people to "take an active and genuine interest in the arts, among other things . . ." but, she claims, "it is impossible . . . to speak of there being *an obligation* to take such an interest." This would require "the compulsion of that which cannot be compelled."[16] I have some doubts, however, about this stronger claim. First, it seems to confuse the question of whether a duty should be held to exist, with the possibility of its "compulsion." People may well have a moral obligation, for instance, to love their children, though it is pretty clear that no such a duty can be compelled on them. The possibility of compulsion just does not form part of the definition of a duty. Secondly, I am doubtful that it is *conceptually* impossible to speak of a duty to share certain values or to take an active interest in something valuable. Duties are based on reasons for action. Therefore, anything which can count as a reason for action can conceptually ground a duty. Since people may well have a reason to share certain values with others, or actively participate in the creation of a common good, as a matter of logical or conceptual truth, they may well have such duties.

Perhaps Rèaume's point is somewhat different. It is true that there are certain values which can only become valuable if they are voluntarily entertained. Consider the values of friendship, or love, for example. People would not want such values to emerge from an obligation since it is part of the very idea of the good in question that it should emerge spontaneously or freely chosen by the relevant agent. Thus, for example, it is probably true that friendship cannot emerge as a valuable type of relationship if it is imposed as a matter of duty.[17] But the scope of this point is very limited; it would not apply to the kind of values which pertain to the creation of a great many types of common good. Culture, national heritage or solidarity, the arts, and many other common goods, do not seem to depend, certainly not entirely, on such spontaneous values. Many aspects of culture are created and nourished by being taught to the young in schools, often to their initial reluctance. National solidarity is often presented as a matter of duty, and at least it is not generally regarded as a kind of value which would be defeated unless it is purely voluntary. The problem with such duties, once again, is a moral one. A duty to value is problematic from an ethical point of view, that is, from the vantage point of moral autonomy.

16 Rèaume, *supra* note 4, 13.

17 It may be worth noting that these things are profoundly affected by culture.

One of the most important commitments of liberalism consists in the profound value it attaches to a person's choices in the values she holds. What people decide to value, and to what extent, is a major constituent of their identity and their conception of their own selves. Liberalism is committed to the view that people should be left to choose their own values because such a choice is what makes an adult person the person she is, and grounds her moral responsibility. Needless to say, it doesn't mean that people should be left to choose *to do* whatever they want. A duty to do something which is valuable is certainly conceivable even if the person who happens to have such an obligation does not recognize the value in question. Moral autonomy does not consist in unrestrained freedom of action. But it does consist in the commitment to let people value whatever they choose to value. A person's choice of the things she values is what makes her the kind of person she is, and substantiates her moral autonomy.[18]

To be sure, none of this entails that a failure to value that which is valuable cannot amount to a moral deficiency. People can be wrong about the values they hold. Being morally wrong about something, however, does not necessarily amount to a breach of duty. Once again, the flaw I find in the idea of an obligation to value is a moral one, not a conceptual impossibility. The imposition of a duty to value is at odds with the values we attach to autonomy; it is morally undesirable to impose such duties on people because it undermines the ideals of choice and personal responsibility in the self-constitution of one's moral views and ethical character. A right to common good, therefore, is morally undesirable, since it involves the imposition of duties to value those aspects of the world which constitute the common good. People should not have a right that involves the imposition of such burdensome duties.

We should be careful, however, to distinguish between people's initial interest in having a common good, and other interests which are related to a common good that already exists. As I have just noted, the initial interest in having a common good cannot justifiably amount to a right, since as such a right, it would require the imposition of a duty on others to share those values which make it a good. However, once a common good actually exists, it may give rise to concerns about

---

18 Perhaps in both of these points Rèaume could rely on something like the familiar thesis that "ought implies can." Note, however, that the "ought implies can" thesis is a moral one. It is not a conceptual truth. Some philosophers believe that one may have a duty to X, even if one cannot actually discharge the duty under the circumstances. Perhaps they are wrong, but if so, their mistake is about substantive morality, not about the conceptual framework of duties discourse.

its fair distribution, and those concerns may ground certain rights in relation to the common good. For example, certain common goods are such that people may have a right not to be excluded from their enjoyment. Furthermore, as I will try to explain in a moment, there are certain common goods which, once they exist, ought to be distributed in a fair way, and then people may well have a right to a certain share in the common good. But again, this is very different from the claim that people have a right *to the good* in question, which would necessarily entail the duty of others to provide it.

Let me first take up the issue of exclusion. Some common goods are also public goods, and therefore they are such that it is typically impossible to exclude some people from enjoying the good in question. However, many common goods are not public, and they do allow for the exclusion of some people from the enjoyment of the good. A community may develop and cherish a certain sense of solidarity, for instance, but at the same time, exclude some subset of the community from this good. People who belong to this subset of the community may well have a right not to be excluded. This right, however, derives from the adverse consequences of the exclusion, and not from the right to the good in question.[19] In other words, even if the creation of a good does not ground an individual right, once the good exists, it may well give rise to the right not to be excluded from enjoying the good. This is so, since the exclusion itself is often a moral wrong, like discrimination and humiliation. Exclusion typically involves a strong message of inferiority to the excluded individuals or groups. Exclusion signals to the excluded people that they do not merit the kind of respect and concern others get, and this is undoubtedly a kind of moral wrong that people may have a right not to suffer.[20]

More importantly, however, there are common goods which, once they exist, give rise to distributional rights. Consider the example of culture. Once a given culture exists, it may well be the case that the cultural resources of the community ought to be distributed according to a just and fair scheme. People may have a right to a fair share of the cultural assets of their community, that is, even if they do not have a right to culture. Or consider the right to democracy, for instance.

19 Rèaume raises a similar point about equality of opportunity in "Individuals, Groups, and Rights to Public Goods" 10.

20 To be sure, I am not trying to suggest that any instance of exclusion is wrong. To some extent, groups need to define themselves by certain forms of exclusion, and I do not want to imply that any group self-determination is necessarily bad.

Democracy, like any other form of regime, concerns the exercise of political power. Now, political power is probably a common good; it cannot be enjoyed in isolation. Political power can become a good only at its communal level, as something that takes place and is valued in a communal context. Therefore, I do not think that people have a right to political power. But they may well have a right to a certain share of it. In other words, democracy can be seen as a commitment to an equal distribution of political power, and therefore, we can speak of a right to democracy, that is, as long as the latter is understood as a right to a certain share in political power. Political power is a common good, but once it exists, it is such that it gives rise to concerns of a just distribution. It is a kind of good that ought to be distributed in a fair manner, and people may have a right to such a fair share of the good as the distribution principle entails.[21]

An analogy may help to make this point. Consider, for example, the idea of friendship. Friendship is not something that people can claim from others; friendship is something that must evolve spontaneously, by the mutual wish and recognition of people who interact with each other in a certain way. However, once it is the case that A and B are friends, and regard each other as such, the relationship of friendship may well give rise to certain claims from each other, claims that it would be wrong to frustrate. Thus, even if A cannot justifiably complain that B does not wish to become his friend, friendship does not involve commitments; and once friendship exists, so to speak, it may give rise to certain obligations. Similarly, I have argued, people may have rights to a certain share of a good, once the good happens to exist, even if it is the case that they do not have the right *to the good* in question.

C. Group Rights and Common Goods

Can groups have rights to common goods? Needless to say, an answer to this question partly depends on the initial question of whether groups, as such, can be right holders at all. Although it is somewhat controversial, I will assume here that an affirmative answer to the question of group rights is not implausible. After all, groups of individuals, such as minorities or nations, may have certain well recognized group interests, and it is possible to hold the view that such interests are

21 I have discussed this issue at length in Ch. 3. The right to democracy is the example Alon Harel used in order to show, contra Waldron, that it makes sense to speak of rights to common goods. See Harel, "Revisionist Theories of Rights: An Unwelcome Defense," 241.

worthy of protection by the imposition of duties on others. Note, however, that the duties which are potentially justified by group interests can be imposed either on other groups or institutions, external to the right-holder group, or on the individuals who happen to be members of the group itself. Let us call them external and internal duties, accordingly.[22] Obviously, internal duties are much more problematic, particularly when we consider nonvoluntary groups, such as ethnic minorities or national groups. But let me consider the question of external duties first.

Thus the first question is this: Can groups have a right to a common good *vis-à-vis* some other group or institution? For example, can it be the case that an ethnic minority has a justified claim to the right to its culture from the dominant majority, or the state? Now this may sound like a worn-out issue; so much has been written on the rights of ethnic minorities to their culture that one does not wish to hear about them yet again. I beg for the reader's patience, however. For the sake of the argument,[23] I am willing to assume that, under certain circumstances, an ethnic minority has a right to maintain its ethnic culture, and that this is a right that holds against the dominant majority and the institutions which exercise its powers. But the question is, what is it exactly *a right to*? Is it a right to a common good? Culture is, of course, a common good. But upon closer scrutiny it should become apparent that minority cultural rights are not rights to have the culture in question. It is not the aboriginal culture itself that aboriginal communities claim to deserve from the state, but the right to the material conditions which render it possible for their culture to flourish in the social and political context of the dominance of the majority culture. Aboriginal minorities claim the right to a certain share of the material resources of the larger community that would enable the minority to maintain its cultural heritage in face of what it claims is an unfair competition over the community's cultural resources.[24] Such rights do not involve the problematic burden of the duty to share the values of the minority culture since it is not the culture that ethnic minorities claim as the object of their rights. Minority cultural rights are rights to those material conditions which would enable such cultures to flourish in face of their inherent inferiority *vis-à-vis* the

22 See, *e.g.*, Will Kymlicka, *Multicultural Citizenship*, 35.

23 I have expressed my doubts about the special rights of minority cultures in my "Equality and Minority Cultures".

24 I rely here on the main argument of Kymlicka for rights of ethnic-cultural minorities, which I take to be the fairly standard stance of liberals who claim for the recognition of such rights. See Will Kymlicka, *Liberalism, Community, and Culture* and *Multicultural Citizenship*.

dominant majority. This is not a right to common goods. It is only a right to the conditions which enable certain common goods to be sustained.[25]

The situation is quite different when we consider the *internal* duties such cultural rights may involve. The rights of minority cultures *vis-à-vis* their own members is much more problematic. It follows quite clearly from our discussion so far that minority cultures cannot have a right against their own members to the common good of the flourishing of their culture. This is important, since there is typically a very strong pressure minority cultures tend to exert on their own members precisely in this direction, namely, a pressure to share those values which constitute the cultural heritage they want to preserve. Many cultural minorities find it very difficult to compete with the dominant majority for the hearts of their members, particularly the young. Such competition, which tends to put the minority cultures in substantial inferiority compared with the majority, often results in a considerable social pressure exerted by the group on its members.[26] It is a pressure of conformity with tradition and a pressure to cherish those values and traditions which constitute the distinct minority culture. The temptation to present such claims of the group with respect to its members in the terminology of rights is understandably strong. Minority cultures, and sometimes even majority cultures, have a strong temptation to claim a right to the preservation of their culture, that is, the group's right *vis-à-vis* its own members. In other words, when we talk about the rights of the group *vis-à-vis* its own members, it is, typically, a right to culture, that is, to a common good, that the group tends to assert. And as we have seen, such rights ought not to be recognized.

To be sure, none of this is meant to entail that groups cannot have any rights *vis-à-vis* their members, whether in the cultural or any other context. The kind of rights groups should not have with respect to their members, however, is the right to the preservation of their culture, since this is a right to a common good, and one which involves particularly burdensome duties. Liberal values cannot be reconciled with *a duty* to value one's culture or ethnic, national, heritage. Once again,

25 A comparison might help here. Consider the Yiddish language and culture, which is, practically, almost extinct. Since there isn't any particular distinct minority in any liberal country that actually practices the Yiddish culture (as opposed to merely speaking the language), it is pretty clear that Yiddish does not deserve the kind of constitutional protection Kylmicka's arguments espouse for, *e.g.*, aboriginal minorities. If there is any right to Yiddish, it would have to be a right to a common good, that is, to the culture itself. My argument entails that under these circumstances, nobody has a right to the Yiddish culture.

26 See, for example, Chandran Kukathas, "Are There Any Cultural Rights?"

though, it should be noted that the absence of such a group right to the preservation of culture against its own members does not rule out certain distributional concerns which may give rise to group rights. If a certain minority culture already exists and deserves special protection, the group may have certain rights to use its group resources in ways which aim to facilitate the preservation of the culture. Such rights to use resources and allocate them in ways which are conducive to the flourishing of the cultures may well be internal rights against the members of the group as well. The right cultural groups should not have with respect to their own members is the right to the common goods which constitute the relevant culture.

The practical implications of this distinction are not easy to draw. For instance, consider the question of whether a group, say an ethnic minority, has a right to impose certain unique dress codes on its members: Is this an attempt to exercise a group right to a culture, and thus to a common good, or is it only an exercise of derivative rights, those which enable the group to allocate its resources in ways which are conducive to its preservation? Presumably, much depends on the way in which the group attempts to impose its demands in practice. The details can certainly matter. For example, if the pressure of the group to impose its unique dress code is a direct social or legal pressure, asserted on behalf on the group's right, then it is clearly not warranted. But there are other, more acceptable means of achieving similar purposes. For example, the group may subsidize certain activities, such as education, or recreational activities, in ways which tie such a subsidy to the dress code it purports to impose. This would seem to be a much more acceptable way of achieving the group's purpose, at least from the perspective of the argument explored in this essay.[27] But of course, the subtle differences between such social instruments are not always so easy to distinguish. Even nuances may turn out to be crucial.

To what extent does the above argument depend on the nonvoluntary nature of membership in one's culture or ethnic group? Is it easier to justify a group right to some common goods with respect to its members if the group is constituted by voluntary membership? I tend to think that voluntary membership makes a moral difference, but in practice, not that much. Certain groups may have a right that

---

27 The overall considerations about the desirability of such practices are much more complex, of course. For instance, the question of feasible alternatives is often crucial.

those who join them voluntarily share the values which the group, as such, cherishes, particularly if those values are an essential ingredient of the communal goods which make it the kind of group it is. A golf club may have a right to impose demands on its members that include the duties to share those values which render it possible to play golf and enjoy it as an activity of its kind. As long as the membership in the golf club is really voluntary, and the costs involved in exit from the group[28] or avoiding membership are negligible, the duty to share the values of the group upon joining it does not seem to be particularly burdensome or problematic. However, voluntary membership in social groups is a tricky idea and rarely as simple as it seems.

Consider, for instance, the question of whether membership in academia is voluntary in the requisite sense. Can we say that academia, as a social group, has a group right *vis-à-vis* its members to share the current academic values, only because membership in academia is voluntary? Two closely related problems can be demonstrated here. First, it is far from clear that membership in academia is as voluntary as membership in a golf club. Joining the academic circles *seems* to be quite voluntary, as it normally takes considerable effort to join, requiring voluntary actions and, so we hope, personal achievements. But for many individuals the cost of avoiding membership in the academic club is very high, as it affects their ability to carry out their life projects and engage in activities which are of great importance to their well-being. For many projects and aspirations, the alternatives to the academic circles are meager and often very expensive. Expecting individuals to share the current values of academia only because there is no external pressure on them to join in may well be too burdensome a duty to expect. And this points to the second problem with the claim to such a group right: Even if the group may have a right to maintain its values, it is far from clear that it should have a right to maintain its *current* values. Why should such a group as academia have a right to preserve the values it happens to have at any given time? Should it not be open to change and innovation? A group right with respect to its members

---

28 This is a very crucial element of the condition of voluntary membership. Most social groups we find ourselves in we do not actually join voluntarily. The costs of exit are crucial in determining whether continued membership is voluntary or not. People can leave, for example, the national group they belong to. But the fact that such an exit from a national group tends to be very costly renders one's continued membership highly involuntary.

to share the group's values, even if warranted to some extent, need not be a right to prevent change, evolution, and even, sometimes, revolution.[29] The less voluntary a group is, the less of a right to its common goods should it have. And as I have tried to indicate, very few social groups are really as voluntary as one might think.[30]

---

29 In one sense, pointed out to me by Chaim Gans, the example is problematic: It is arguable that the values of academia are not only the business of the academic circles, as it may well be in the interests of outsiders, that is, the community at large, that the academic institutions share certain values and instantiate them. This may well be true of some other quasi-voluntary social groups as well. The question to what extent such external interests should count is a very difficult one, but I cannot go into the details here.

30 I am indebted to Chaim Gans, Elizabeth Garrett, Alon Harel, and Denise Rèaume for invaluable comments and suggestions.

CHAPTER 11

On The Right to Private Property and Entitlement to One's Income

In their book on the justice of income taxes, *The Myth of Ownership*, Liam Murphy and Thomas Nagel argue that people do not have a right to their pretax income. This, they say, is the basic conviction that determines their approach to the entire book. There are two main paragraphs in which they purport to explain this conviction, and in this essay I want to discuss the difference between these two formulations. I will label them the "first quotation" and the "second quotation," respectively. The first runs as follows:

> The conviction that determines our approach to all more specific questions is that there are no property rights antecedent to the tax structure. Property rights are the product of a set of laws and conventions, of which the tax system forms part. Pretax income, in particular, has no independent moral significance. It does not define something to which the taxpayer has a prepolitical or natural right, and which the government expropriates from the individual in levying taxes on it.[1]

In the next paragraph on the very same page, the following formulation is offered:

> People do have a right to their income, but its moral force depends on the background of procedures and institutions against which they have acquired that income—procedures that are fair only if they include

---

1 L. Murphy & T. Nagel, *The Myth of Ownership, Taxes and Justice*, 74.

> taxation to support various forms of equality of opportunity, public goods, distributive justice, and so forth. Since income gives rise to clear moral entitlement only if the system under which it is earned, including taxes, is fair, entitlement to income cannot be used as an assumption to evaluate the fairness of the tax system.[2]

Let me say from the outset that I fully agree with the main moral insight of the second quotation. Nor is it my main purpose here to argue that the content of the first quotation is misguided. (Part of it is, as I will explain at the end, but not necessarily the main part.) My main purpose here is to point out the fact that there are two very different philosophical insights at stake here, and that we may gain a much better sense of the philosophical debate if we disentangle them.

In the first quotation, Murphy and Nagel seem to be making a very familiar yet highly contested point about the nature of the right to private property: namely, that the right to private property is *not a natural right*. They do not say whether or not they think that there are other rights which may be "natural." However, even if there are some rights which may be deemed natural in a traditional sense, the right to private property is not one of them. "Property rights are the product of a set of laws and conventions," they say. This would seem to deny precisely what Locke in his famous argument on the origins of the right to private property strove to establish, viz., that it is a prepolitical natural right (at least under certain conditions).

Now consider the second quotation. Here there is no question about the naturalness of the right to private property. Instead, the claim is that people's right to their income (whatever that right is) can only be justified if it forms part of an entire system of norms and institutions which yield morally acceptable distributional procedures and outcomes. In other words, the claim here is that an entitlement of the kind under consideration is just, or fair, only if it forms part of a fair system. I will argue that this may be quite right, even if the content of the first quotation is wrong. In other words, I will argue that the conclusion about the nature of the right to private property is neither necessary nor sufficient to establish the validity of the moral argument that is espoused in the second quotation.

---

2 *Ibid.*

As a first step, we must clarify what is it that philosophers mean when they claim that a right to X is *a natural right*, and what would be the meaning of denying this. There are at least two, partly overlapping, possibilities:

1. A natural right is the kind of right people can acquire in a hypothetical "state of nature."

2. A natural right is a right people have by virtue of being human beings, or persons, or moral agents.[3]

Let me briefly explain each one of these ideas in turn. Following Locke's famous argument, the first option is the traditional meaning of a natural right that is associated with the right to private property. Locke's argument is open to various interpretations, but at least a few points are clear enough. As a first step, we try to envisage a *state of nature* that is meant to capture the idea of the world without political organizations, that is, without a state and a legal system. At the second stage, we ask ourselves whether people in that hypothetical state of nature would have certain rights. The point of Locke's "mixing of labor" argument, I take it, is to answer *this* question in the affirmative with respect to the right to private property. Thus, to the extent that something like Locke's argument succeeds, a right to private property would be a natural right in the sense that it is the kind of right people could acquire in a state of nature. Obviously, a lot depends here on how we characterize the hypothetical state of nature. But this is not the point I want to focus on. Rather, for our purposes, the question should be a different one: what is the moral significance of the conclusion? Why would it matter that a certain right, say to private property, can be acquired in this hypothetical state of nature, and other rights, for example, the right to due process of law, cannot? It is not difficult to surmise what Locke's answer is: Locke assumed that if he can establish the "natural" aspect of the right to private property, namely, that it is the kind of right people can acquire in a state of nature, then it follows that the state, once established, as it were, must respect the right and protect it. But this move is actually a *non sequitur*. Even if there is a certain right that people can acquire in the state of nature, once a state is established, the right may be lost or superseded by other concerns. Suppose, for example, that in a state of

3 This conception of a natural right roughly accords with the traditional Marxist distinction between human rights and civil rights. Human rights are those people have by virtue of being human beings, and civil rights are those people have by virtue of being subjects of a political entity.

nature people would have the right to defend themselves by, *inter alia*, punishing anyone who transgresses their rights. Surely, such a right to punish must be rescinded with the establishment of a state that maintains a legal system.

There is an obvious response to this point: It may be admitted that the establishment of a state may, indeed, transform the nature of the relevant natural right, but the state must nevertheless protect the interest that grounds the right in question. Even if people should lose their right to punish with the establishment of a state, that is only because the role of punishment is now undertaken by the state, thus protecting the same interest by other, presumably more efficient, means. This is quite right. But it does not undermine the simple point that at a political stage, as opposed to a state of nature, individual people no longer have a right to punish. It is at least possible, then, that a similar fate befalls the right to private property. Perhaps the interests and other moral concerns that ground the right to private property in a state of nature are better protected by the state in other forms, that is, without upholding an individual right to private property.

I am not suggesting that this is necessarily the case. But it is a possibility one must consider, and the fact that such a possibility exists quite simply proves that even if people, as individuals, have a right to x in a state of nature, it does not necessarily follow that the state, once established, must recognize an individual right to x. Since it is quite clear (and was clear to Locke himself[4]) that the conditions which may give rise to the right to private property in the state of nature do not obtain at the political stage, it remains a bit of a puzzle why so much attention has been paid to Locke's "mixing of labor" argument. In any case, the naturalness of the right to private property has no clear implications with respect to the nature and scope of the right to private property in the political society. Perhaps the argument can show that there are certain human concerns that the state must attend to and protect, but the question of whether these concerns must be protected in the form of an individual right to private property is clearly underdetermined by the natural-right argument.

The second interpretation of the idea of a natural right seems more promising in this respect. There are certain rights, it can be argued, that people have just by virtue of being humans, or persons, or moral agents, or such. (Obvious examples

---

4 There is a clear indication in the text that Locke was aware of this difficulty in his argument, since he was at pains to show that at the political stage, there is an additional argument for the right to private property that he attributed to a form of tacit consent, associated with the introduction of money.

of such rights would include, for instance, the right to life and perhaps the right to a minimal level of subsistence; the right not to be subject to humiliation, torture, etc.; perhaps the right to freedom of conscience, and so on.) The existence of such rights, therefore, does not depend on the existence of a state or a legal system. Furthermore, it is plausible to maintain that if there is a certain right that people have just by virtue of being, say, human beings, then the state must recognize the right and protect it.

Arguably, the Hegelian argument about the right to private property is a natural-right conception in this second sense. Hegel has argued that the ownership of property is essential for a minimal level of human flourishing and that it is essential for the healthy development of personhood and personal freedom.[5] It seems possible to interpret this type of argument as the kind of claim which maintains that the right to own property is a right people ought to have just by virtue of being humans or persons. Even if one accepts this Hegelian reasoning, however, nothing follows from it about the extent of property one should own, or about the ways in which property rights may be gained, transferred, or lost. The Hegelian argument is rather abstract, and it only shows that people ought to be allowed to own some private property. Perhaps it, or another similar argument, can also show that there is a certain *minimal* level of ownership that is essential for human flourishing, and thus the state should provide for each and every individual a minimal amount of goods to own, so to speak. But again, no details about the scope of the right to private property can follow from the Hegelian argument.

Let me pull these two points together. If the right to private property is deemed a natural right in the Lockean sense, then it is far from clear that such a natural right must be recognized and protected by the state. If, on the other hand, the right to private property is deemed natural in the sense that it is the kind of right people have just by virtue of being humans, or persons, or such, then the right in question is far too abstract to yield any conclusions about its desired scope in any particular political state.

If this is correct, then it becomes very unclear what is to be gained by denying that the right to private property is a natural right. Recall that Murphy and

5 Hegel, *Philosophy of Right*. For an excellent account of Hegel's argument see J. Waldron, *The Right to Private Property*, Ch. 10.

Nagel want to substantiate the conclusion that people do not have a right to their pretax income. Since they do not want to deny that individuals do have a right to own property, there is nothing in their argument to suggest that they would object to the Hegelian conception of the right to private property.[6] Thus, they need not deny that the right to private property is a natural right in this second sense. If it is the Lockean sense of the natural right thesis that they wish to deny, then the move is moot since there is nothing in the Lockean argument that could possibly support a denial of the Murphy/Nagel conclusion.

In one sense, however, this last point is not accurate. There is a crucial *part* of Locke's argument that may be very relevant to the dispute here, but it is not the natural right to private property. One crucial premise in Locke's "mixing of labor" argument is the moral thesis that people have a natural right to the fruits of their labor, which is supposed to be derived from the idea of self-ownership. As Locke put it:"[E]very man has a property in his own person . . . [therefore] [t]he labor of his body and the work of his hands, we may say, are properly his."[7]

Evidently, it is *this* premise of Locke's argument that Murphy and Nagel strive to undercut, and that is precisely the point of their normative thesis in the second quotation. They claim that even if people have a right to the fruits of their labor, the moral force and scope of such a right cannot be determined in isolation from the entire distributive system which prevails in the society at large. I think that they are quite right about this.

Consider Locke's premise again: understood literally, the moral point of it is almost too silly to be taken seriously. Surely, from the fact (if we generously grant that it is a moral fact) that I own my hand, it does not follow that I own everything that I do or transform with it. (If I use my hand to rub your head, does it mean that I can come to own your head, or that I have any justified claim to it?) As has been pointed out before, Locke's moral intuition here can only be understood in terms of an entitlement people may have to the fruits of their labor, if the latter is understood in terms of the *added value* of their product or the impact

6 In fact, they actually indicate an acceptance of the Hegelian line of thought. See Murphy & Nagel, *supra* note 1, 45. Furthermore, the Hegelian argument is compatible with the thesis that the right to private property is a product of laws and conventions.

7 J. Locke, *Second Treatise of Civil Government,* § 27.

of their labor.[8] But the problem for Locke, and for contemporary libertarians who followed him, is that the very idea of the added value of labor makes *moral* sense only against the background of a system of norms and practices which guarantees fair bargaining and fair pricing. Libertarians take it for granted that there is an objective measure for the added value of labor that is simply the price that could be earned on it in an ideally free market. But this can only make moral sense if we also assume that the conditions of a free market, *ipso facto*, are fair, and there is very little reason to make such an assumption or take it for granted.[9] In any case, Murphy and Nagel are quite right to maintain that whatever one's views about fairness are, it is the fairness of the entire system that necessarily conditions the specifics of one's entitlement to the fruits of one's labor, since it is only on the background of the entire system that we can determine what the added value of one's labor, morally speaking, is.

My conclusion is this: In order to establish their main moral conclusion, Nagel and Murphy need not deny that the right to private property is a natural right. There is nothing to be gained for their argument by insisting that the right to private property is not a natural right. Nor do they have to deny the moral intuition that people have a right to the fruits of their labor. On the contrary: the plausibility of their normative argument in the second quotation relies on the premise that people do have a right to the added value of their labor. The argument maintains, and rightly so, I think, that there is no possible conception, morally speaking, of what such an added value is, independent of the system of legal and social norms that constitute the terms of fair bargaining, just pricing, and so on. In other words, people can only have a right *to a fair assessment* of the added value of their labor, and the latter cannot make any sense independent of the entire system of norms prevailing in the relevant society.[10]

---

8 That is how Marx also understood, and actually subscribed to, this moral insight. Thus, his famous doctrine about the surplus value of labor that the capitalist steals from the workers. It is also how Nozick understood Locke's premise. See his *Anarchy, State, and Utopia,* 175. See also G. A. Cohen, *Self-Ownership, Freedom and Equality.*

9 In fact, the libertarian position is even more dubious: Not only must it hold that the pricing of an ideally free market is necessarily fair, but libertarianism must also hold that any other alternative system that may attach different pricing to the added value of labor is necessarily not fair.

10 The Marxist argument is very instructive here: Since Marx believed that it is inherently wrong for some people to own the means of production, he was able to claim that the capitalist actually steals the surplus value of the laborer's work and therefore free-market pricing of labor is necessarily unjust. I am not suggesting that Marx expressed himself in these moral terms. But there is a moral argument here that, even if wrong, is not necessarily absurd.

Nagel and Murphy might argue that I have missed a crucial element in their argument in the first quotation. The reason for denying that the right to private property is a natural right, they could claim, resides in the following idea: People cannot have a property right in their pretax income because property rights are essentially defined by legal norms and conventions, and the latter must comprise elements of taxation. As they put it: "Property rights are the product of a set of laws and conventions, of which the tax system forms part." (I take it that they mean "necessarily forms part.") I think that this is not a convincing argument, and for two reasons. First, libertarians need not insist that people's right to their pretax income is necessarily a *property* right. Instead, they could claim that it is their natural right to the fruits of their labor, which is a moral claim that perhaps underlies the natural right to property but is not identical with it. In other words, even if the right to private property is basically artificial, people may still have a right to the fruits of their labor. As I have argued above, the real disagreement is about the conditions which can determine what the fruits of one's labor, morally speaking, are.

Secondly, even if we accept the premise of Murphy and Nagel's argument that the right to private property is entirely artificial, constituted by legal norms and conventions, it seems to me groundless to claim that such norms must necessarily include the institution of taxation. It is not difficult to envisage a state that has a well developed system of private property that does not impose any taxes whatsoever. The state may, for instance, finance its operations and the maintenance of its legal system by controlling some of the country's natural resources (e.g., oil, or diamonds, or such). Perhaps this is not a viable option for most countries, or perhaps this is not an efficient or a fair system of financing a state, but I do not see any conceptual link between a legal system of private property and a system of taxation. To the extent that such a link exists, it is entirely contingent. So this argument fails. But as I have tried to argue above, the main moral insight of the second quotation is valid, regardless of the non-naturalness of the right to private property.[11]

11 I am indebted to Scott Altman, David Enoch, Marshall Cohen, and Ed McCaffery for comments on previous drafts.

CHAPTER 12

The Intrinsic Value of Economic Equality

Why should we care about economic equality? Some philosophers, prominently Joseph Raz and Harry Frankfurt, claim that we shouldn't, that is, at least not if we think of economic equality as intrinsically valuable. They claim that economic *equality* has no moral value in itself. Harry Frankfurt formulated this point succinctly in saying that "what is important from the point of view of morality is not that everyone should have the same but that each should have *enough*."[1] But there is a serious question that arises here: Can it be the case that people have enough of what they need if others have much more? The immediate suspicion that perhaps this cannot be the case stems from the fact that needs are profoundly relative to the norms of flourishing in one's society. A great many needs, for example, are relative to culture. People's needs, and the criteria of sufficiency for those needs, are determined to a very considerable extent by the culture they live in. This, I take it, is widely recognized. But needs are also relative to the actual possessions of others in the same society, or, at least, so I shall argue here. Roughly, the basic idea is this: Above the level of bare subsistence, the resources people need, and mainly to what extent they need them, is something which is partly, but significantly, determined by the actual availability of those resources to others within an indeterminate distance around them.

If this is true, then it is not so clear anymore that claims of need, and more generally, our concern for people "having enough," is essentially distinguishable from having not much less than others. In any case, this is precisely what I shall try to argue here, namely, that part of what having *enough* economic resources *means* is that one does not have much less than most others. This will show that the

1 H. Frankfurt, "Equality as a moral ideal," reprinted in his *The Importance of What We Care About*, Ch. 11. Frankfurt has reaffirmed this line of thought in his recent article, "Equality and Respect." Joseph Raz makes essentially the same point (among others) in his *The Morality of Freedom*, Ch. 9, 240.

value of economic equality is actually derivable from those same considerations which were meant to show why equality, as such, has no intrinsic value, namely, the basic moral concern with the satisfaction of people's needs. In the first section I will try to substantiate this claim. In the second section, I will try to show why this value of economic equality is an intrinsic one. Finally, I shall say a few words about the kind of equality which is entailed by the discussion.

A. Needs, Sufficiency, and Equality

The ultimate concern of humanist moral-political ideals is with people's lives. Ultimately, what matters is how well each individual's life is going. What makes one's life go well depends on innumerable things. The possession of economic resources is only one of many factors which contribute to people's well-being. How crucial economic resources are, as compared with other factors which affect people's chances of leading a good life, also depends on a great many things, partly on specific cultural circumstances. It would be safe to assume, however, that the relative significance of the possession of economic resources in the modern world is increasing steadily. For better or worse, the predominance of Western capitalism in the world creates an increasing dependence of people's well-being on their economic resources.

Furthermore, I will assume here that the relation between people's well-being and the resources they possess is both instrumental and intrinsic, or constitutive. Obviously, people need economic resources in order to be able to realize their life plans and the projects they regard as valuable. In this sense, the possession of resources is instrumentally valuable. But I will assume that there is also a deeper, noninstrumental relation between the possession of resources and well-being. What one has and what one is are not totally detachable aspects of one's life and personality. In other words, my assumption is that the satisfaction of people's needs and interests in material resources is, at least to some extent, intrinsically valuable.[2]

Another assumption needs to be spelled out: Throughout the discussion, I will assume that there is a distinction between the moral grounds for seeking a desirable state of affairs, and the grounds for taking measures to attain it. In particular,

---

2 It is safe to assume that both Frankfurt and Raz would not object to this last point. Frankfurt, in any case, seems to pre-suppose it.

a certain state of affairs may well be morally desirable, even if there is no particular agent, private or official, whose responsibility it is to try to bring about such a state of affairs. My argument about the intrinsic value of equality will not assume that if a certain form of equality is valuable, intrinsically or otherwise, then it automatically follows that the state, or anyone else, must take measures to accomplish it. The argument that follows is about values, concerning things we should care about. It leaves the questions concerning the implementation of those values entirely open.

Now, when we look at the societies we know, and that, I will suppose here, include the world at large, we see that at least from an economic perspective, many people can lead a decent life. Some people have much more than that; they have more resources than the vast majority can ever hope for. And then, there is a huge number of people at the bottom of the socioeconomic scale whose lives are pretty miserable. These poor people suffer from real deprivations; they don't have enough resources to be able to conduct a decent life. Frankfurt, Raz, and others, who object to the intrinsic value of equality, ask us to realize that it is the urgency of poor people's needs which calls upon our attention, and not the quantitative discrepancy between their possessions and others'.[3] But why, exactly, do we think that certain needs are urgent? What is it that constitutes needs and "having enough" resources?

The notion of "need" is often used to indicate something like *fundamental*, or *basic*, interests. My use of the term "need" is much broader than this. Need, as I shall use the term here, is tantamount to any interest in material resources one might have. But it is crucial to note that interests differ from wants and desires. People can wish to have things they don't need, even things it would be against their interest to have, and *vice versa*.[4] They may not be aware of, or be aware of and not want, things they actually do need, things that are in their interest to have. Furthermore, it is possible to distinguish between what a person needs and what he thinks that he needs. People may think that they need something which, in fact, they do not need.[5] Does this make needs an objective matter?

---

3 See also Amartya Sen, "Poor, Relatively Speaking," 325–343.

4 See, *e.g.*, D. Wiggins, *Needs, Values, Truth*, Ch. 1.

5 This is actually not so simple. Though people can certainly be mistaken about their needs, it is far from clear that colossal mistakes are possible. Most common mistakes about one's needs stem from mistakes about facts. We may all think, for example, that we need a low-cholesterol diet, and this may turn out to be a big mistake: It may turn out to be that cholesterol is actually good for us. But it is less clear that we can *all* be mistaken about the nature of our needs, if it does not involve mistakes about facts.

Perhaps it does. But even if needs are objective, metaphysically or otherwise (though I am not suggesting that they are), needs are still relative, and in several respects.

First, as I have mentioned above, it is generally recognized that at least some needs are culture-dependent.[6] There are, however, several ways in which culture affects people's needs, and not all of them are important for our discussion. The influence of culture is most evident in shaping the various ways in which people satisfy their needs. One and the same kind of need may be satisfied differently in different cultures. This, however, does not render needs themselves relative to culture. But there are needs which are partly constituted by culture, though typically indirectly. In order to see this, it is essential to realize that above the level of biological needs and bare subsistence, needs are inherently relative to what is considered as prosperity, flourishing, etc. (and its opposites, i.e. harm, wretchedness, etc.), in one's society. Needs, after all, are always *for* something. People need things in order to avoid harm and to attain some forms of flourishing. What constitutes human flourishing is, to a considerable extent, culturally determined.[7] Some cultures value forms of human flourishing which other cultures regard with disdain. To be sure, I am not trying to deny that there are universal human needs, transcending cultural differences. But I believe that it is equally clear that a great many needs are not universal, but relative to culture.

In a similar, but I think much less recognized way, needs are also relative to the socioeconomic opportunities which prevail in one's society. Roughly, again, what people need, and mainly to what extent they need them, is something which is partly, but significantly, determined by the actual availability of those resources to others within their social vicinity.

In order to clarify this point, let me distinguish, though somewhat artificially, between several levels of needs. We can construct a simple scale along the following lines. At the very bottom, we would find those needs which are absolutely essential for one's survival. These needs are determined by our biological makeup and environmental realities. We can say that these biological needs are *absolute*, in that they are entirely determined by necessities of survival. Such needs

---

6 The cultural dependence of needs has often been stressed by the Frankfurt school. See, *e.g.*, H. Marcuse, *One-Dimensional Man*, 4. Marcuse, however, also believed that there are "real" needs transcending cultural contingencies.

7 See Wiggins, *supra* note 4, 11.

are obviously not relative, either to culture or to socioeconomic scales. Now, one step above the bottom, we will find those things people need without which their lives are doomed to be wretched, miserable, almost unbearable. Let us call these "urgent needs." These would be the things people need in order to be able to maintain something like a *minimally decent* life. Farther up the scale we can identify those things most people need in order to conduct a decent life. Let us call them "reasonable" or "average" needs. Satisfaction of such reasonable needs is what would provide most people with the kind of resources they need in order to conduct a decent, prosperous, fulfilling life. Finally, there are things people may want to have, though, in one clear sense, it would be awkward to say that they need them. We can call them "luxuries," indicating the fact that the satisfaction of such "needs" is not really required in order to conduct a decent life. In other words, having luxuries is what distinguishes the rich, or the very rich, from the well-to-do.

Now, my basic claim is that above the level of absolute needs, this scale of needs is profoundly sensitive to the actual division of resources in the society. Whether someone is warranted in holding that her need of x is urgent, reasonable, or less than that, crucially (though not exclusively!) depends on the actual availability of x to others. The more readily x is available to others, the more urgent or important its possession may become, and *vice versa*, of course. In other words, what I am trying to suggest is, that the scale of needs is basically a matter of social constructions, because there is no truth of the matter about it which is independent of the division of possessions in one's social vicinity.

Let me clarify: I do not wish to claim that just about anything which is readily available to most people becomes, *ipso facto*, a reasonable need. People can have a great many things which they do not need. In order to need something, other conditions would normally have to obtain; relative availability does not form a sufficient condition of something being a need. Needs relate to things people would normally want to have, and they would normally want to have them for reasons. Some of those reasons may be agent-relative, and others may not. In any case, the argument under consideration does not depend on *a definition* of "needs." Nor is such a definition intended here. The moral intuition of the Frankfurt–Raz argument concerns the *sufficiency* of the satisfaction of needs; it does not depend on any precise definition of what "needs" are. Frankfurt and Raz claim that we should be concerned with people having enough of *whatever* they need, and the main question I want to raise here is whether we can know what this "enough" means, in a nonrelative manner.

As a rough illustration, consider this example. Imagine that we discover life on a remote planet, very similar to earth, which is comprised of two groups, the "rich" and the "poor"; imagine that the differences between the economic resources of these two groups are considerable, but, nevertheless, the "poor" in this imaginary alien society are actually better off than most of us. That is, judging by *our* standards of living, the "poor" in this imaginary society are not poor at all. They are poor, however, relative to the "rich" in their society. Suppose further, that the "poor" in this imaginary society do feel poor; judging by the only standards familiar to them, they do feel deprived of many opportunities which are available to the "rich." They think that they have some urgent needs, and a great many reasonable needs, unsatisfied.

Now, according to the view that denies the relativity of needs to the actual socioeconomic gaps, one would have to maintain that the "poor" in this imaginary society suffer from some kind of false consciousness; they only think that they have unsatisfied needs, but as a matter of fact, they actually have enough. But this is quite implausible. After all, nobody would think that the poor people in *our* society should suddenly think of themselves rich and content if we discover yet another, opposite, remote planet, where even the "rich" are much worse off than they are.

A similar way to think about this is this: Take a poor segment of our society, that is, think of people whose biological needs are met, but beyond that, they have very little. Imagine that they are the only ones around, that is, imagine that the whole world is exactly in their situation. Whatever they have is all that there is to have for everybody else. Would you still think of these people as "poor"? Would you still insist that they have urgent needs? I don't see how you could.

It may be objected that this relativity of needs to the actual distribution of resources in society is only an empirical generalization concerning typical human reactions, and a contestable one at that. This is true about one aspect of the relativity of needs, and false about another. We must distinguish between two questions: how people *actually form* their conceptions of their needs, and how we judge their *sufficiency*. People form their own conceptions of what they need on the basis of a very complex combination of factors, some which are culturally determined, and others which are personally variant. The general norms of flourishing in society form an essential part of such need-formations, but only a part, and the extent to which such cultural factors figure in individuals' conceptions of their needs is a contingent matter. It varies between different cultures and between individuals in the same culture.

The relevant question, however, is not about the way people come to form their own conceptions of their needs—which is, indeed, largely an empirical matter—but about the criteria of sufficiency: Can we have *objective criteria* for judging that people have enough (or plenty, etc.) of what they need that are not relative to the possessions of others? A negative answer only to this last question is what I am trying to defend here. And it is not an empirical question. It is a philosophical question about the concept of needs, and particularly, about what it means to have enough, or plenty, etc.

Now, we know what it means to have enough food, since food is needed to satisfy certain biological needs. In such cases, needs are determined by some absolute standards which are simply there, given by the realities of life. But most needs are not like that. People don't need to go to the opera, or have cars, washing machines, television sets, personal computers, etc., in order to survive. These are "reasonable" needs in our society only because nowadays a great many people can afford them. One who cannot afford most of such standard consumer items would rightly feel that she is unable to conduct a decent life. Such a self-conception of deprivation, however, would be totally out of place if the items in question would have been considered luxury items. Whether they are luxury or reasonable items crucially depends, however, on who can afford what. The more people can afford x, the less of a luxury it may become (that is, assuming that x is something that people actually want to possess).

Consider, for example, the possession of cars. Just a few decades ago, automobiles were considered luxury items because very few people could afford them. Nowadays, however, we no longer think of the private possession of a car as a luxury. In present developed societies, the possession of cars is something most people need in order to be able to conduct a decent standard of living, and those who cannot afford such a consumer item as a private automobile are, indeed, deprived of something they might reasonably need.[8]

---

8 Once again, though, it should be emphasized that widespread availability of an item does not necessarily render that particular item one in need. Relative availability certainly does not constitute a sufficient condition of needs; it only figures in our criteria of what it means to have *enough*.

Amartya Sen claims, however, that such examples do not really show that poverty is a relative matter. Poverty, Sen claims, is an absolute notion in what he calls "the space of capabilities," though it would often take a relative form in the space of commodities, that is, with respect to people's interests in a specific material resource.[9] Admittedly, there is something very important in this distinction. It is certainly true that the widespread availability of cars has actually changed the world, so to speak, in the sense that people can no longer function in society as they could have functioned without cars at the beginning of the twentieth century. Therefore, Sen concludes, the relative deprivation of those who cannot afford a car these days is a failure only in the commodity space, leaving the space of capabilities constant.

This conclusion, however, is overstated. The fact that the same kind of functioning capability may require different commodities in different cultures does not show, by itself, that capabilities remain constant.[10] In order to deny the relativity of needs, Sen would have to show that we can articulate an absolute, nonrelative list of capabilities which are constant across cultures, irrespective of the commodities which are available in them. This seems to me very unlikely. Even less plausible, however, is the thesis underlying Sen's argument here, that the notion of poverty, and more generally, the notion of "standard of living," is best defined solely in terms of capabilities to function.[11] Such a view entails, for example, that the Bedouin peasant, who needs only a camel to move around, and the suburban American Yuppie, who needs a car, are equally well off if the Bedouin gets his camel and the Yuppie gets his car. Surely we must allow for the intuitive idea that the Bedouin is poor, and the Yuppie is rich.

---

9 Sen, "Poor, Relatively Speaking," 335.

10 Here is a similar example Sen himself provides to illustrate this point. Citing research which showed that children in Western countries might not be able to follow their school program unless they have access to television, Sen claims that a child in, say, England, without a television set is actually worse off than, say, a child in Tanzania without a television, who presumably does not need the television in order to fulfill his educational needs. In other words, the widespread availability of televisions in the West, and their role in education, has not created a "brand new need," Sen claims, but that to meet the same need as that of the Tanzanian children in education, the British child must posses more commodities. See *ibid.*, 336–337. In a limited sense, this is true; but of course, it does not entail that one would be indifferent between growing up in England or in Tanzania. Even if there is a loose sense in which education in both countries serves the same functioning capabilities, those are, nevertheless, quite different. The fact that the English child needs a television to accomplish her tasks is rather indicative of the fact that both the quality of her education and her standard of living are, quite simply, much higher than the quality of education and standard of living in Tanzania.

11 *Ibid.*, 334.

Admittedly, there is an obvious way in which one could support something like Sen's argument: One could claim that needs are generally satiable. That is, whatever one needs, one can reach a point where one has enough of it in the sense that having more of it would not constitute any improvement. Surely some needs are satiable in this sense. Nourishment, fresh air to breath, etc., are satiable needs. But it seems extremely unlikely that economic resources, in general, are satiable. One's economic situation can always be improved. This does not mean, however, that there is no such thing as having *enough* economic resources. Only that any judgment about the sufficiency of economic resources is bound to be relative to the actual socioeconomic scale which prevails in one's society.

Now it is, of course, only the objective judgment about sufficiency that concerns us here. The fact that we can easily envisage very poor people who are content with what they have is beside the point. Only according to rather crude versions of Utilitarianism is the subjective state of mind of people about such matters decisive of anything, and it tells more against such versions of Utilitarianism than against the argument offered here.[12]

Another serious objection, however, might go as follows: People need things for certain *reasons*. Now, according to the objection, whatever the reasons are for needing something, those reasons are also reasons for having a certain amount of it. If x is a reason for A's needing y, then x may provide the grounds for judging how much of y is enough for A. And if this is the case, it would seem to be a decisive argument against the relativity of needs to the possessions of others. But the conclusion is premature. The reasons which underlie a particular need are typically *indeterminate* about the criteria of sufficiency of that need. In other words, even if the reason for needing something is independent of any considerations about what others have, the criteria of its sufficiency may well be relative to others' situations. Consider, for example, people's need for lodging. There are good reasons for this need, but those reasons do not entail any particular standard of lodging which could be considered appropriate in any given set of circumstances. The appropriateness, or sufficiency, of one's lodging condition is

12 For example, such versions of Utilitarianism are committed to the view that if it turns out to be cheaper to convince poor people, say, by indoctrination, to be content with what they have, than actually to improve their economic situation, then such indoctrination is warranted and more desirable than trying to improve people's economic situation. This, I take it, is a very implausible moral stance.

bound to be relative to the general availability in one's socioeconomic vicinity.[13] Similar considerations apply, I believe, to most economic resources. Their criteria of sufficiency are underdetermined by the reasons for having the economic resources one needs. This is so because the basic criterion of sufficiency of economic resources is essentially a comparative matter, largely determined by the norms of flourishing in one's society.

Admittedly, it is very difficult to answer the question what the relevant society is here. Though the argument assumes that standards of flourishing are relative to a given society, it does not assume that those standards are parochial. Mexican farmers, for example, do not form part of the North American society, but presumably they are affected by the standards of flourishing which prevail in the U.S. and Canada. Perhaps nowadays we may safely assume that the world at large is so intertwined by mass media and economic ties that it is the one society that matters.[14]

There seems to be a further, serious objection that might arise here, with respect to the irrationality of envy. Rawls famously claimed that rational people do not suffer from envy: A rational person "is not ready to accept a loss for himself if only others have less as well," that is, "as long as the differences between himself and others do not exceed certain limits . . . ."[15] Now, it may be objected that the kind of relativity of needs I have assumed here goes against this fairly standard assumption about the irrationality of envy. That is so, because if it is true that people cannot really have enough economic resources if others have much more, then it may often be rational for a person to forgo a certain economic gain just in order to prevent an even greater gain to somebody else.

---

13 For example, think: Why would it be so ridiculous if someone said that she "needs to live in Buckingham Palace"? Well, obviously, because most everybody lives in a much humbler residence. But it is worth keeping in mind that for millions of poor people around the world, our residences are not unlike Buckingham Palace compared to their lodging conditions. Appropriateness of residence conditions is profoundly a relative matter.

14 It is a difficult question whether the argument depends on people's knowledge, or awareness, of the others' situation. I tend to think that such knowledge is only relevant if we think about the empirical question concerning the ways in which people come to form their own conceptions of their needs. It is not required for purposes of assessing the sufficiency of their needs. We can form our objective judgment about the poor condition of the Mexican farmers in comparison to their North American counterparts, even if the former are totally unaware of the condition of the latter.

15 Rawls, *A Theory of Justice*, 143.

There are several complications here. To begin with, there is an important distinction between individual comparisons and those which relate to socioeconomic classes. Although it may be irrational for an individual, as such, to forgo a certain expected gain only to prevent others from gaining more, such a strategy may well be quite rational when the comparison relates to socioeconomic classes. For example, if the dean offers one of his professors an increase of 5% to his salary while increasing the salary of another professor by 30%, the former would probably behave irrationally if he declines the offer just in order to prevent his colleague from getting a higher increase to her salary. But if the government offers an increase to the salary of university professors, say by 5%, conditional upon a much higher increase say, of 30% to the civil service employees, the situation is quite different. Creating, or substantially increasing, a socioeconomic gap between classes of people involves moral costs regardless of envy. It may create a class difference which had not previously existed, and this difference may be detrimental to the disadvantaged class in many ways, even if, as is often the case, each and every individual in that class would have personally preferred the modest gain.

Second, there is the issue of limits. As Rawls himself admitted (see the quotation above), if the expected difference in gains between the parties concerned exceeds a certain limit, the so-called envy principle turns out to be quite rational. Now, this threshold proviso may well be quite intuitive, but it is far from clear what its grounds are; why does the *quantity* of the expected difference matter? If the principle of rationality assumes that one should only be concerned with one's own possessions, and one's own expected gains, why does it matter *how much* more the others are going to gain? Where does the threshold come from?

Note, however, that if the argument about the relativity of needs is correct, the rationality of the threshold proviso is rendered pretty clear. My rational concern with others' expected gains can stem from my concern with my own situation—if others gain *much* more than I do, then my own gain can easily turn out to be a relative loss.

In other words, Rawls's principle is not necessarily a principle of envy. Envy is a type of motivation, or reason, and there is no swift move from Rawls's principle to the real motivation behind it. A motivation is based on envy only when it is essentially not self-regarding, that is, when the loss which is intended to be inflicted on the other party contributes nothing to the situation of the envious party. A motivation is envious only when it is intended to prevent the other from gaining something which the envious party is in no position to gain himself.

This, however, is not necessarily the case whenever one is willing to forgo a certain expected gain just in order to prevent somebody else from gaining even more. And this is particularly the case when we concentrate on the differences between classes of people, not individuals. If it is true that people cannot have enough if others have much more, the reasons against increasing economic gaps are self-related ones, based on real interests of the disadvantaged party. Thus, the following conclusion seems to be warranted: On the one hand, it is true that the argument about the relativity of needs entails that it can be rational sometimes to forgo certain possible gains only in order to avoid increasing the gaps between the parties concerned. (There is, of course, little wonder about that: It is something which is entailed by all egalitarian principles.) On the other hand, such sacrifices are not necessarily motivated by envy.[16]

Another difficulty that seems to present itself is this: How can we explain the fact that we seem to be much less concerned with the inequalities between the well-to-do and the rich than with the poor and the rest? Harry Frankfurt claims, not unreasonably I think, that "we tend to be quite unmoved . . . by the inequalities between the well-to-do and the rich. . . . The fact that some people have much less than others is morally un-disturbing when it is clear that they have plenty."[17] Does this not show, then, that people can have quite enough even if others have much more? I don't think that it does, and for three different reasons. First, it should be kept in mind that if my argument so far is correct, then "having plenty" is simply not a judgment we can make irrespective of what others have. From an objective vantage point, "having plenty" can only mean something like having more, or at least not less, than the average. Secondly, I venture to guess that we are typically unmoved by the discrepancies between the rich and the well-to-do, partly because there are much fewer of the former than the latter. In a society where there are many rich, few poor, and few in between, I am not so sure that we would not be concerned by the discrepancy between the rich and the well-to-do. Relative numbers may matter.[18]

---

16 Economists often take it for granted that nobody can really object to Pareto improvements. But this is far from clear. Pareto improvements, particularly in successive stages, can easily increase the gap between the rich and the poor to such an extent that the gains to the poor are outweighed by the cost of the increased gap. This, perhaps, may have been the intuition behind Rawls's proviso.

17 Frankfurt, "Equality as a moral ideal," 1,147.

18 See, *e.g.*, L. S. Temkin, *Inequality*, Ch. 1.

Most importantly, however, the reason for being much more concerned with the relative disadvantage of the poor than that of the well-to-do stems from special, *additional* disadvantages of being poor, over and above one's relative place on the socioeconomic scale. The status of being poor, though essentially a relative matter, is particularly degrading, for reasons which have to do, for example, with the way in which poor people see themselves in relation to the society they live in. Poor people typically feel alienated from their society. At best, they tend to feel excluded from the general advantages of living in society. More often, they also feel humiliated. Such understandable feelings of alienation, exclusion, and humiliation add an especially urgent demand on our attention, and this provides one important reason to be much more concerned with the discrepancies between the poor and the well-to-do than with discrepancies between the latter and the rich.[19] There are, of course, many more disadvantages to being poor compared to the other socioeconomic segments of society, but we need not go into this here.

To sum up so far: I have tried to argue that the value of economic equality derives from the basic moral concern with the sufficiency of people's needs. From a moral point of view, it is important that each person should have enough resources to be able to conduct a decent, autonomous, fulfilling life. The argument was that this concern cannot be realized without a considerable amount of equality, since the criteria of the sufficiency of needs are essentially relative to others' possessions. People cannot have enough if many others have much more. A crucial question remains open about this argument, however, and it is whether the value of equality which is entailed by it is intrinsic, or merely instrumental. I take up this issue in the next section.

B. Intrinsic Values

What is the significance of saying that something is merely of instrumental value? The typical case is the following: Suppose there is a state of affairs, say A, and we hold that A, as such, is not good in itself; that is, we have no reason to pursue A for its own sake, but, combined with circumstances Ci . . . n, the pursuit of A is

---

19 It may be useful to compare our intuitions with respect to the poor in our society, and the urgency of their needs, with the way we react to very poor, but also very isolated, communities. I think we are much less concerned with the predicament of the latter, because we assume that their poverty does not involve such feelings of alienation and humiliation.

likely to bring about some good consequences B, and B is such that it is something we value for its own sake.[20]

Note that there is a good reason for saying that in such cases, the pursuit of A is *merely* of instrumental value (i.e. positive or negative). This normally indicates the fact that things could have been otherwise, that is, that the connection between the pursuit (or the avoidance) of A and the things we really value in life, is only contingent. If the circumstances change, the consequences following from A may change as well. It is this element of contingency which warrants our reaction to instrumental values as "merely" instrumental. Furthermore, contingency, in a sense, admits of degrees. Things can be more or less contingent, depending on the probability that we attach to the occurrence of the relevant causal chain.

Given this line of thought, it is natural to assume that valuable things in our lives can be either instrumentally or intrinsically valuable. If we attach a certain value to A, then it must mean that A is either something we value for its own sake, or else it is something we value only because its pursuit (or realization, etc.) is likely to bring about something else which we value for its own sake.

Compelling as this dichotomy may be, it is in need of much further refinements. For our purposes, however, we only need to distinguish between several categories of intrinsic values. Raz's distinctions are very useful here. He suggested three such categories: Things can be intrinsically valuable if they are valuable in themselves, regardless of anything else. Some of these things may be of ultimate value. The relation between these two categories is, as Raz explains, a justificatory one. "Ultimate values are referred to in explaining the value of non-ultimate goods."[21] Thirdly, there are "constituent goods," and these are "elements of what is good in itself which contribute to its value, i.e. elements but for which a situation which is good in itself would be less valuable."[22]

It is on this, third category, that I want to concentrate, suggesting that constituent goods can be of two kinds. Things may be valued in this sense because they are instances, or realizations, of goods which we value intrinsically. These are the

---

20 The same structure can be put in negative terms: We can say that A is not bad in itself, that is, if A obtains, by itself, there is nothing to complain about, but, combined with circumstances Ci . . . . n, the fact that A obtains tends to bring about bad consequences.

21 Raz, *The Morality of Freedom*, 200.

22 *Ibid.*

things which instantiate, noninstrumentally, something which is good in itself. If friendship is of intrinsic value, then my friendship *with Sarah* is a constituent good in this sense. There is, however, another important category, where the constituent good is an *essential ingredient* of something which we value for its own sake. The main difference between these two subcategories of constituent goods is that nonessential constituent goods are, typically, substitutable. My friendship *with Sarah* is not an essential ingredient of friendship, though it instantiates friendship noninstrumentally.

As an example of the second subcategory, consider the complex relations between the value of choice and the value of personal autonomy. As Raz famously formulated it, "The ruling idea behind the ideal of personal autonomy is that people should make their own lives. The autonomous person is a (part) author of his own life. The ideal of personal autonomy is the vision of people controlling, to some degree, their own destiny, fashioning it through successive decisions throughout their lives."[23] Clearly enough, the value of choice figures in this picture as an essential ingredient. That it is only an ingredient can be clearly seen from the fact that there is much more to the value of personal autonomy than an aggregate of choices. Furthermore, not all choices are relevant to personal autonomy. Only certain types of choices, and under certain circumstances, form part of the realization of an autonomous life. And it is equally clear how *essential* an ingredient choice is to the ideal of personal autonomy. Part of what it means to be an autonomous person is that one has made certain choices in one's life. Choice is not something that only contributes, instrumentally, to personal autonomy; it actually forms part of what it is to be an autonomous person. Its value consists in being an essential ingredient of personal autonomy.[24]

Similarly, I want to suggest, the intrinsic value of economic equality is in its being an essential ingredient of the kind of general moral concern Frankfurt has in mind, namely, our moral concern with people having enough of what they need. We should not value economic equality as such, but only as an essential constituent of the value of having enough of what one needs to conduct a decent life.

Let me summarize in brief. I agree with Frankfurt and Raz that the fundamental moral concern is with the idea of need: what we should really care about is

---

23 Raz, "Autonomy, Toleration, and The Harm Principle," 314.

24 By this I do not mean to exclude other values we may attach to choice, values which do not derive from choice being part of autonomy.

people having enough of what they need. A considerable amount of economic equality, however, forms an essential ingredient of this general concern. Generally speaking, people cannot have enough of what they need in a society where many other people have much more. Part of what "having enough" means is that one does not have much less than most others. Equality, on this account, is not of instrumental value; its value lies in being an essential ingredient of the general concern with people's needs, which *is* something we should value for its own sake.[25]

C. Two Types of Ideals

What kind of economic equality is entailed by our discussion so far? There are two distinctions, or contrasts, that I would like to dwell on in order to answer this question. First, it is noticeable that the kind of economic equality which is entailed by the considerations I have mentioned in the first section is very rough. If the basic moral concern is with people having enough of what they need, and all we have shown so far is that people cannot have enough if others have much more, it certainly does not follow that total economic equality is required. Only a very rough amount of economic equality is what is needed. Now, many egalitarians would be happy to concede that equality is, anyway, only an ideal. Part of what we mean when we say that P is a moral-political ideal is that P need not, or cannot, be implemented in full. Note, however, that there is an important difference between "need not" and "cannot," and that there are, accordingly, two categories of *ideal* principles. Let me call them *guiding* ideals, and *limit* ideals, respectively.[26]

A guiding ideal principle is one which does not require, on its own moral grounds, full implementation. Limit ideals, on the other hand, would require full implementation, if only that would be possible. That is, anything that falls short of full implementation does so because of the obstacles imposed by the realities of life. A good example of a limit ideal principle is the principle of equality of opportunity. This principle, on its own moral grounds, requires the elimination of *all* possible factors which would give anyone an unfair advantage or disadvantage compared with another. But in most contexts, we know that life is too complicated,

25 None of this, of course, excludes the possibility that equality is also of great importance in terms of the instrumental values it serves, in, *e.g.*, containing the relative political power of some people over others, and the like.

26 I use the term "limit" here in deference to the Renaissance notion of *idea limis*.

and no matter what we do, some people will have an unfair advantage over others, since it is simply impossible to eliminate all the relevant factors. The principle sets an ideal limit that we can only try to approximate.

Guiding ideals, on the other hand, do not require full implementation. That is, not because we have given up on something in advance, but because the grounds of the principle itself are such that they do not call for strict implementation. What such principles do require, however, is that there be no gross deviations from the standards they set. Furthermore, such guiding ideals are typically non-perfectionist principles, in that attempts to implement them in full tend to be self-defeating, neurotic, or ridiculous. Consider, for example, ideals such as "reasonable care" (i.e. the avoidance of negligence), charity, authenticity, or spontaneity. Only that much of spontaneity is enough; one who tries to be spontaneous whenever possible tends to look rather ridiculous. Similarly, excessive caution is not always a symptom of rationality.[27]

The ideal of economic equality which is entailed by our discussion in the first section belongs to this latter category. It is a guiding ideal. On its own grounds, it does not call for full implementation of economic equality. It only tells against gross deviations from economic equality, since such deviations undermine the basic moral concern we should have for people's needs. The argument was that people cannot have enough of what they need if others have *much more*; but surely they can have enough if others have just a little more, or perhaps even if very few people have much more. Rough economic equality is all that the principle requires.

In order to introduce the second contrast, it may be useful to draw on Derek Parfit's distinction between two main kinds of egalitarian concerns: The Telic and the Deontic views.[28] On the Telic view, inequality is bad, regardless of how it came about. On the Deontic view, inequality is unjust, injustice being a special kind of badness, one which necessarily involves wrongdoing. On this rough dividing line, the value of economic equality I have argued for above certainly belongs to the Telic view. What is bad about inequality is not that it results from some injustice that had been done, but from the fact that it is a *bad state of affairs* if people don't

---

27 The Kantian distinction between "perfect" and "imperfect duties" is very similar to the idea I have in mind here. But I don't think we need the specific Kantian grounds for it.

28 See D. Parfit, "Equality and Priority," 1.

have enough of what they need, combined with the fact that people cannot have enough if others have much more. Thus, if we care about people having enough of what they need, we should also care about economic equality. Needless to add, economic equality is not the only distributive concern we should care about. Furthermore, the implementation of equality, even as a guiding ideal, is often a wasteful policy, and it certainly may happen that the waste is too big to be ignored.[29]

29 I am very grateful to Omri Ben-Shachar, Meir Dan-Cohen, Chaim Gans, Amy Gutman, Leslie Green, Alon Harel, Frances Kamm, Martha Nussbaum, Joseph Raz, Donald Regan, Philip Soper, and Mike Seidman for their illuminating comments on previous drafts of this paper.

Bibliography

ALEXY, R., *The Argument from Injustice: A Reply to Legal Positivism* (Oxford, 2003).

—"A Defense of Radbruch's Formula," in D. Dyzenhaus (ed), *Recrafting the Rule of Law: The Limits of Legal Order* (Hart, 1999), 15.

AQUINAS, T., *Summa Theologica* (Dawson trans, ed. d'Entreves, Blackwell, 1970).

ARENDT, H., *The Human Condition* (Chicago, 1958).

ARNESON, R. "Democracy is not Intrinsically Just," in K. Dowding, R. E. Goodin & C. Pateman (eds.), *Justice and Democracy* (Cambridge University Press, 2004), 40.

ARROW, K., *Social Choice and Individual Values*, (2nd ed.) (Yale, 1970).

AUSTIN, J., *The Province of Jurisprudence Determined* (London: Weidenfeld & Nicolson, 1954).

BAKER, HAREL, & KUGLER, "The Virtues of Uncertainty in Law: An Experimental Approach," 89 *Iowa L. Rev.* 443 (2004).

BARON OF BURY HEWART, (1870–1943), Remark, Nov. 9, 1923. "Rex v. Surrey Justices," vol. 1, *King's Bench Reports* (1924).

BERLIN, I., *Concepts and Categories* (London, 1978).

BRIGHOUSE, H., "Egalitarianism and Equal Availability of Political Influence," *4 The Journal of Political Philosophy* 118 (1996).

BROOME, J., "Is Incommensurability Vagueness?," in R. Chang (ed.), *Incommensurability, Incomparability, and Practical Reason* (Harvard, 1997), 67.

BROWN v. BOARD OF EDUCATION, 347 U.S. 483 (1954).

BUCHANAN, J.M. and G., TULLOCK, *The Calculus of Consent: Logical Foundations of Constitutional Democracy* (Michigan, 1967).

BURGE, T. "On Knowledge and Convention," 84 *The Philosophical Review* 249 (1975).

CAMPBELL, T., *The Legal Theory of Ethical Positivism* (Dartmouth, 1996).

CHAPMAN v. UNITED STATES, 500 U.S. 453 (1991).

CHISOM v. ROEMER, 501 U.S. 380 (1991) (Scalia, J., dissenting).

CHRISTIANO, T., *The Rule of the Many* (Westview, 1996).

COHEN, G.A., *Self-Ownership, Freedom and Equality* (Cambridge, 1995).

COHEN, J., "Deliberation and Democratic Legitimacy" in J. Bohman and W. Rehg (eds.), *Deliberative Democracy* (MIT, 1999), 67.

COLEMAN, J., *The Practice of Principle* (Oxford, 2001).

COOTER, R., *The Strategic Constitution* (Princeton, 2000).

DAHL, R., *Democracy and Its Critics* (Yale, 1989).

DAN-COHEN, M., "Decision Rules and Conduct Rules: On Acoustic Separation in Criminal Law," reprinted in his *Harmful Thoughts* (Princeton, 2002), 37.

DARWALL, S., "Two Kinds of Respect," 88 *Ethics* (1977), 36.

DELLMUTH v. MUTH, 491 U.S. 223 (1989).

DICKSON, JULIE, *Evaluation and Legal Theory* (Hart Publishing, 2001).

DRIVER, J., "Caesar's Wife: On The Moral Significance of Appearing Good," LXXXIX *The Journal of Philosophy* 331 (1992).

DWORKIN, R.M., *Sovereign Virtue* (Harvard, 2000).

—*Law's Empire* (London: Fontana Press, 1986).

—"Rights as Trumps," in J. Waldron (ed.), *Theories of Rights*, Oxford Readings in Philosophy (Oxford, 1984), 153.

—*Taking Rights Seriously* (London: Duckworth, 1977).

EASTERBROOK, F., "Statutes' Domain," 50 *U. Chi. L. Rev.* 533 (1983).

ELSTER, J., *Ulysses Unbound* (Cambridge, 2000).

ELY, J.H., *Democracy and Distrust* (Harvard, 1980).

ENDICOTT, T. A. O., *Vagueness in Law* (Oxford, 2000).

ESKRIDGE, FRICKEY, & GARRETT, *Cases and Materials on Legislation* (West, 2001).

ESTLUND, D., "Political Quality," in Estlund (ed.), *Democracy* (Blackwell, 2002), 175.

—"Jeremy Waldron on Law and Disagreement," 99 *Philosophical Studies* 111 (2000).

—"Beyond Fairness and Deliberation: the Epistemic Dimension of Democratic Authority," in Bohman & Rehg (eds.), *Deliberative Democracy* (MIT, 1999), 173.

FINNIS, J., *Natural Law and Natural Rights* (Oxford, 1980).

FRANKFURT, H., "Equality and Respect," 64 *Social Research* 3 (1997).

—"Equality as a Moral Ideal," in *The Importance of What We Care About* (Cambridge University Press, 1988), 134.

FULLER, L., *The Morality of Law* (Yale, 1964, 1969).

GALLIE, W. B., "Essentially Contested Concepts," *Proceedings of the Aristotelian Society* (1956), 167.

GARDNER, J., "Legal Positivism: 5½ Myths," 46 *American Journal of Jurisprudence* 199, (2001).

GARRETT, E., "The Purposes of Framework Legislation," 14 *Journal of Contemporary Legal Issues*, 717 (2005).

—"Issues in Implementing Referendums in Israel: A Comparative Study in Direct Democracy," 2 *Chicago Journal of International Law* 159, 2001.

—"Legal Scholarship in the Age of Legislation," 34 *Tulsa L.J.* 679 (1999).

GEORGE, R., "Reason, Freedom, and the Rule of Law: Their Significance in the Natural Law Tradition," 46 *Am. J. Juris.* 249 (2001).

GREEN, L., "The Concept of Law Revisited," 94 *Michigan L. Rev.* 1687 (1996).

—"The Political Content of Legal Theory," *17 Philosophy and Social Sciences* 1 (1987).

GREENAWALT, K., "How Empty Is The Idea of Equality?" 83 *Colum. L. Rev.* 1167 (1983).

HAREL, A., "Review Essay: Free Speech Revisionism: Doctrinal and Philosophical Challenges" 74 *Boston Univ. L. Rev.* 687 (1994).

—"Revisionist Theories of Rights: An Unwelcome Defense" 11 *C.J.L.J.* 227 (1988).

HART, H.L.A., *The Concept of Law* (Oxford, 1961); 2nd ed., with Postscript, Bulloch & Raz (eds.) (Oxford, 1994).

—*Essays in Jurisprudence and Philosophy* (Oxford, 1983).

—*Essays on Bentham* (Oxford, 1982).

—"Rawls on Liberty and its Priority" in Daniels (ed.), *Reading Rawls* (Blackwell, 1975), 230.

HARTNEY, M., "Some Confusions Concerning Collective Rights" 4 *C.J.L.J.* 293 (1991).

HASEN, R.L.,"Vote Buying," 88 *Calif. L. Rev.* 1323 (2000).

HAYEK, F., *The Road to Serfdom* (Chicago, 1944, 1972).

HEGEL, G.W.F., *Philosophy of Right* (T. M. Knox trans., Oxford 1967).

HERSHOVITZ, "Legitimacy, Democracy, and Razian Authority," 9 *Legal Theory* 201 (2003).

HOHFELD, W.N., *Fundamental Legal Conceptions* (W. W. Cook, ed.), (Yale, Press, 1919).

HOROWITZ, D., *Ethnic Groups in Conflict* (University of California Press, 1985; 2nd ed. 2000).

KANT, I., *Groundwork of The Metaphysics of Morals*, (M. J. Gregor, ed.) (Cambridge, 1997).

KAPLAN, D., "Demonstratives" in *Themes from Kaplan*, (Almog et. al., eds.), (Oxford, 1989), 481.

KELSEN, H., *Pure Theory of Law*, 1st ed., [*Reine Rechtslehre*, 1934], translated into English as *Introduction to the Problems of Legal Theory* (Paulson and Paulson trans.), (Oxford 2002).

—*Pure Theory of Law*, 2nd ed., (Knight trans.) (University of California Press, 1967).

—*General Theory of Law and State*, (A. Wedberg trans.) (Harvard, 1949).

KUKATHAS, C., "Are There Any Cultural Rights?" *In* W. Kymlicka, ed., *The Rights of Minority Cultures* (Oxford, 1995), 228.

KYMLICKA, W., *Multicultural Citizenship* (Oxford: Clarendon Press, 1995).

—*Liberalism, Community, and Culture* (Oxford: Clarendon Press, 1989).

LARMORE, C., "Public Reason," in S. Freeman, ed., *The Cambridge Companion to Rawls* (Cambridge, 2003), 368.

LEVMORE, S., "Voting With Intensity," 53 *Stanford L. Rev.* 111 (2000).

—"Voting Paradoxes and Interest Groups," 28 *J. Legal Stud.* 259 (1999).

—"Bicameralism: When Are Two Decisions Better Than One?" 12 *International Rev. of Law and Econ.* 145 (1992).

LEWIS, D, *On Convention: A Philosophical Study* (Oxford, 1968).

LIJPHART, A., *Patterns of Democracy, Government Forms and Performance in 36 Countries* (Yale, 1999).

LOCKE, J., *Second Treatise of Civil Government* (Prometheus, 1986).

MACCORMICK, N., "A Moralistic Case for A-Moralistic Law," 20 *Valparaiso L Rev.* 1 (1985).

—"Rights in Legislation," in Hacker and Raz (eds.), *Law, Morality, and Society* (Oxford, 1977), 189.

MACPHERSON v. BUICK MOTOR CO., 217 N.Y. 382 (N.Y. Ct. App. 1916).

MANNING, J., The Absurdity Doctrine, 116 *Harv. L. Rev.* 2387 (2003).

—"Textualism As A Nondelegation Doctrine," 97 *Colum. L. Rev.* 673 (1997).

MARCUSE, H., *One-Dimensional Man* (London: Routledge, 1964).

MARMOR, A., "Deep Conventions" (forthcoming in *Philosophy & Phenomenological Research*).

—"Constitutional Interpretation" in *Interpretation and Legal Theory,* revised 2nd ed. (Hart Publishing, 2005).

—*Interpretation and Legal Theory*, (Oxford, 1992); revised Second ed., (Hart Publishing, 2005).

—Book review of *Law and Disagreement*, 112 *Ethics* 410 (2004).

—*Positive Law & Objective Values* (Oxford, 2001).

—"Equality and Minority Cultures," 3 *Democratic Culture* 149 (2000).

—"On Convention" 107 *Synthese* (1996).

—"Pure Theory of Law" in *Stanford Encyclopedia of Philosophy, http://plato.stanford.edu/entries/lawphil-theory/*

MILL, J.S., *Considerations on Representative Government* (London, 1861).

—*On Liberty* (London, 1859).

MOORE, M., "Hart's Concluding Unscientific Postscript," 4 *Legal Theory* 301 (1998).

MUELLER, D., *Public Choice II* (Cambridge, 1989).

MURPHY, L., and T., NAGEL, *The Myth of Ownership, Taxes and Justice* (Oxford, 2002).

NAGEL, T., "The Fragmentation of Value," in his *Mortal Questions* (Cambridge, 1979), 128.

NOZICK, R., *Anarchy, State and Utopia* (Blackwell, 1974).

PARFIT, D., "Equality and Priority," in A. Mason, ed., *Ideals of Equality*, (Blackwell, 1998), 1.

PERRY, S., "Hart's Methodological Positivism" *in* Coleman, ed., *Hart's Postscript* (Oxford, 2001), 311.

—"Interpretation and Methodology in Legal Theory" in A. Marmor (ed.), *Law and Interpretation* (Oxford, 1995), 97.

PETERS, C., "Equality Revisited," 110 *Harv. L. Rev.* 1211 (1997).

POSTEMA, G., *Bentham and the Common Law Tradition* (Oxford, 1986).

—"Coordination and Convention at the Foundations of Law," *11 Journal of Legal Studies* 165 (1982).

PUTNAM, H., *Mind, Language and Reality* (Cambridge, 1975).

RAWLS, J., *Political Liberalism,* (Columbia, 1993).

—*A Theory of Justice* (Oxford, 1971).

RAZ, J., *Engaging Reason* (Oxford, 1999).

—"Autonomy, Toleration, and The Harm Principle," *in* R. Gavison, ed., *Issues in Constitutionalism: Philosophical Foundations* (Cambridge, 1998), 314.

—"On the Authority and Interpretation of Constitutions," in L. Alexander (ed.), *Constitutionalism: Philosophical Foundations* (Cambridge, 1998), 152.

—"Incommensurability and Agency," in R. Chang (ed.), *Incommensurability, Incomparability, and Practical Reason* (Harvard, 1997), 110.

—*Ethics in the Public Domain* (Oxford, 1994).

—"The Relevance of Coherence" in his *Ethics in the Public Domain* (Oxford, 1994), 261.

—"Liberalism, Skepticism, and Democracy," 74 *Iowa L. Rev.* 761 (1989).

—*The Morality of Freedom* (Oxford, 1986).

—"Right-based Moralities" in J. Waldron, ed., *Theories of Rights* (Oxford, 1984), 182.

—"Authority and Consent," 67 *Virginia L. Rev.* 103 (1981).

—*The Authority of Law* (Oxford, 1979).

—"Law and Value in Adjudication," in his *The Authority of Law* (Oxford, 1979), 180.

—*Practical Reasons and Norms* (Hutchinson, 1975).

RAZ, J., and MARGALIT, "The Right to Self Determination," in J. Raz, *Ethics in the Public Domain* (Oxford, 1994), 110.

RÈAUME, D., "Individuals, Groups, and Rights to Public Goods," 38 *U.T.L.J.* 1 (1988).

RECTOR, HOLY TRINITY CHURCH v. U.S., 143 U.S. 457 (1892).

RICHARDSON, H., "Democratic Intentions," in Bohman and Rehg (eds.), *Deliberative Democracy*, (MIT, 1999), 349.

SCHACTER J., "Metademocracy: The Changing Structure of Legitimacy In Statutory Interpretation," 108 *Harv. L. Rev.* 593 (1995).

SCHAUER, F., *Playing by the Rules* (Oxford, 1991).

SCHWYZER, H., "Rules and Practices," 78 *Phi. Rev.* 451 (1969).

SEARLE, J., *Speech Acts* (Cambridge, 1969).

SEN, A., "Poor, Relatively Speaking," reprinted in his *Resources, Values and Development* (Harvard, 1984), 325.

SHAFER-LANDEAU, R, "Vagueness, Borderline Cases and Moral Realism," 32 *American Philosophical Quarterly* 83 (1995).

SMITH v. U.S., 508 U.S. 223 (1993).

SOAMES, S., "Drawing the Line between Meaning and Implicature – and Relating both to Assertion," forthcoming in *Nous*.

—"Direct Reference, Propositional Attitudes, and Semantic Content," 15 *Phil. Topics* 47 (1987).

SYPNOWICH, C., "Utopia and the Rule of Law," in D. Dyzenhaus (ed.), *Recrafting the Rule of Law: The Limits of Legal Order* (Hart, 1999), 178.

TEMKIN, L., *Inequality* (Oxford, 1993).

WALDRON, J., "Normative (or Ethical) Positivism," in Coleman (ed.), *Hart's Postscript* (Oxford, 2001), 410.

—*The Dignity of Legislation* (Cambridge, 1999).

—*Law and Disagreement* (Oxford, 1999).

—*Liberal Rights* (Cambridge, 1993).

—*The Right to Private Property* (Oxford, 1988).

—"A Right to do Wrong," 92 *Ethics* 21 (1981).

WALUCHOW, W., *A Common Law Theory of Judicial Review: The Living Tree* (Cambridge, 2006).

WESTEN, P., "The Empty Idea of Equality," 95 *Harv. L. Rev.* 537 (1982).

WIGGINS, D., *Needs, Values, Truth*, 2nd ed. (Blackwell, 1991).

WILLIAMS, B., "Conflict of Values" in *Moral Luck* (Cambridge, 1981), 71.

WILLIAMSON, T., *Vagueness* (London, 1994).

WRIGHT, G.H. von, *Norm and Action* (New York: Routledge, 1963).

ZEPPOS, NICHOLAS S., "Justice Scalia's Textualism: The "New" New Legal Process," *12 Cardozo L. Rev.* 1597 (1991).

Index

Note: page numbers followed by n refer to footnotes.

M